Advan‹

"In my opinion, Tomer is one of the top five minds for Amazon selling strategies in the world. His keyword research and listing optimization techniques are absolutely next level."

—**Bradley Sutton**, Director of Training and Chief Evangelist at Helium 10

"Tomer is one the OGs of the Amazon ecosystem and one of the smartest guys out there. He has been a pleasure to work with over the years!"

—**Ryan Gnesin**, CEO at Elevate Brands

"Tomer's name is brought up regularly within Amazon seller circles. He's thought of as a thought leader, strategist, and mentor to seven- and eight-figure sellers. It is possible to grow from zero to a million dollars in revenue using the strategies in this book combined with hard work and a little capital. But to scale to an eight-figure brand, you need the insights and guidance of someone like Tomer."

—**Brandon Young**, eight-figure seller and CEO at Data Dive

"What makes Tomer different is his ability to combine his stellar knowledge and experience of Amazon together with his deep understanding and insights into people, leadership, and management. To be successful on Amazon is not only about the expertise but also about understanding the human factors. If you want to accelerate on Amazon, you must read this book!"

—**Pierre Poignant**, Co-Founder and CEO at BRANDED

"When Tomer speaks, I listen. I remember staying up until 4:00 a.m. in the hotel lobby of a conference in Hawaii a few years ago, listening to Tomer drop nugget after nugget on how he was crushing it on Amazon. He may be a magician at heart, but he is a master seller and business builder in knowledge and execution. You'd be crazy not to pick up his book and treat yourself to a treasure trove of tips and strategies for selling on Amazon."

—**Kevin King**, creator of Billion Dollar Seller Summit

"What stands out when Tomer speaks is his stagecraft; this is something that can only be developed over a long period of time, and it comes from his former life as a magician. When we are on the road together, he is always ready to entertain with some tricks. When it comes to business, there are no tricks. He takes his work very seriously and is very good at what he does. He knows a lot about what buyers want and how to scale teams, and he is highly respected in the community."

—**Danny McMillan**, Seller Sessions

"Not only does this brilliant man cover all the aspects of growing an Amazon business, but he does it masterfully so that the reader feels less like they are being lectured and more like they are going on an exciting adventure with Tomer. Along with actionable resources, Tomer weaves stories and life lessons that are relatable and ease the reader into a powerful mindset that makes a believer out of anyone that gets their hands on this masterpiece. This book is for dreamers, believers, and doers and will surely prepare you for this exciting entrepreneurial e-comm journey."

—**Izabela Hamilton**, CEO at RankBell

"When it comes to pre-exit preparation, Tomer is one of the leading professionals in our industry. We've seen many of our clients go through his masterminds and grow their business significantly, which eventually led to higher valuations in the sale. The title 'magician' still fits after all!"

—**Yael Cabilly**, Co-Founder of Fortunet

"I've been lucky enough to hear Tomer speak at various events around the world. Over the last few years, I've attended his presentations in China, London, and Las Vegas. Not only is it evident that Tomer has incredible knowledge in e-commerce and Amazon, but he also has a creative flair for breaking down complex situations into very simple solutions. The way his mind works is incredible, and to be able to have this book as a resource will be a massive help for anyone in e-commerce, no matter if you are a beginner, intermediate, or advanced seller."

—**Kian Golzari**, CEO at Sourcing with Kian

"When you talk to Tomer, you know you are getting straight-up, no-BS, actionable material. I went to many events and met many Amazon speakers. No one can compete with Tomer: straight to the point and no fluff."

—**Moshe Neuman**, Amazon Seller

"Tomer Rabinovich is an expert who imparts valuable knowledge to e-commerce entrepreneurs and provides wisdom that can only be gained through real life experience. That's advice you can trust. I recommend Tomer as your go-to guy for this vital Amazon seller knowledge."

—**Steve Simonson**, Founder, *Awesomers.com* podcast

"You know how a magician would do Amazon FBA? Meet Tomer. He already blew my mind with his tricks."

—**Alex Huditan**, CEO at Amazonienii

"When you are involved with as many events, masterminds, and general educational collaborations as I get to be a part of in the e-commerce space, it is easy for all content and strategies to start to blend together. And then a guy like Tomer steps up and reminds you that there is always something new, interesting, and impactful to learn! Tomer has gained his respect by giving great info, exhibiting true thought leadership, and creating results. Tomer is the real deal."

—**Tim Jordan**, Founder of Private Label Legion Community

"When I first heard Tomer speak at a live event, he definitely had my attention because he was able to talk strategy and tactics with no fluff while making perfect sense. I was impressed enough that I signed up for his mastermind, and our brands benefitted from his insights and listing optimization methodology. He's on the cutting edge and always coming up with practical ways to simplify operations and optimize processes. He's also extremely well connected in the e-commerce space and a great go-to resource."

—**Sanjay Chandiram**, CEO at Kaliber Global

"If you're still using Amazon sales methods from 2015, if you feel you haven't been able to launch a good product in a while or, well, ever, you'll want to get your hands on this book.

"If you ever wondered how seven- and eight-figure sellers seem to consistently knock it out of the park and catapult their businesses to each next level, this book is required reading."

—**Chelsea Cohen**, Co-Founder of SoStocked

"Tomer is an authentic and well respected figure in the Amazon seller community. An expert in Amazon FBA, he provides tremendous value as a speaker. Best of all, Tomer always backs up his strategies with data from his own direct experience in the trenches."

—**Rich Goldstein**, e-commerce patent attorney at Goldstein Patent Law and author of *The ABA Consumer Guide to Obtaining a Patent*

"We've invited Tomer to speak at our biggest live e-commerce events multiple times because he's one of the best at Amazon marketing strategies. If you want to learn what's working to sell more on Amazon, listen to Tomer."

—**Matt Clark**, CEO of Amazing.com, Inc.

RIDE THE AMAZON WAVE

THE PRO SELLER'S GUIDE TO PRIVATE LABEL SUCCESS

TOMER RABINOVICH

LIONCREST
PUBLISHING

RIDE THE AMAZON WAVE

The Pro Seller's Guide to Private Label Success

ISBN 978-1-5445-3304-9 Hardcover

     978-1-5445-3305-6 Paperback

     978-1-5445-3306-3 Ebook

     978-1-5445-3345-2 Audiobook

This book is dedicated…

*To every seller who's drained their savings to fund a product,
ignored their family for weeks before a product launch,
and refreshed Amazon's Seller Central over and over again,
believing they are making sales magically appear…*

*Every seller who's begged their family, their friends, their family's friends,
and their friends' families for five-star reviews…*

*To every seller who's run out of stock, overstocked, and who checks
their sales every morning before they even get out of bed.*

To every seller who's reached 500 percent ACoS with their PPC…

*To every seller who's lost reviews, gotten their listing shut down,
or gotten suspended for no real reason…*

*And to every seller who ignored all the people who said
they couldn't do it, said they were crazy, said they should give up
on their dream and get a real job…every seller who believed in
themselves more than they believed other people and is
living their dream right now—this book is for you!*

CONTENTS

INTRODUCTION

Congratulations on picking up this book. Whether you bought it, borrowed it, or just clicked on "Look Inside," I hope you'll keep reading because I have a lot to tell you about selling products on Amazon. First, let me tell you how this all started—and why you should keep reading.

I have met many, many Amazon sellers. Here's how it usually works for them: They get into the business, launch a few products, and have some success. Then they get excited, but instead of figuring out how to do more of what they're doing—and do it better—they get complacent. Some get, well, lazy. They launch a bunch of new products without the same due diligence they applied with their first products. Or they get distracted. They want to try something else, so they start a website, thinking it will be easier to sell their products on their own site than selling on Amazon. Or they decide to go into retail, thinking they can sell more products in a store than online.

Maybe those people who set up their own sites forget that Amazon is the most popular online shopping site on the planet. Those distractions sound stupid when you see them in writing, but Amazon sellers make these kinds of choices every day.

I chose to sell on Amazon for the convenience of it, not to sell on retail or my own website. I chose Amazon for the freedom it provides.

I can joke about this now because I made mistakes like these—and worse. I stopped doing what was already working and did a bunch of stuff that didn't work. And as you've probably guessed, I had some major failures. But the failures showed me what not to do, and they showed me how to refocus on what worked. Not just what worked some of the time or most of the time, but what worked every time.

I used to be a professional magician. No, really. I stood onstage in front of hundreds of people and performed all kinds of magic. I was very good, very experienced. Every magician has a specialty. Mine was close-up magic, like card tricks. Some magicians can read minds. See if I got this right:

You're a private label Amazon seller who's launched a few products. So you know how to launch, and you know something about inventory management and PPC. You're just not sure where to go from here. Do you keep launching product after product?

Here's the deal: You can keep doing what you're doing, but you'll never scale your business until you do something different. You have to build a real business and go from "product launcher" to "business owner." That means creating systems and processes, just like the big sellers. You can get there from here, and that's what this book is about—leveling up to a whole new stage where, instead of focusing on launching, you're focused on running a business that meets all your goals. Granted, launching products is part of that, but it's not everything and it won't get you where you want to go.

There are a lot of books out there about launching products and being an Amazon seller. This book is different. Whether you've launched a few products that were successful or weren't successful, whether you're doing well or not doing well:

WHEREVER YOU ARE AS AN AMAZON SELLER, THIS BOOK WILL TAKE YOUR BUSINESS TO THE NEXT LEVEL. EVEN IF YOU'VE NEVER SOLD ANYTHING ON AMAZON, THIS BOOK WILL HELP YOU—THOUGH I WROTE IT MAINLY FOR ACTIVE SELLERS.

When an amateur magician goes to the magic store, he asks the storekeeper, "What's hot? What's the newest trick out there?" When I was a magician, I never asked that question. Instead, I asked, "What do you have that always gets a *wow* reaction from the audience?" I wanted to know what worked—what got that *wow* response—every single time. When I left the magic business and became an Amazon seller, I learned to ask the same question: "What always works? Not some of the time or most of the time, but every single time?" That's what I had to learn to achieve my goals, and it's what I will teach you in this book.

But before I could sell anything, I had to answer another question: "What's my motivation?" I had to take a step back and think about why I was working so hard to be an Amazon seller. What did I want out of this? I wrote down all the reasons—everything I wanted from this venture, and everything I didn't want. That exercise helped define my path and motivated me to avoid the distractions and stay on track.

I didn't start my business so I could work more, and I'm guessing you didn't either. If you did, then maybe this book isn't for you. But if you want to stop working for other people, build a business, and create your own brand on Amazon, then we have something in common and I can help you. If you want to do all that and work less, I can help you too.

What do you want? What do you hope to achieve as an Amazon seller? Where do you see yourself in three months? Six months? Five years? Eventually, you'd probably like to be a seven-figure-a-year seller (or more), or maybe even sell your business and start a new one. Or never work again.

Now here's the million-dollar question: When are you going to get there? And why aren't you there now?

If you don't know the answers to these questions, then you can't see your destination. You don't know how close you are or how far you have to go. You need to know where you're going. Then you can refocus your business on the path that takes you there.

Are you already doing this? Do you have a clear destination, and are you headed in the right direction? Congratulations, once again, because that's a major accomplishment that the majority of business owners aren't doing at all.

If you aren't doing these things, you're going to love this book. And if you are, you're still going to love it because I can help you get there even sooner, or help you sell even more along the way. I can be your guide, showing you the most efficient path, and you can decide whether or not you want to follow me. Because being an Amazon seller can be really hard. It can be a lonely business if you let it. But done well, with the right focus on the right areas, and some hard work in the beginning, it can be the best gig in the world. Not just a gig, but really, the best opportunity that's come along in our lifetime. Being an Amazon seller can get you whatever freedom you want out of life. It's the most scalable, most profitable, and hands-down best business model in the world. And you don't even have to put on pants to do it. Or pull a rabbit out of your hat. Amazon's done all the heavy lifting for you, and you just have to figure out how to use what they've given you.

You're probably wondering who I am to think I know so much about selling on Amazon, so let me tell you. I began studying business as a teenager in high school, drawn to the subject and knowing that someday I'd have a business of my own. In Israel, where I grew up, you join the military right after high school. I was in intelligence for three years, then I took a year off to travel before going back to school. In college, I studied business and economics, and in my senior year, I volunteered to be the head of the student body. That was more demanding than it sounds, working till three in the morning and getting just a few hours of sleep because I had to be in meetings and in class early the next morning. I met my wife, Shani, there and ended up moving in with her and her parents after I graduated. I was working a nine-to-five job, and after working around the clock in the military and all through college, a regular job left me with a lot of free time. I wanted to do something, but what? I had always wanted to own my own business, so I started there.

I began studying how to sell on Amazon, and I was intrigued. This looked like something I could do, and I wouldn't have to quit my regular job, at least not at first. So, after talking with Shani about my idea, I took my entire life savings, $3,500, and spent it all on inventory for my first private label product on Amazon. In March 2015, I launched my first product. You never forget your first product, but more about that later.

On July 12, 2016, Amazon celebrated their second annual Amazon Prime Day. I remember that day very well, because the next day, I quit my job. Rather, I tried to quit. I told my boss that the day before, I had made enough profit selling on Amazon to match my current salary and I didn't need to work for him anymore. He convinced me to stick around for another year working from home, but in 2017, I made it official: I quit being an employee, started working 100 percent for myself, and never looked back.

I thought the best way to keep learning was to go to events and seek out the experts, so I did. I learned from some of the best people in the industry and spent six figures on different masterminds and events. The people I learned the most from weren't always onstage though; more often, they were other sellers I met by networking at various events. I found people in the audience who were doing what I was doing, and after a while I started holding my own events called Top Dog Summits and inviting those sellers to speak. This way, I could invite people who were interested in the same things I was interested in, and we could trade notes and compare what worked for all of us. On top of those events, I've created masterminds, talking with just a few sellers at a time while being transparent with what works for me in my own business.

Along this journey, I also interviewed Amazon coaches and other experts to find out what worked for them and their clients. I compared that with my own experiences and figured out what we had in common that worked every time. I came up with a number of areas to focus on and realized that when I got certain areas of my Amazon business right, everything else fell into place. Those are the areas that I focus on in this book. I also figured out what *not* to focus on. Like those distractions I told you about. Because running a business can get so complicated that even minor distractions can pull you away from the most important parts.

From there, I began to realize that all this experience and learning had put me in a position where I could coach other sellers, so I started my own masterminds, where I facilitated a group, coached them, and helped them grow their businesses and reach their goals. I still do this. I coached one seller from $50,000 a month to $400,000 a month. I coached another seller from working 16-hour days to just 4 hours a day. I've had more than a thousand one-on-one coaching sessions with Amazon sellers and spoken to many more thousands of sellers in person, online, and at various events over the past few years, and of course, I've grown my own private label business exponentially. In just five years, I went from initial launch to running multiple, hugely successful businesses. My success made me a sought-after speaker at events around the world, from Tel Aviv to Guangzhou, and from London to Las Vegas.

In the process of leading masterminds and sharing what I know, I learned that I enjoy helping Amazon sellers reach their goals. I love teaching. And while I still speak at events, my preference is to work directly with sellers. But my masterminds are small—I keep them to just a few people, because I believe that's most effective. The question then was, how could I get everything I know out to more people, not from a stage, but in a more personal setting? If you're holding this book, the answer is in your hands. By writing a book, I could put everything I teach in my masterminds in one place to share with anyone open to learning. What you have in your hands is everything I've learned about Amazon over the last six years, from the collective experience of myself and hundreds of my students.

There are no tricks in this book. It's just packed with solid advice for building a business that gets you where you want to go. The areas that I focus on aren't secret hacks or clever shortcuts—they're what expert sellers talk about when they get together. They know that the key to riding the Amazon wave is simply about identifying the basics, then nailing them.

Although this book is Amazon-seller-centric, most of the concepts apply to online selling in general and can be applied to any online retailer. You'll recognize some of the topics in here like product selection, sourcing, launching, and inventory management. In each of these areas you will notice some things that you already know, but probably many things that you didn't really think about in the same way. This book is not a "how to sell on Amazon book"; it's the book for people who are already selling and looking to get to the next level. But I'll tell you about some other things that you may not be familiar with, like having the right mindset to run your business.

This book is also not a "here's the best software to run your business" book. New tools and technologies are developed all the time, and a solution that's cutting edge one day may be outdated within a year's time. This book is meant to be timeless, as timeless as a book about selling on Amazon can be, so I focus on those concepts that will serve you, the seller, today and into the future.

You don't have to read this whole book from start to finish. I recommend reading the sections that interest you most. The first six chapters, comprising roughly half of the book, lay the foundation with guidance on having the right mindset to be an Amazon seller, along with choosing the right products to sell. You can read only these chapters and have a successful business, but I encourage you to keep reading.

Chapters 7 through 10 take you from product launch through pay per click (PPC) and inventory management, plus insider information on key performance indicators (KPIs) that will change the way you think about return on investment (ROI)—all topics that can take your business to the next level.

Chapters 11 through 14 are about the next step in your Amazon seller's journey, from creating a structure where the business practically runs itself to selling your business.

Chapter 15 is a bonus chapter about deciding what's next for you—not as a seller, but as a human who has achieved their dream as an Amazon seller. What do you do once you've reached your goals? Because just being a successful online seller isn't everything. There's more to life, and you'll want to explore the possibilities. Some of them will make you a better seller, or a better business owner. Some will just make you a better person.

By the way, I've worked with many sellers and other business owners over the years, and I've taken the liberty of recounting their experiences in this book. Their stories make good lessons. I changed the names of these people to protect their identities, even though most of them had good outcomes and probably wouldn't mind being mentioned!

After you read this book, I hope you put what you learn to work. I also hope you reach out to other sellers like yourself. Form your own mastermind and learn from each other. Being an Amazon seller is a constant process. You don't just get there and stop learning, because the business is always changing.

Most sellers, including myself, tend to forget why they started this business in the first place. They get sucked into selling and before they know it, they're working around the clock. Never forget why you started. Whatever you envisioned is entirely possible, but it doesn't happen by accident. You must intentionally build what you want, and that starts with having the right mindset.

How do you get that mindset? Let's talk about it in Chapter 1.

CHAPTER I

THE AMAZON SELLER MINDSET

"Absorb what is useful, discard what is not,
add what is uniquely your own."

—BRUCE LEE

Thinking like an Amazon seller didn't happen for me immediately. It happened somewhere between my career as a magician, selling products to strangers in the mall, and finally figuring out that I needed to change my mindset.

Israelis like to travel after they leave the military. Before starting college, I decided to visit the United States. Eager to get a head start in business—and following the traditional advice that I should sell something I'm passionate about—I ended up selling magic tricks in US malls. You may have seen these: kiosks where, as you walk past, a magician does some tricks to lure you in. Then they sell you the magic kit and a DVD that shows how to do the tricks yourself. I was a professional magician, not a professional salesperson, and it was a good gig for a while because it taught me the basics of marketing and selling.

When I started selling on Amazon, I thought about that earlier experience. Selling products that represented my own interests had worked well for me in the past, so I decided to try it again, this time selling magic kits online. But selling on Amazon was different, and I quickly realized that, when it came to product selection, following my passions wasn't the best strategy! I had to develop better methods for choosing products and identifying niches that made sense for the Amazon business model. This led to discovering and developing techniques that capitalized on the online platform, leveraging the tools and technology Amazon provides to sellers. Along the way, I fell in love with the business, the lifestyle, and everything that came with it. I became a private label seller, meaning I sell products under my own brand. And while I believe in my brand, and I stand behind every product, I found a new passion, one that captivated me, and eventually compelled me to write this book. That passion is selling on Amazon.

That passion didn't develop immediately. It took me a while to figure out the potential of the business. When I took my first Amazon seller's course and saw the money people were making, I was skeptical. I wasn't a believer, and my expectations were low. But the business model made sense to me, so I gave it a try. At the time, I had no idea how much that decision would change my life. Though selling on Amazon turned out to be my passion, your reasons for being an Amazon seller may be completely different, and that's OK. Everyone's "why" is unique and personal. Take the time to identify it. Knowing why you're doing this will motivate you to keep going and inspire you to do more.

Why Amazon Is a Seller's Best Friend

I promise to tell you more about my business, but first let's get back to the Amazon mindset because it will be critical to your success. When I sold magic tricks, I was attached to the product and to the customer. These were my customers, and I didn't want anyone getting between me and them. When I started to sell on Amazon, I felt the same way: my business, my products, my customers.

I had learned the importance of developing that close customer relationship when I was a kid. Every summer, I worked at my grandparents' electronics store in Tel Aviv. Their customers came back again and again to buy, and my grandparents knew them all by name. They gave them honest advice on what to buy, and their customers trusted them. They were even honest by telling them they didn't need the more expensive equipment if that was the case. I could see how this was the right way to treat customers and the best way to run a business.

They had dedicated many years to building a business that people trusted. So as long as I maintained those same principles, I could sell products there too. The customers trusted my grandparents and the business, and so they trusted me.

It's the same with Amazon. They have built a company that people trust, and so I had to learn to step away from the belief that I had created this successful business and attracted all these customers and instead give Amazon credit for that. Then I had to hold up my end of the deal by treating their customers right.

Thinking this way can be difficult for people who have always seen their customers as "their customers," but it's critically important. Instead of seeing Amazon as the competition or even the enemy, embrace the company for the amazing platform they've built. Recognizing and respecting these people as Amazon customers will put the company in a whole new light and make your selling experience so much better. Look at it from the customer's point of view. They don't know you. They don't know your product. Yet, they trust that when they purchase one of your products on Amazon, they will be satisfied, because Amazon has created that trust. These people are not your customers—they're Amazon customers, and that's a good thing.

SELLING OUTSIDE OF AMAZON | SELLING ON AMAZON

Amazon has done all the heavy lifting for sellers, and from there, we can launch our products, build a brand, and leverage what they've done to attract customers to our brands. It's like being invited to put your products in my grandparents' store: you don't have to worry about whether anyone will buy them—you know they will, because they're in my grandparents' store. The only difference is that Amazon has a lot more customers. Hundreds of millions of them.

Some sellers try to pull customers away from Amazon. They want their email addresses so they can market to them outside of the website, thinking they can do a better job and make more money. That's like taking a product out of my grandparents' store and trying to sell it from a kiosk at the mall. Instead of trying to compete against Amazon, make it your partner. Embrace it. Appreciate all it can give you—which is much more than you will get trying to sell products on your own. Amazon is not the enemy; it's actually the best partner you could ever ask for.

You Reap What You Sow

If you want to ride the Amazon wave, you need a well-designed company that supports all the challenges of running a successful online business—not just new product launches, but competing with other sellers' products, and scaling too. The more effort you put in upfront, the easier it will be to compete and scale your business, and the more you will profit—while working less!

As an Amazon seller, you don't make any money right away. You're working for yourself and not drawing a salary. During this time, you will have to support yourself with a regular job, live off savings, or rely on a partner to pay the bills for a while. As you begin to make sales, keep track of how much money you are making and how many hours you are working. Be honest with yourself about this. Track your time with an online timer or by writing it down. The hours can get away from you when you work for yourself, and during what you think was a full day of work, you may have actually worked just a few hours.

Keep tracking your seller's income and your time, and when you start earning a good "hourly wage," say $200 an hour, think about all the tasks you're doing. Your time is valuable now, so don't spend it on tasks that you could hire someone else to do for much less money than your own time is worth. Put a person, process, or system in place to do those tasks so you can focus your time on actions you can't delegate. If you don't do this, you are leaving a lot of money on the table. Instead of riding the Amazon wave, you'll burn out and drown.

Building your business this way will allow you a lot of freedoms. You'll be able to take time off without sales coming to a standstill. Your customers will be taken care of, and you'll continue to earn money. You won't have to be there every single day doing all the work yourself. Again, you have to build it that way, and that means putting in the effort upfront.

As you build your Amazon business, if all you do is keep launching more products, you'll just end up working more and more. That's a common trend—not only among Amazon sellers but all business owners. They believe that to make more money, they have to offer more products or services, which leads to more hours of work. Before you fall into that trap, take a step back and remind yourself of the reasons why you started the business. Keep that goal in mind to guide your decisions as your business grows.

Most people want some type of freedom. They want more time, more money, and more opportunities, which means more freedom from constraints on their time, money, and choices. Consider the freedoms you're after and focus not on what you want right now, but what you must do to have those freedoms. For me, this means always thinking long term and being willing to work hard right now so that I can have all the freedom I want in the future. I put in the time, the money, and the effort now, and am willing to make sacrifices because I can clearly see the end game and am willing to work for it.

This is the opposite of being an employee at someone else's company, where to make more money, you have to work harder and longer, and the hard work and longer hours never end. As an Amazon seller, your job gets easier—but only if you build your business in a way that makes it easier.

Becoming an Amazon Seller Must Be the End Goal

Being an Amazon seller is a commitment. It's a career. If you like your day job, then keep it. Don't be a seller. You may be able to launch a few products and still do your day job, but this is a business, not a hobby, and it should be your end goal. You are changing professions and going from employee to business owner. You will need to make it a full-time career, at least initially, in order to scale.

This is a major decision and one not to be taken lightly. Give it the serious thought it deserves and make sure you are prepared to take the leap. If you decide it's the right decision for your life, then go for it.

Get Comfortable with Being Uncomfortable

I invested $3,000 in my first product launch. That doesn't seem like a lot of money now but at the time, it was my life's savings. I doubled the amount in a short time, then doubled it again. Today, I might invest $30,000 or $50,000 in a shipment. That uncomfortable feeling I got back then—investing thousands of dollars into a business venture, with no promise of making a profit or even breaking even—never goes away. I know I'm not alone, because other sellers tell me they feel the same way. Aiden, a seller who participated in my coaching program, spent $1 million on restocking a single product. This is an eight-figure seller, and he told me he couldn't sleep at night because of it. I thought I might get to a point where putting that kind of money into inventory wouldn't bother me, but I was wrong. The uncomfortable feeling never went away, so I had to get comfortable with being uncomfortable. I had to grow.

As long as your business keeps growing, you have to grow with it. You have to change your ideas around what's acceptable risk. You have to be brave and willing to take chances. Not stupid chances, but carefully weighed ones, where you've done all the research and are confident that you're making the right choice—yet there are still no guarantees, and you could lose a lot of money.

I got over my fears by networking with people who were bigger sellers than I am. I read books about successes and failures written by heavy hitters in the business world. I learned about selling and about people and about myself. I had to grow as a person so I could lead my growing business.

I changed in my personal life too. Instead of sticking to my usual habits and routines, I looked for new experiences that could expand my horizons. Going different places, seeing new sights, and trying new things gave me experiences that made me think differently about the world and myself, and they also helped me see my business differently. Innovation and growth don't happen in a bubble or a vacuum. To have new thoughts and ideas, you have to expose yourself to new things. Like cliff jumping, ax throwing, and taking your infant son for a ride in a helicopter.

You don't really have to do those things, but you get the idea. I actually did those things, and more, and it changed my perceptions about my life and made me a better business owner. These events were organized by and for Amazon sellers. The experiences helped me connect with other sellers, probably due to the extreme emotional impact of engaging in activities so far beyond my usual day-to-day life. They took me out of my comfort zone and helped me manage the usual nerves and fear associated with business risks.

Whenever I spoke at an event, I'd have some anxiety. Whether I was flying to a new country and a new event or speaking at one I'd spoken at before, the crowd was always new, and I was always worried. It's like going up to a complete stranger to introduce yourself, except I was saying hello for the first time to hundreds—sometimes thousands—of strangers, all at once. They were all staring at me, hoping to glean some new magic that they could instill in their business. I still get anxious, but the more I do it, the easier it gets. I feel like I've grown as a person, and that's helped me grow my company.

I'm not suggesting you do anything drastic. Start small and see how far you can go with new experiences, meeting new people in new places. You've probably heard that a good exercise routine is to do a pushup every day. Once you're on the floor, you won't stop at just one pushup—you'll do 5, or 10, or 20. It's the same with expanding your experiences. Each step takes you further from your comfort zone, and gradually, you'll get used to venturing into uncharted territory.

Baby Steps

I attended an event for advanced sellers in Majorca, off the coast of Spain. The last day was all outdoors and included cliff jumping. Professional instructors supplied all the gear: helmets, harnesses, and so on. The first jump was just 3 meters high (for those of you who don't speak metric, that's almost 10 feet). The next one was 5 meters, then 10 meters. If they had told me to jump 10 meters the first time, I wouldn't have done it, but working up to it made the jump much easier. They showed us how to step off the cliff, and some people were hesitant. So we had to line up and go one at a time. When it was your turn, you had to jump without thinking about it. The instructors explained that the more you thought about it, the less likely you'd be to jump. If you stood there too long, you'd get shaky and scared.

It reminded me of the analysis paralysis that some sellers deal with before a product launch. They're so worried about what's going to happen, they never take that step off the cliff and into online selling.

Being an Amazon seller may seem brand new to you. Learning a lot of new skills can be daunting. But if you've ever held a job or owned a business, you have many skills that will transfer to your new role. When I was a magician, I specialized in card tricks. At 20 years old, I was introduced on a TV show as "the fastest hands in Israel." But no matter how much I wowed my audiences, I was always looking for ways to take the wow factor a step further and give them something totally unexpected. Believe it or not, that turned out to be a valuable skill in my selling business (and when you get to Chapter 4, you'll see why!).

I have a friend, Alex, who's a seller on Amazon. Alex also runs marathons. He has trained himself to focus for long periods of time so he can complete a marathon within a specified time. Lapses in focus can cost him time in the race. Alex's ability to focus, he tells me, has helped him become a better seller because he can focus on problems for long periods of time without getting distracted. And just like training for a marathon, he works toward the long-term goal of building a business instead of looking for quick tricks or hacks to shortcut his way to the top. Alex knows that strategy doesn't work on the road, and it doesn't work in business.

Just like Alex the marathon runner, you also have skills that you can use as an Amazon seller. No matter what you've done in previous jobs or what your life experiences have been, you have a lot of knowledge, wisdom, and expertise that you can transfer to your position as a business owner and online seller. You won't recognize these skills at first, but you will over time.

Be OK with not being able to do everything right away. Especially, get comfortable with not knowing everything. No one in this business knows everything—we are all still learning. You will learn and grow as your business grows.

Get Out of Your Element—
And Out of Your Own Way

Look outside yourself and outside of this industry for more learning and different ideas. Study other industries, read books from people in different kinds of companies, and listen to thought leaders in other businesses and from other parts of the world. These resources might spark something that helps you solve a problem or improve what you're currently doing in your Amazon business. Adopt the mindset of a person who is always curious, always learning, always open to new ideas.

If you can develop and maintain that mindset and give me a chance to prove to you the business you want is totally within your reach, you will be well on your way by the end of this book. The only thing missing is you, your commitment, and your willingness to do the necessary work to get there.

Do you have the Amazon mindset? I hope you do, but whenever you start to question why you're doing all this, please come back and read this chapter again. The Amazon mindset will keep you from getting distracted or lazy. It will keep your head in the game.

So, mindset. Do you have it? Yes—check! The next big question is this: "What the hell am I going to sell?"

Funny you asked! That's the subject of the next chapter.

BREAKERS

This is the first Breakers box in the book, and you'll see a new one at the end of each chapter. I call this a Breaker because it is both a break from the book to watch more content on a topic and a wave breaker, which is fitting for the theme of the book. Each Breakers box is a reminder to check out my Breakers site, tomerrabinovich.com/breakers—an online resource filled with free podcasts, full lectures, worksheets, tool recommendations, and other materials specific to the topics in each chapter. I'm always updating my Breakers site with fresh content, and I want you to have it so you can keep learning beyond this book.

You don't have to wait for the next Breakers box, though. Take a quick break right now and check out all the cool free stuff that's waiting for you at tomerrabinovich.com/breakers.

CHAPTER 2

THE PRODUCT TREE

"Someone is sitting in the shade today because
someone planted a tree a long time ago."

—WARREN BUFFETT

B efore you open an account on Seller Central, the backend platform to manage your sales on Amazon as a seller, you need a product. Before you launch your business, before you do anything, you have to find not just any product, but the right product to sell. You already know this because every Amazon seller book, course, and expert starts with the same message: find the right product.

Everyone says that, and every seller has the same question when they hear it:

"How the hell do I do that?"

Great question. There are a lot of products out there. Which one is right for you?

The traditional strategy for choosing a product is to narrow your search based on certain criteria like product category, price range, sales range, and weight. You find a product based on that criteria, you look for a supplier, and you prepare to launch your product. You make sure your page has beautiful-looking images, great copy, and an explainer video. Eventually, you launch.

But the product doesn't sell. You have no sales. Zero. Zip. Zilch. Nada. And you don't know why.

What's going on?

The launch is a bust because even though you did everything right, you still picked a bad product. You did what everyone else is doing, and that doesn't work anymore because Amazon has changed. It's more saturated. With everyone choosing products the same way, they're all choosing the same ones. And nothing you can do at this point will save your product.

That's the bad news. The good news is that you can do just about everything wrong, but if you pick a good product, people will still buy it. You can be a complete Amazon idiot or have only basic skills and little knowledge of more in-depth concepts like listing optimization or PPC, and still sell well. Having a good product increases your chances of success more than anything else you can do.

This is why product selection is number one when it comes to selling on Amazon. And why you have to use a different strategy than everyone else's to pick that product. Your strategy needs to be broad—not defined by narrow criteria. It has to be timeless—not something that works for six months. This isn't a theory. I didn't come to this conclusion in a dream. I figured out why the traditional method for choosing products doesn't work anymore, tried something new, tested it extensively, and proved that it works not just in my own business, but it has also worked hundreds of times for my students. It also happens to make sense.

BSR, SBA, FBM, and FBA—and Why They Matter

Before I tell you the details of my strategy, let's cover some basic acronyms that you may or may not be familiar with. If you already know what BSR,

SBA (AMZ), FBM, and FBA mean, then feel free to skip these sections and go straight to "A Different Strategy."

BSR

Every product category has a BSR, or best seller rank, and every product's ranking within its category appears on the product's listing. To see what I'm talking about, open any listing and scroll down to the section titled "Product Information." You'll see an entry called best seller rank and the ranking of the product in one or more categories. If a product is ranked number one in the electronics category, that means that right now, more units of that product are being sold than any other products in the electronics category. The lower the BSR, the more sales, and the better for the seller.

Some categories have many more products than others, so a number one BSR in a category with few competitors could denote hundreds of sales per day, whereas a number one BSR in a category with many competing products could denote thousands of sales per day. However, Amazon does not show you how many units of an item have been sold or are currently being sold. Again, a product with a number one BSR may seem like a hot item, but it could be one of only a few products in the category, with few sales—just more than any of its competitors.

A product's BSR one day can represent 10 sales, and another day, it can represent 100 sales. Take for example a product in the *toys* category. During the holiday season, having a number 100 BSR in the *toys* category represents many sales, because people buy a lot of toys as gifts for their kids during this time. But a number 100 BSR in the toys category in January will mean much fewer sales, because fewer toys are purchased after the holidays.

Though category sales information isn't available on Amazon, you can find out how many units are sold in any category with tools made specifically for sellers. Visit my Breakers site, where you'll find a list of tools

I recommend. Some of these tools are free, and others come with a fee. With this information, you can estimate how many units of a product are selling, based on that product's BSR, and once you have a product listed, you can get an even better idea of how many units your competitors are selling by comparing your BSR with theirs.

When you list a product, you choose a main category. For books, the main category is (surprise!) *books*. Within that category are many subcategories that you can assign to your book product. When your product reaches the number one BSR spot in a category or subcategory, Amazon attaches a best seller badge to your listing for that category/subcategory. Another example of categories and subcategories are babies and baby monitors. You might have the top-selling baby monitor and get a best seller badge for that subcategory, yet your product is only the 1,000th bestselling baby product.

You want to be as clear as possible about the product's categories. Don't try to manipulate the system. To make it easy for people to find your product, you have to make it easy for Amazon to identify your product. The platform learns your product by only a few criteria: the listing title, the bullet points, the categories, and the sales you're generating from different keywords. It doesn't scan your images to learn about your product, so if you associate misleading categories to it, Amazon will have a more difficult time showing your product to the people who are looking for it—potential customers. You won't get properly ranked for your keywords, and the people you're trying to attract may never even find your product.

BSR is based on sales. That's it. Amazon tracks sales at regular intervals and updates the BSR, so you may have a number one BSR and drop to 100 the next day. Hold onto that thought for a few minutes while I tell you about SBA, FBM, and FBA. We'll get back to BSR and how you can use it to drive your product selection strategy in just a few paragraphs.

SBA (AMZ)

Your products can get to customers three different ways. Most major brands go with SBA, or "sold by Amazon." Companies sell their products to Amazon and Amazon sells them to the customer. SBA is also referred to as AMZ, which of course stands for Amazon.

SBA (AMZ) doesn't apply to private label sellers—you just need to know what it is and how it impacts your product selection strategy. For the rest of this book, I'll use the acronym AMZ in place of SBA, as it's more commonly used among sellers.

FBM

With the second option, FBM or "fulfilled by merchant," you store your products in-house (in your garage, for example) or at a warehouse and ship them yourself. With this model, however, Amazon Prime customers don't qualify for Prime (free) delivery. They have to pay for shipping. This is a general rule, but there are exceptions. For example, a seller can have product shipped to their home and still qualify for FBA shipping (described below), but they must guarantee two-day shipping. The process is a bit more complicated, and if you choose to use this method, I recommend you research the topic more fully before committing to it.

FBA

Alternatively, you can go with the "sold by FBA" method, or "fulfilled by Amazon." This means that you put your products in an Amazon warehouse, and they take care of the storage and shipping the product to the customer. This is the way most private label sellers sell their products, and the approach we will use throughout the book.

A Different Strategy

Now that you understand best seller rank and best seller badge, let's look at the traditional product selection strategy. This is the typical guidance that many sellers follow:

- Select a product that sells for between $15 and $60.
- Select a product with a BSR range between 2,000 and 5,000. The range varies between product categories, but the idea is that you are selecting a product that's popular enough for you to sell a lot of units, but not so popular that you have a lot of competition.
- Select a product that is just one piece, small, and weighs two pounds or less; isn't complex or electronic; is easy to package; and doesn't require FDA approval.
- Select a product where, if you do a search for it, every competitor on the first results page has less than 1,000 reviews.
- The keywords for the product need to have a high search volume on Amazon (even though I'm not recommending this strategy, you can visit my Breakers site for information on tools that provide this information).

Does this sound like what you've been hearing the past couple of years? At one time, this strategy may have guided you to that one "perfect product." It doesn't work anymore. If you use this strategy to select a good product today, it will be saturated by the time you bring it to market, because so many other sellers are using the same approach, and they're going to land on the same product.

AT ONE TIME, THIS STRATEGY MAY HAVE GUIDED YOU TO THAT ONE "PERFECT PRODUCT." IT DOESN'T WORK ANYMORE.

I don't follow that strategy, and I don't teach it. There's a better way—a strategy that finds products that no one else has found. Products that sell.

When it comes to product selection, I don't look for reasons to eliminate products; I look for reasons to sell them. I don't disqualify them; I qualify them. In other words, I look for everything those other sellers are trying to avoid.

I go for cheap products—and expensive ones. Bulky products that are hard to package and heavy ones that are hard to ship. I go for products that are complex, complicated, regulated, and that may need FDA approval. I go for other products too. My goal is to find products that customers want, that other sellers don't want to sell, and that won't have a lot of competition long term.

Dealing with these types of products may seem like a lot of work, and it is. Here's the thing, though: no matter how much work it takes to figure out the details of sourcing, packaging, shipping, and selling a product, I only have to figure it out one time. Once I do that, I'm golden. I can sell that product over and over again. So I don't look at the work as a challenge—I see it as barriers to the competition. A barrier I am willing to deal with, while they are not.

Should you choose your first product this way? Probably not. You might get discouraged. Feel free to go the traditional route for your first product or several products, while you're learning the business. Once you're comfortable selling on Amazon, challenge yourself to do the work it takes to sell those products that no one else is selling.

Sellers tend to avoid products that are too big, too expensive, and too complicated, and they also avoid products that turn up a lot of AMZ sellers on the first page of a search. For example, type "yoga mat" into the search bar on Amazon. Many yoga mats appear on the first page, and many of them have thousands of reviews. These are typically AMZ products and Amazon is giving them preference on their site, so naturally, more people see them, buy them, and leave reviews for them. This causes a snowball effect, with even more people seeing, buying, and leaving reviews for them. Products like this tend to scare off sellers who think, "How can I compete with a yoga mat that has 60,000 reviews?" But you can, and I will show you how.

This all goes back to my methodology for selecting products: don't look for reasons to disqualify a product; look for reasons to select it. Instead of looking for negatives, seek out positives. This will not only guide you toward better product selection, but it will also make the work a lot more enjoyable.

I have other strategies for selecting products, too, and I'm going to step you through all of them in this chapter.

The Restaurant Theory

Say I'm going to open a restaurant—no, a coffee shop: Tomer's Coffee. I'm thinking of opening this shop in a busy downtown location. There's a Starbucks on every corner, and they're all doing well. So I know that a major coffee shop like Starbucks can succeed in this location, but there are no smaller, locally owned coffee businesses on the street.

Is this a good location for Tomer's Coffee?

What do you think, yes or no?

Maybe?

Maybe, but maybe not. People are already coming to this part of town for coffee, so I may be able to grab a small piece of the pie—the foot traffic that's being driven by those larger coffee shops. But if someone comes to the area specifically for a Starbucks coffee, they will likely pass up my little shop and head to Starbucks. Then again, if I were willing to differentiate Tomer's Coffee with a lot of marketing and advertising dollars, this location could pay off.

Here's a second scenario: I want to open a pizza place. I'm looking at a location where there are a lot of restaurants, but no pizza shops. Is this a good location?

Again, what do you think? Yes...or no?

The truth is, I don't know. You could argue that the locale is already attracting people who want to eat, which would be good for my pizza place. On the other hand, maybe the people visiting the area don't like pizza, or are seeking healthier options. I would have to invest in marketing research to learn more. If I discovered that a pizza place would do well in the area, then I would have to invest in advertising to let people know that they had a new restaurant option in the area: Tomer's Pizza.

The bottom line for these two scenarios is that I don't know if opening Tomer's Coffee or Tomer's Pizza will work in these locations. People could be flocking to the first location because they like Starbucks, not because they're big coffee drinkers. They could be eating in the second location because they happen to like what's offered there now, and they have no taste for pizza (hard to imagine, but you never know). If I'm going to invest my time and money in a café or a restaurant, I want a sure thing.

The third scenario is for a place called Tomer's Burgers. Again, the location is home to many restaurants, including a Burger King, a McDonald's, and an In-N-Out Burger. But unlike the coffee scenario and the pizza scenario, this location has other small, locally owned burger joints that aren't part of a restaurant chain. Some have been there for a few years and others are fairly new. Most of them seem to be doing very well. In fact, every time I drive down that street, I notice lines out the door at some of these places. What do you think about this location for a Tomer's Burgers?

Yes? No?

Don't be afraid to answer. There's no one here but you and me!

Here's my answer: I'd need to do a little more research to see how well the smaller burger joints are doing. If they're all staying very busy, then there's room for Tomer's Burgers. If some of the new ones aren't catching on, or the older ones are losing business, then that tells me the market is saturated in that area and there is no room for Tomer's Burgers. I need to look for another location.

What do coffee, pizza, and burgers have to do with online selling? I'm glad you asked, because the answer is everything.

Low-Hanging Fruit

To explain the Low-Hanging Fruit product selection approach, let's look at the coffee shop example again. If I open Tomer's Coffee, I would not be competing against Starbucks. My direct competitors would be other small, privately owned coffee shops. However, the fact that Starbucks exists tells me that a lot of people visit coffee shops. That's a good thing for Tomer's Coffee.

It's the same with Low-Hanging Fruit on Amazon. When I select products with this method, I look for other FBA products just like mine. That's my competition. And if there's an AMZ product just like it, that's not necessarily a bad thing. This tells me that a lot of people are buying this type of product. It's a big pie—maybe big enough for me to get a little slice. Let's say the competing FBA products are making $200,000 a month combined, and the AMZ product is making $1 million a month. I'm not going head-to-head with Starbucks here, but I could take a little slice of the pie.

The issue with Tomer's Coffee is that there are no small players, and that's why it's not a good option.

In the restaurant theory example, you can see that Starbucks and In-N-Out Burger are not my competition. Likewise, AMZ products aren't my competitors either. But they are like bait that attracts customers to a certain place—and that's the place that I want to be. But only if there are two other types of sellers in that same market, who are past the launch phase and have been selling for at least 100 days: (1) those with a low number of reviews that are doing well (selling a lot of product) and (2) those with a lot of reviews that are doing even better. If those two types of sellers are in that market, there is still room for Tomer's Restaurant. The newer FBA products with few reviews show me that I can enter the market and start selling very quickly, while the long-term products show me that, over time, I can get to where they are. And since I have the advantage of a better product and listing, I could get to where they are quickly.

This is not what most sellers do. They see a product with many AMZ sellers and thousands of reviews, and immediately click away in search of a different product. Not me. I zero in for a closer look. I find a product with a number of FBA sellers, some who have been on Amazon for a while and others who are new. They are all getting reviews and based on BSR, they are getting sales, some of the sellers have been on Amazon for a while and a few that are new. I other words, I'm looking for reasons to qualify the product and not to disqualify it.

The most important criteria for choosing Low-Hanging Fruit is revenue per month. I figure that out by looking at the BSR to figure out the sales per month and multiplying the sales by the price. That gives me the monthly revenue for the product.

If you are just starting out or you're doing less than a million a year in sales, your goal should be to launch products that will generate at least

$10,000 a month in sales within the first year. You may be able to get to that figure with a product in as little as three months, or it could take longer. Focus on products that will continue to generate that kind of revenue every month. That equals 20 to 50 percent profit in your pocket—a nice steady income, especially when you have multiple products delivering these results.

When you're identifying the Low-Hanging Fruit, look for competing FBA products with fewer than 350 reviews. If the competition has thousands of reviews, yours won't stand out enough to get the attention it needs to make sales.

Let's say you have an idea for a product that you'd like to sell. Alternatively, you can use tools (and do the math) to filter for products that are making $10,000 or more in revenue every month. In this example, I decided to research yoga mats. By the way, there are more products on Amazon besides yoga mats, obviously, but I like this example because most people know what they are, and they know the general price range.

To decide whether this is good Low-Hanging Fruit, I type "yoga mat" into the search bar on Amazon. I use a tool to scan the first page of results to see the BSR information and monthly revenue for all the products on that page. I'm looking for at least two FBA products that have been online for more than 100 days to make sure they aren't still in their launch phase, have fewer than 350 reviews, and are doing more than $10,000 a month. This tells me that I can get to that level in revenue with my product within a year, and more likely within three to six months, because again, I will have a six-star review product and an optimized listing.

I make sure there are at least two products that meet this criteria, to avoid making an assumption based on one product that succeeded due to some fluke that I'm not aware of, and if there are more than two, that's even better. Two is just the minimum. There may also be AMZ and FBM products, or FBA products with thousands of reviews, but as long as there are at least two products that meet my criteria, I'm going to continue the qualification process. Remember that we're qualifying products, not disqualifying them.

Getting to a couple hundred reviews with a Low-Hanging Fruit product will take a few months. So you need a strategy for generating revenue in the meantime. While you're still looking at that first page of results, look for two additional products that are also FBA, have been on Amazon for more than 100 days, have fewer than 100 reviews, and are generating at least $2,000 in sales per month. That shows me that even with just a few reviews, I can start generating revenue. From there, my organic sales via PPC or through customer searches will begin to pick up and increase my sales to $10,000 in a reasonable amount of time.

These numbers—100 days, 350 reviews, $10,000 per month—are subjective. They work for many sellers, but your figures may vary based on what you're comfortable with, and your goals. If you want to look at products with fewer than 20 reviews and regular sales of $2,000, even after many months of selling, that's fine if it gets you to your goals. Sellers who are already doing $1 million or more a year may want to increase these numbers, looking at products with fewer than 1,000 reviews that are doing $50,000 in monthly sales. Also consider that for more expensive products, you might want to lower the number of reviews you're after.

These are US numbers, and if you're selling on Amazon's UK, Canada, or any other Amazon marketplace, you'll want to adjust them and go with what makes sense for your business. The bottom line is that you should be comfortable with the investment of time and money you put into the launch and the ongoing sales, with the probable initial monthly revenue, and the potential to scale. You should be looking to move into a higher tier of sales with the product. If that possibility isn't strong (or doesn't exist), then don't waste your time on the product.

Finally, I do disqualify certain products in the Low-Hanging Fruit research process, but only if the market is saturated. This means there are so many sellers offering the product that there's no room for me. To check whether the market's saturated, again, I look at all the products on that first results page.

Say I find products that meet my criteria. But I also find products with a lot of reviews and few sales; then I know that those products have been out there a while, and though they had good sales initially, those sales are dropping off either due to lack of demand or to increased competition. Before making a final decision, I might click through several pages to see if this is a problem. If it is, I move on to another product.

Summary of the Low-Hanging Fruit Method

▶ Two products over 100 days on Amazon, selling through FBA, under 350 reviews, and generating over $10,000 in monthly revenue

▶ Two additional products over 100 days on Amazon, selling through FBA, under 100 reviews, and generating over $2,000 in monthly revenue

▶ Make sure the market is not saturated: you don't see products that have thousands of reviews, with a 4.5-star rating or higher, good listings, and the products are not making over $10,000 in monthly revenue. When you see this, you want to skip the product because it's already saturated.

▶ These numbers are adjustable with whatever you feel comfortable with. The point is that you're looking for two sets of products, one for when you launch and the other for when you scale. When you launch, you just want to get a few reviews to start seeing organic sales. I feel comfortable with 100 reviews; you might feel comfortable with 20 or 200. And instead of just getting to $10,000 a month, you might want to reach $50,000 or $100,000 a month, so that should be your higher tier.

The Low-Hanging Fruit method may be the most valuable piece of information that you get out of this book. That's not to say the rest of it isn't worth reading, but if you learn just this, you can do very well as an Amazon seller. So if you don't understand how this works, go back and reread the section. I promise you—it will pay off!

Apples to Apples

Many big sellers—those in the seven-figure range—don't sell as many different products as you might think. More often, they have identified a great-selling product, optimized the product and the listing, and then sold more products that are just like it. Their products may come in different colors, sizes, and materials, but they're basically the same product. Those sellers are experts in just a few product niches—maybe just one— but they've figured out how to dominate that market. That's how you build a big business on Amazon. Not by launching a bunch of different products in many markets that you don't fully understand, but by being successful with one product and launching more of it. This is the Apples-to-Apples approach, and it should be your next step after launching several Low-Hanging Fruit products.

If you have a good yoga mat launch, why not sell more yoga mats? If your yoga mat is black, for example, you could launch red mats, blue mats, and multicolored mats. If your yoga mat is the standard size, what about launching a longer one, or a wider one? You could launch an extra-thick yoga mat for people who need extra cushioning, or a mat with a nonstick backing for people with slippery floors. As long as you're still targeting the same general audience, you have a lot of options.

Some sellers have a good Low-Hanging Fruit launch, and they immediately look for complementary products to sell. They sell a lot of yoga mats, so they decide to sell yoga blocks, yoga balls, or yoga towels too. The problem with this approach is that a yoga block is not a yoga mat. It's a completely different product. The customer may be the same, sure, but everything else is different, so you'll need different keywords, different images, and probably a different supplier. That's a lot of work—especially when you've just done a lot of work to launch your yoga mats.

Launching new products with the Apples-to-Apples method saves a lot of time and research. You already know the right keywords and have the pay-per-click piece figured out. It may still work as-is, or you may just need to tweak it. You may have to update your images. The point is, you're not starting from scratch. You might not even need to find a new supplier or figure out the packaging and shipping again either. You've already done all that work, so why not use what you know to launch and sell more products?

Another huge benefit to launching this way is that you can fill containers with the new products. Again, I'll tell you more about shipping in Chapter 9, but for now, you should know that when you ship by sea, you have to fill a container with your own products or consolidate them with other sellers' products. Filling a container with your own products is easier, and it's easier to fill a container coming from the same supplier and leaving from the same port than trying to fill one with products from multiple suppliers. This way, you have just one supplier providing you with black yoga mats, red yoga mats, and green yoga mats, and they're all leaving from the same port, in the same container.

Big sellers often use this strategy to save time and money, and to dominate searches on Amazon. Think of this strategy like the branches of a tree with many types of apples—red ones, green ones, and yellow ones. I call this strategy Apples to Apples because you're selling many types of apples, but they're still all apples, and it's easier to sell many apples than it is to sell apples and oranges. Or bananas, for that matter.

At the same time, you probably want to expand your product line. This is where looking at yoga blocks, balls, and towels makes sense. You can build a brand—your private label—this way, while taking advantage of Amazon's "frequently bought together" feature. Go wide with more products within your brand, and use the Apples-to-Apples method to go deep, building a "root system" of more of the same products.

Amazon Wants You to Build a Brand

Amazon wants sellers to do well. They want your customers to keep buying from you, whether they're buying similar products (wide) or more of the same product (deep). They want you to keep targeting the same market with your brand. They want you to trademark your brand, get on Amazon's Brand Registry, and build a storefront for your brand. Being in the Brand Registry opens a lot of doors on Amazon, too, like Brand Analytics, which gives you a lot of information about your products and how they're performing; and Project Zero and Transparency by Amazon, which help you protect your products from hijackers and other people who try to take over your listings.

If Amazon didn't want you to build a private label brand, why would they give you all these great tools to do it? Of course, they want you to sell your products on their site and using their tools embeds you in the platform. But there is no downside, because trying to create all these tools on your own—and attracting the volume of buyers to your site that Amazon attracts every day—is probably not even possible.

You don't have to sell similar products to just one market. You can sell very disparate products—say, yoga mats and electric drills. You just won't be able to build a brand around those products or take advantage of the cross-selling opportunities that are available, because the same customer is not interested in buying both from you. Building a brand allows you to scale your business faster and with less effort.

Generally speaking, Apples-to-Apples product selection works very well, but you want to avoid offering "too much of a good thing." Having a dozen different-colored yoga mats may work well, but having 25 different colors and patterns may actually hurt your sales. You're giving your customer too many options and instead of trying to decide, they may just click away to another yoga mat page. You also have to deal with all those colors on the backend too—the inventory. What if your black mats are selling like hotcakes, but no one's buying the pink ones? Now you're stuck with a bunch of pink mats. To find out how many choices to offer, take a look at what your competitors are doing. See if they're selling other colors, sizes, and materials, the types of colors, sizes, and materials they're selling, and how many choices they're offering. What complementary products have they added to their initial offering to build out their brand?

Look at what they're doing and what's working. How are their sales on these items?

Once you decide which variations of your product to offer, you have another dilemma. You're probably asking yourself right now, at this very minute:

"OK Tomer, you've convinced me. I'm going deep! Sooooo do I need a new listing for each variation of my product? Or can I add them to my existing page?"

Let's talk about the advantages of creating a new listing versus adding the variations to your existing listing. When you create a new listing for each variation, each listing will contain just one variation of the product, and all the listings will appear in the search results. So, five variations, for example, each one has just one color yoga mat, and all five listings show up in the search results. On the other hand, if you put all the variations in one listing, then just one listing shows up in the search results, but your customer can see them all by clicking on just that one listing instead of searching through many listings.

Another advantage to including all the variations in one listing is that all the reviews are counted together. So if you have 100 reviews for the black yoga mat and you add a red yoga mat to the listing, you automatically have 100 reviews for your red yoga mat too. Likewise, the sales from every product (variation) on a listing is combined to calculate the BSR. If you sell 100 black yoga mats and 100 green ones, Amazon counts that as 200 sales—getting you closer to that best seller badge in your subcategory.

There is a third option: create a new listing for each variation, and also add the variations to your existing listing. My preference is to put variations under only one listing, and I have a theory that Amazon prefers this, too, because they don't want search results to show many listings of all the different variations of what is essentially the same product.

However, there is no one best way to do this for all products, and you'll figure out the best way for your product by trial and error. To save time and sell more faster, again, look at what your competitors are doing in the same market. Look at what they do, and how it affects their sales. Find out which method is giving the best results and try a similar approach with your listings.

Expand Your Product Line
to Mitigate Risk

A seller I know, Audrey, was selling Chinese lanterns. These are the paper lanterns that you put candles in and use as decorations for weddings and other events. The candles illuminate the lanterns from within, creating a colorful display. Audrey went wide and deep with her Chinese lanterns. It was her only product, and she offered them in every color, size, style, and quantity imaginable. Audrey had lanterns for every occasion, and she dominated the market, doing $200,000 a month in Chinese lanterns. Then one day someone decided that paper lanterns with candles inside were a fire hazard, and one by one, states in the US stopped allowing them to be sold. At some point, Amazon decided they didn't want to take on the fire hazard risk, either, so they stopped allowing people to sell them via FBA. Audrey, with her booming business that relied on just one product, went from $200K a month to zero—and was stuck having to get rid of a lot of unsold lanterns.

Going deep makes a lot of sense and can be very lucrative, but it can also be risky. No matter how successful you are by going deep with a product, mitigate the risk by continuously going wide by researching new products and launching new products.

To review: There is very little effort involved in Apples-to-Apples product selection other than looking at other sellers to see what's working for them. Research the competition. See what kinds of products they're selling. What colors of the product are they selling? What sizes? You'll be able to get Apples-to-Apples products in different colors and sizes from your current supplier (which I'll describe in plenty of detail in Chapter 5), and the packaging and shipping will be the same. Don't be surprised if your variations of a product end up outselling the original product. That's a bonus, but it would never happen if you didn't try the Apples-to-Apples method.

Summary of the Apples-to-Apples Method

▶ Launch Low-Hanging Fruit products first.
▶ Once you get a hit with a product, launch more of the same of that product: colors/sizes/quantities/etc., based mainly on what is already working for the competition.
▶ At the same time, look for your next "different" product; for example, if your product is a yoga mat, then look at yoga balls, yoga blocks, etc.

It's best to follow Low-Hanging Fruit with Apples to Apples, but my next product selection method doesn't follow any particular order. You can try this approach anytime at all. Get ready to take a bite out of the Big Apple.

The Big Apple

Big Apples are products that are in an already saturated niche. Think bath bombs (who knew so many people took baths?), yoga balls, and Bluetooth headphones. Everybody seems to have a slice of these Big Apples—a product in these markets—so it doesn't make sense to even try to compete, right? Not exactly. Because the audience for these products is huge.

When there is a big demand for a product—any product—more companies start offering that product. Take McDonald's for example, which was one of the first fast-food restaurant chains. Once they opened their doors and people got a taste for fast food, the demand grew, and fast-food restaurants started popping up everywhere. Sure, there were plenty of McDonald's restaurants, but there were also fast-food places that targeted different audiences. Some featured chicken instead of burgers, while others focused on tacos or deli-style sandwiches. So while they were, and still are, capitalizing on the popularity that started decades ago, each fast-food restaurant chain has a different offering that appeals to a particular audience. Every chain found its niche.

This happens with every high-demand product. When cell phones first came out, they all looked very similar (remember the Blackberry?). Now you can buy a smartphone in every color, style, and size imaginable for every audience imaginable. Smartphones for adults, for kids, for seniors. But when the original cell, and later the smartphone, was introduced, there weren't that many different types. It wasn't until the demand grew that companies began offering a variety to suit every audience.

> **THIS IS WHY AMAZON WILL NEVER GET SATURATED.**
> **WHEN A NICHE BECOMES SATURATED, THERE ARE**
> **NEW OPPORTUNITIES IN NEW SUB-NICHES.**

Which brings us to bath bombs. When bath bombs first came out, the target audience was women. But kids liked them, and so did men, and as the demand grew, bath bomb makers started making bath bombs designed especially for these markets. If only a small number of men or children liked them, manufacturers wouldn't have bothered. The key is that the demand within each of these niche markets was great enough to warrant introducing a new product. The greater the demand for a product, the more niches (and sub-niches) open up for that product.

Do you see where I'm going with this? That's right. You're going to identify a product that's in high demand, and you're going to put a dent in it. You're going to take a bite out of the Big Apple—not by entering someone else's niche, but by carving one out all for yourself.

The great thing about the Big Apple method is that you don't do all the hard work of launching a new product that isn't already in high demand. The buyers are out there, obviously. You just have to carve that niche, and you do it with branding.

"Branding" is a word that confuses some people. They don't quite know how to describe it—but they know it when they see it. Let me tell you what I mean by branding: it's simply narrowing down a bigger audience. With branding, rather than competing with everyone else for Low-Hanging Fruit, you're competing with no one because you have your own targeted niche.

When you decide to build a brand, and brand your products, you're making a decision to sell to a certain audience, which means you are also making the decision to not sell to other people. You're narrowing your audience. That may sound counterintuitive to someone who wants to sell more products, but done right, your brand will attract people who may have purchased somewhere else, they'll be more likely to buy from you again, and they'll be more likely to buy other products within your brand. You won't have to continuously be searching for new customers as much, because you'll develop a dedicated following of customers. And the best way to do this is by taking a bite out of a Big Apple—creating that niche in a saturated market.

Take bath bombs, for instance. When I first looked into selling bath bombs, I saw that the market was supersaturated. So saturated, that many sellers weren't doing well. But what if I could differentiate my bath bombs to attract an underserved audience? And who might that audience be?

To find out, I had to do some research. Before I explain the process, remember that Amazon is a big search engine. The only products that will ever sell on Amazon are products that people are searching for with that search engine. So if you introduce a brand-new product on Amazon, since no one's searching for it, no one will ever buy it. Those types of products make more sense for Kickstarter campaigns.

Only sell products on Amazon that people are already searching for on Amazon. Your product may be "new" in the sense that no one is selling that exact product, but if people are still searching for something just like it, then you can sell it—even if no one else is selling it yet. A good example is bath bombs for men. There are a lot of bath bombs on Amazon, but before there were bath bombs for men, people were searching for that particular item. They knew they could buy bath bombs for women on the site, so why not bath bombs for men? They'd type a phrase into the search bar, but no one had the product for sale. Since the demand exists, you would know there's a market for bath bombs for men and it makes sense to sell them.

One way to see what people are searching for is by typing a word or phrase into the search bar and looking at how Amazon autocompletes it. In this case, typing "bath bombs for" (plus the spacebar) may show auto-completion choices like "bath bombs for seniors," "bath bombs for women," "bath bombs for kids," and of course, "bath bombs for men." That tells you immediately that people are searching for those products.

In that example, you can see how autocompletion showed you a variety of markets (or target audiences) for bath bombs. It can also show you a variety of uses, such as "bath bombs for big bathtubs." Click through each autocompleted phrase to see what shows up. You may be surprised by the results.

In another example, type "Bluetooth headphones for." The autocompletion might show something strange like "Bluetooth headphones for sleep," but when you click into the results, you'll see things like face masks with built-in headphones that help people fall asleep. This is an example of another use for a product that you may not have considered.

In addition to autocompletion, tools like Brand Analytics can also help you identify new audiences and new uses for your product, and opportunities for narrowing your niche with branding. In Brand Analytics, typing in "bath bombs" will display all the keywords people are typing into the search bar along with "bath bombs." You can also use tools to see the volume of searches for those terms, or keywords.

This is how I figured out the different types of bath bombs that people wanted to buy. By looking at the autocomplete options, I could identify the various bath bomb audiences and uses. Typing "bath bombs" into the search bar first returned "bath bombs for women," which is a huge market. I wanted a smaller audience, such as the next autocomplete entry: "bath bombs for kids." This was obviously a much smaller niche than just "bath bombs" or "bath bombs for women." The bombs were different too. The colors were different. Some had surprises inside, such as small toys. The listing, including the images and the copy, differentiated these bath bombs from the typical ones. They were obviously made for kids.

Big brands attract anyone because of the name recognition. You can't compete with them head-on, but you can get a slice of that Big Apple by differentiating your product and listing to target a smaller, niche market. And you don't need a big brand name to do it. A seller who knows their customer well and can personalize the product to speak to a specific market can have great success with this method. So can a confident seller willing to take the time to figure out exactly what their target customer wants. A bonus for the seller willing to take a bite of the Big Apple is this: customers will pay a little more for your differentiated product than they would for a product on a more generic listing because they feel that it speaks to them and their needs.

You may not find a slice of the Big Apple to target on your first try. Say bath bombs for kids is also saturated; then what? Well, look at what else the search engine tells you: "bath bombs for men," maybe? Take a look at the products that appear and see how sellers differentiate those products for that market. They might have bath bombs that look like baseballs, or smell like Scotch. With a little imagination, the possibilities are endless. The key is, if it shows up as an autocomplete option in the search bar, people are searching for it. That product has an audience!

Again, in your research, look at the competition. See how they're doing with bath bombs for kids and for men. And if there are very few sellers—or no sellers at all—don't be discouraged. If customers are searching for it, there's a market and a demand. So look at what people are searching for on Amazon and decide whether it makes sense for you to sell it.

Even though the Big Apple method takes some time to establish, if you do it well, you may be able to charge a higher price, have bigger margins, and a higher ROI—while having few or no competitors—for many years to come.

New sellers often lament, "I can't sell on Amazon—it's too saturated. There's no room for my product!" By now, you can see the problem with the disqualifying product selection method that so many sellers use. With the three methods above, you could find dozens of fresh product opportunities in just a few hours of research.

One Tree, Many Leaves

Have you ever searched for a product on Amazon, and the listing showed many, many variations of that product? Think towels, bathrobes, and bed sheets. Just like the many colors and sizes of leaves on a tree, these products come in a lot of different colors and sizes.

When I look for product opportunities, I prefer products with no more than three to five variations on the same listing. The more variations you have, the more stock you have to order, and you don't always know which variation will be the most popular. It can get complicated quickly and can be especially difficult to launch. However, I've seen and consulted many sellers who do this successfully. I believe the key is to choose products carefully and be willing to invest the time and money necessary to make it work.

Before you try this method, get a feel for the opportunities. A good example is bed sheets. Search "bed sheets" on Amazon and you'll see that in just one listing, you have a number of sizes and colors. These are the two standard variations of many products. But with just those two sellers, you can get to more than a hundred variations, or different combinations of color and size, on just one listing. It's a lot to manage. The upside is that selling just one of each combination every day—say, 100 individual sales—boosts your sales and your BSR.

My advice is that if you want to go with this product selection method, first sell only this product, or maybe two or three products at the very most. Whatever you can reasonably handle. Don't have multiple launches and multiple different products. I know eight-figure sellers who rely solely on this method, with just a few listings. It can be done.

Second, if you're going to do this, you have to offer many variations. That's what your competitors are doing, and you won't match their sales with just a few options on your listing. You won't get the cumulative reviews or the BSR ranking either.

Think about how people shop. If a buyer searches "gray bed sheets," the first listing they click on won't have only gray sheets; it will have many variations—gray sheets, blue sheets, red sheets, maybe even variations of gray (light gray, blue-gray, etc.). That customer is not going to click away to check out another listing. They're going to find what they need on that first listing. By the way, that's the listing with many variations, a great BSR, and thousands of reviews. Of course they're going to click on it.

Start with the most popular variations, then add more. Tools are available that allow you to divide the reviews by variation, so you can find out which ones are getting the highest and most reviews, and which ones are getting the lowest and fewest.

So, to review: this method works if you can commit the time, money, and effort to managing all the variations, which means you will have fewer product launches. If it works out for you over time, then just one listing with 10 variations can be much easier to manage than 10 listings for 10 different products.

It also only works if you maintain all—or at the very least, many of—the variations. If you don't do it this way, good luck. You're going to get overwhelmed with the work and buried by the competition.

By the way, I'm not advocating for this method. It's a lot of work initially, but done well, with the right product, it may actually be easier than managing multiple launches. Mostly, I want you to understand the commitment that's involved if you decide to launch a product that other sellers are selling with many variations. So even if you use one of the other methods I've proposed in this book, before you settle on a product, make sure it isn't offered in a hundred different colors, sizes, patterns, and materials by other sellers.

Finally, if you choose the One Tree, Many Leaves method, understand the risk. You are putting all your eggs in one basket and if it fails, you're out of business. On the other hand, with several products and launches, you can manage the risk. If a product fails, you still have the others to tide you over until you find a replacement.

The difference between this method and the Apples-to-Apples method is that you're not launching just one or two variations and only expanding to more if it's working. Your entire strategy here is to launch dozens of variations of a product. Basically, it's a different type of product and launch that most sellers stay away from—which is exactly why you should pay close attention to it.

One Tree, Many Leaves works best for seasoned sellers who have had a number of successful launches and understand Amazon selling very well. It's not for beginners.

One Tree, Many Leaves Method Summary

- ▶ Get some experience with other products and launches within your brand first.
- ▶ Make sure you have the cash flow required for many variations of a new product.
- ▶ Look at products in your niche with at least 10 to 15 variations.
- ▶ See if there's an opportunity there in terms of monthly revenue, as well as low enough reviews so it's not too competitive.

Apple Picking for Success

To recap what you've learned so far: As a newer seller, start with the Low-Hanging Fruit, going wide with products that will generate at least $10,000 per month once established. Then add to your product line by going deep with Apples to Apples. Once you get some experience, take a bite out of the Big Apple. You can research products for all three methods simultaneously; for example, while you're going deep with Apples to Apples, be aware of going wide with Low-Hanging Fruit opportunities and products that may fit your brand and your niche—your bite of the Big Apple. And if you're an experienced seller and you have the desire, the time, and the resources—you might consider the One Tree, Many Leaves method.

You can be successful with any of these methods. Be honest with yourself about your level of experience, how well you understand selling on Amazon, and how well you know your product and your customer. Consider how much time and money you have to invest in your chosen product selection method. Then go with the right one for you.

> **REMEMBER, THE FACT THAT YOU HAD SUCCESS WITH ONE PRODUCT DOESN'T MAKE YOU AN EXPERT AND DOESN'T MEAN YOU'RE GOING TO HIT GOLD EVERY TIME.**

And again, look for what everyone else is doing to see what works. But also look at what other sellers aren't doing—the products they're staying away from—because those could be huge opportunities. Products that are above and below the typical price range. Those that are heavy or oversized, hard to ship, or that are electronic. Figure it out once, solve the problem, and start selling.

TOMER'S TIP:
Impressions, Sessions, and Conversions

Impressions, sessions, and conversions are critical metrics. They can affect your product choices—specifically, the One Tree, Many Leaves method. We'll get into more detail in later chapters, but for now you need to know:

▶ *Impressions* are views of your listing in search results. *Sessions* are clicks on a listing from those impressions. *Conversions* are sales from those sessions.

▶ If you have 100 sessions in a day and 5 of those sessions turned into sales, you have a 5 percent conversion rate.

▶ A high conversion rate tells you that a high percentage of people who click on your listing are buying the product. Think about what customers see before they click on your listing: an image, a price, and reviews (how many, and the average). If you want people who click on your product to purchase your product, those three factors must be in line with what they're looking for. They must be good enough for the buyer to make a decision.

▶ Alternatively, you can have a high conversion rate with a product in the One Tree, Many Leaves method, especially if your product shows up on the first page and you have many variations of the product from which to choose.

▶ Conversion rates vary between products. In other words, a good (high) conversion rate for a particular product, like yoga mats, might be a bad (low) conversion rate for another product, like jumper cables.

- All things being equal, the more "personal" an item, the lower the conversion rate. Expect your yoga mat customers to click and compare more products than your jumper cable customers.
- Expensive products also tend to have lower conversion rates. When a customer shops for a new laptop, for example, they're more likely to look at many options before finalizing their choice. You may have to make a larger investment in pay-per-click (PPC) ads to make up for the low conversion rate, but the bigger profit margin on a more expensive product helps make up for the cost.
- The bottom line is that I don't advise going after a product with a low price point or a mix of price points that tend to have a low conversion rate, unless you intend to launch many different variations that cover all the bases in the same listing. Recall the bed sheet example!

The Product Tree Checklist

At this point, you know several methods for choosing products. Continue researching them, using whatever method or methods work best for you, and compile a list of possibilities. You're not ready to launch yet; you're still in research mode. But you are ready to move to the next stage.

If you've read this far, you're probably eager to launch. Not so fast. There's more to learn, and taking the time to read the next four chapters can mean the difference between a successful launch and a product flop. We'll get to launching in Chapter 7, but trust me, you're not ready yet.

Always remember that you are not committed to a product until you give the supplier the go-ahead and make a payment. Until then, you should continue your research to make sure you're picking the best product you can find for your business. The next four chapters are part of that research. Don't skip these chapters; they'll help you make better product choices and set you up for a better launch.

Here are some final notes on growing your Product Tree. We'll explore some of these topics in upcoming chapters:

- Whichever product selection method(s) you use, keep your business simple. As a new seller, or even an experienced one, you don't want to be juggling dozens of products. Work on getting a product up to $10K a month, and add products until you're doing about $1 million a year. The reason for this is because you don't want to invest a lot of cash while you're still learning. It will be easier to recover from a small investment loss than from a large one so you can keep selling (instead of going out of business). Scale slowly and methodically to avoid failed launches, and set yourself up for steady success.

- Once you're nearing $1 million a year in sales, go after $20,000, $30,000–$50,000 a month products. It's easier to launch and sell one product that makes $50,000 a month than it is to sell five products that each make $10,000 a month. You'd be surprised by the number of sellers who never make that shift. I was working with a seller named Angelo who sold five different motivational journals and was doing $50,000 a month, or about $10,000 per journal. He wanted to launch five new journals, thinking that would take his business from $50,000 a month to $100,000 a month. That sounded great, until you considered all the work that went into making the journals. On top of that, Angelo was already dominating his niche, and introducing new journals would cannibalize the market. It wouldn't attract new buyers—it would just draw his existing buyers to a different product than the one they were already buying from him. I told Angelo to take a different approach. Instead of producing and selling more $10,000-a-month journals, he should create water bottles that complemented the journals, with the same branding and similar motivational quotes on them. They would be a lot easier to develop than customizing five new journals. Angelo could do another $50,000 a month with just one water bottle, perhaps in several colors and with several motivational quotes on them, and those would be much easier to produce—and manage—than five new journals. The water bottles also wouldn't cannibalize his audience. His customers would continue buying Angelo's journals and now, have matching water bottles.

- Only choose products that work. Products that deserve and get five-star reviews. We'll get to that more in the next chapter.
- Choose products that are profitable. If the margins are slim, you'll have to sell a lot of products, and that's OK if you can sell a lot of products. If the product has a sizable margin but is tougher to sell, make sure you're prepared to make the necessary investment to make it a winner. I'll talk more about this in Chapter 5.
- Choose products that align with your cash flow. In the simplest terms, if you have $5,000 to invest, don't invest all of it in one very pricey, untested product. You could bankrupt your business before you even get started. It's safe to say that whatever you spend for your initial investment, you need two and a half to three times that amount in the bank. More on cash flow in Chapter 9.
- It's OK to focus on products that interest you, but don't feel like you have to. You can be just as successful selling drain plugs as you would be selling your favorite type of ice-climbing gear. People buy products that you're passionate about, and they also buy products that you're not passionate about—but they are.
- On the other hand, maybe building a brand around a particular line of products that you're passionate about is your dream. In that case, go for it. I happen to be passionate about selling on Amazon. That delivers the time, money, and lifestyle I want and makes reaching my other goals possible.
- The time it takes to choose a product varies. A lot of big sellers launch a product every month—sometimes several times a month. This doesn't mean they research and identify a winning opportunity every month. They are researching a number of products all the time, and they launch when they're ready. One product may take only a short time to develop because the seller found an

existing product at a supplier that isn't on Amazon—or is on Amazon but isn't being sold well—and that they can sell "off the shelf." At the same time, the seller may be developing other products that require customization, or they're having a unique mold or design created and patented, which could take months or years (more on this in Chapter 5). In the meantime, they're researching, talking to suppliers, ordering samples, and figuring out how to make the product competitive and make the finances work. Some products will eventually get a Green Light and others won't, and that's OK. It's all part of the process.

- Don't rush into product selection. Getting samples doesn't mean you're ready to launch. Neither does improving the product, or figuring out the sourcing, packaging, and shipping. Until you've paid the first deposit to the supplier and given them the Green Light to start production, you're still just researching products.

- Before you take that step—paying the supplier—check the numbers again. A product that made financial sense two months ago may not make sense today. Check the market too. A market that was underserved when you started your research may now be saturated. Also make sure the product works. We'll talk about this more in Chapter 5, but for now, assume the sample you got from the supplier is the best version of that product. You need to make sure the ones that go to your customers are of the same high quality before you spend a dime. Make sure everything—the finances, the market, and the product—works and that this is the product you want to launch. Until you make the payment, you can always change your mind. Take your time and get it right.

- Another reason to check your numbers is because you may have made improvements to the product that drive up the cost to the point that it's no longer profitable for you to sell. Be aware of this as you make those improvements and check the numbers again before you pay the supplier.

- Don't dwell on all the time and effort you've put into a product that no longer makes sense. And don't feel like you have to move forward with it. You'll regret that decision. You're learning, always learning. Every seller has samples in their closets. Every seller has winning opportunities that suddenly went sour. The difference between the losing sellers and the winners is whether they moved forward with a bad choice, or they pulled the plug. Experienced sellers still make this mistake, even though they know better. It's hard to back off a product you're invested in, but the wise seller—the one who knows how to ride the Amazon wave—feels no shame in returning to shore instead of drowning in bad product choices. This should never be an emotional decision. It should be data driven. If you need help with this, download my Batch spreadsheet, which you can find on my Breakers site, and run the numbers to see if it makes sense.

Taking a product from research to launch is the most time-consuming and complex process in the Amazon selling business. You've probably done it multiple times. These chapters step you through that process, right up to Chapter 7.

Figure 1, "The Product Tree," displays the big-picture view of that process, but for now, we're focused only on the gray bubbles in the diagram: Product Research to Green Light.

THE PRODUCT TREE

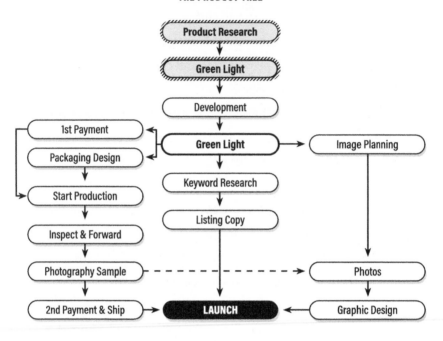

Figure 1: Product research is the first step in the product launch process.

After you've researched and selected a product, you need to validate that the product is worth pursuing financially. Talk to a few suppliers or look at websites like Alibaba to get a general idea of the cost. See if there are other FBA sellers on Amazon with similar products. I'll have a lot more to say about product cost in upcoming chapters, but for now, at least take a few minutes to make sure the product has enough margin (the difference between cost to you and the price you charge the customer) to make it worth pursuing. After you've done that, you can move to the development phase, starting with the Six-Star Formula.

When we give a product the Green Light, we don't start production. The Green Light only means we have completed this initial research and are ready to move to the next steps, which I'll cover in the following chapters.

Once you've selected your products, there's more work to do. Even though you're learning from what other sellers are doing well—and from what they're *not* doing well—you still need to differentiate your products further. You don't want to sell the opposite of what everyone else is selling, but you don't want to sell *exactly* what they're selling either. You're going to give customers a reason to choose your product over another seller's, and you're going to do this by providing a true customer experience.

BREAKERS

Want to see my full, live lecture on The Product Tree? You can watch it on my Breakers site at tomerrabinovich.com/breakers.

CHAPTER 3

THE SIX-STAR EXPERIENCE

*"If you make customers unhappy in the
physical world, they might each tell 6 friends.
If you make customers unhappy on the internet,
they can each tell 6,000 friends."*

—JEFF BEZOS

T he above quote by Jeff Bezos is true for negative experiences, but it's also true for positive ones. That's what this chapter is about: creating that positive experience that your customers will want to share with their friends—and with thousands of total strangers. How do they do that? With reviews.

Reviews are the social proof of our products on Amazon. It's one of the main factors that influence people to buy, or not buy, our products. Consider this:

- 79 percent of consumers check reviews on Amazon before making a purchase.
- When making a purchase on Amazon, only 6 percent of shoppers "rarely" or "never" read product reviews.[1]

---

[1] "The 2019 Amazon Consumer Behavior Report," Feedvisor, March 19, 2019, https://fv.feedvisor. com/rs/656-BMZ-780/images/Feedvisor-Consumer-Survey-2019.pdf.

- 76 percent of consumers say they trust the reviews they read online as much as personal recommendations.[2]

Sellers are always looking for ways to get reviews. The problem most of them make is waiting until *after they've launched*—by then, it's too late: "My product is live! How can I get five-star reviews?"

Well, you have to go back in time several months and make a plan for getting great reviews from real customers before you launch your product, *that's how*. You do the work that's necessary so that when you launch your product, customers *want* to leave you a review—preferably, a five-star review.

[2] Rosie Murphy, "Local Consumer Review Survey 2020," Brightlocal, December 9, 2020, https://www.brightlocal.com/research/local-consumer-review-survey-2020/.

Forget about putting this off until later. Forget about trying to "hack the system" after the fact. Neither of those options is anywhere near as effective as setting your product up for success before it's even listed on Amazon. If you're struggling to get five-star reviews, it's probably too late. You have to start this process early.

Your goal is to get as many five-star reviews as possible. Expect to get some fours and maybe a few threes, but the majority of reviews should be fives. Anything else drags down your overall score. Your score may occasionally drop to 4.5, but if it starts to plummet, you may have a problem, and if it drops to four—depending on the product—you may be losing sales.

If your review average drops to three, you would probably stop selling.

Your goal is five stars.

Do a Google search on "how to get reviews" and you'll find all kinds of advice. Amazon provides tools to help you get reviews by asking for them. Here's the problem: people are seldom motivated to take the time and make the effort to write a review. They have better things to do with their time. Think of the average online buyer who may be getting several packages a month, a week, *daily*—do you really think they are going to write reviews for all those products?

A seller has to differentiate their product from all those other deliveries and impress the customer so much that they want to leave a review. They can't wait to leave a review. Your product blew them away so much, changed their life, made them so happy, they can't wait to tell anyone who'll listen how wonderfully amazing this new thing they bought is. They have it, and they want to talk about it. It's the best purchase ever, the best decision they ever made, and they want to shout it from the rooftops: *Look what I bought! It's great! You should own one too!*

Even the biggest sellers tend to overlook the importance of reviews. They focus on sales, revenue, and other indicators of success. They seem to be oblivious to one critically important fact: *reviews are the one of the best ways—if not THE best way—to get ranked on Amazon.* But not just any old reviews. *Organic, five-star* reviews, from *real* customers, on an ongoing basis.

I'm talking about reviews that you didn't pay for or do any favors to get. They're not from your mom, or your sister, or your neighbor. You didn't give away a free product to get them. Organic reviews are from real customers who liked your product so much, they took time out of their busy day to log in to Amazon and tell everyone about their wonderful experience.

"So, Tomer, if five-star reviews are so important, why did you name this chapter 'The Six-Star Experience'?"

Great question! I see that you're paying attention. Here's the answer: if you shoot for five stars, you'll get five stars some of the time, but you'll also get four-star reviews, and even (gasp!) some threes. And you do not want three-star reviews. To get all the organic five-star reviews you will ever want, on an ongoing basis, you need the Six-Star Formula.

THE SIX-STAR EXPERIENCE

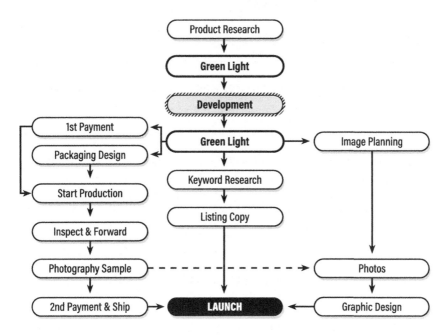

Figure 2: After you've researched your product and given it the Green Light, check with a few suppliers or other sources to get an idea of whether the product is financially viable before moving to Development and the Six-Star Formula.

The Six-Star Formula

I know what you're thinking: *Amazon doesn't even have six-star reviews!* You're right. But remember that to get five-star reviews, you have to aim for six. This is my way of saying, "Shoot for the stars to land on the moon."

The Six-Star Formula is designed to deliver five-star reviews in six steps—or rather, stars. Are you ready to uncover the mystery of great reviews? Keep reading.

The First Star: The Product Must Do What It's Supposed to Do

If you claim that your product does something, it must actually do that. A bicycle tire repair kit must actually repair a tire. A hairdryer must actually dry hair. The product has to work, and it has to work well. Not some of the time or even most of the time. It has to do what it's supposed to do—and do it well—all the time. If it doesn't, you will get one-star reviews. Get this one right and you'll avoid the dreaded, easily avoidable, one-star review.

I say "easily avoidable," yet sellers often get this wrong. They get samples and realize the product doesn't quite do what they expected, but they move forward with production anyway. If you notice your product doesn't function the way you promised in your listing, your customer is going to notice too. Test the product, get familiar with it, and know your customers' expectations. Live up to those expectations. Exceed them. Only sell bulletproof products that won't disappoint people. If you fail to do this, you will get a lot of negative reviews. You will have done all that work for nothing and will have to start all over again. Plus, think about it: Did you become an Amazon seller because you wanted to sell inferior products that disappoint people? Is that the best way for you to reach whatever goals you set for yourself when you started this whole journey?

Here's something else to think about: Before you choose a product, think about the potential for negative reviews. Even if the product functions well, will it function well for everyone? Some products, such as apparel, come in a lot of different sizes. You can add a sizing chart to your listing, but odds are, customers will still choose the wrong size. They'll either give you a bad review or they'll return the clothing for another size, and then you have to deal with returns. I'm not saying you shouldn't sell apparel, but I avoid it for this reason. Unless you want to commit time to managing returns and working harder to get a lot of good reviews to outweigh the bad ones, it doesn't make sense.

Sellers used to get away with selling products that didn't work well. Prior to 2016, you could offer products to customers for free in exchange for a review, as long as they noted in the review that they had received the product for free and their review is not biased. As you can imagine, this prompted many dishonest reviews. People liked getting free products—even bad ones—and were more than happy to leave five-star reviews for products that didn't perform well. But in 2016, Amazon changed the rules. They got rid of those reviews. Some sellers were very upset when this happened because they lost thousands of reviews. They didn't know how they would ever sell another product. The truth is, Amazon did everyone a favor, including sellers, because it forced them to stop manipulating the system and start relying on honest reviews. This action prompted sellers to learn more about their customers and their customers' expectations. It encouraged them to source better products. By making it harder for sellers to sell inferior products, it made Amazon a more reputable site. That helped everyone: Amazon, customers, and sellers.

I changed my product line when this happened. I had a few 4.5-star products that were probably, if I'm being honest, three-star products. For example, I sold lawn aerators that were basically spikes that you strapped onto your shoes like crampons. The idea was that by walking around your yard with these things on, you could aerate your lawn. The problem was that they didn't work well—in fact, they were horrible. But since I had given a bunch of them away to people in exchange for reviews, I had a lot of great reviews. When Amazon changed the rules, instead of trying to figure out how to maintain 4.5 stars—for example, by manipulating the system in some other way—I stopped selling them. I pulled all of my inferior products off of Amazon and decided I would only sell truly five-star products.

Amazon wants sellers to do well. They want their customers to be happy. Sellers who fight the Amazon way, or who think they can outsmart the Amazon system, are fooling themselves. You're here to ride the Amazon wave, not swim against it. Like I said in the introduction, being an Amazon seller is the best opportunity that's come along in our lifetime. Grab onto that opportunity and use that system to your advantage.

The Second Star: Product Installation and Use Must Be Crystal Clear

In the customer world, patience does not exist. The instructions for installing and using your product must be stupid-proof. The customer should be able to use your product right out of the box, with minimal set up. They should be able to use it immediately. If it's a complex product that requires a bit of set up, include clear written instructions. These can be a paper insert, or you can allow the customer to download a PDF or watch a video demonstration.

Make the packaging easy to open too. Don't frustrate your customer with blister packaging that they have to wrestle with to get to the product. Consider the whole experience, from receiving the product, to opening it, to learning how to use it, to using it, to what they do with the product after they've opened it, and after they've used it. Be aware of bulky packaging that the customer now has to dispose of, either by recycling or throwing away. Be aware of what happens to the product when it's not in use. For some products, this might mean including a container for storing the product.

If a customer can't figure out how to use the product right away, they'll return it or worse—leave a one- or two-star review. Avoid this scenario by testing the product or multiple products before choosing one to launch. When I researched baby monitors, I was traveling to China at the time and had more than 20 samples sent to my hotel room. There, I set every one of them up. Most of them came with apps that I had to download to my smartphone. Some of the apps worked well, but others were confusing. One baby monitor didn't require an app at all because it worked on radio waves—I plugged it in, and it worked. Can you guess which monitor I chose to launch? Of course, I wouldn't say to avoid products that require downloading an app completely. Some great products come with great apps. Just make sure the app that goes with your product is easy to download and use. If your product works and it's easy to install and use, you will avoid one- and two-star reviews.

The Third Star: The Product Must Be Better than the Competition

The product must be better than whatever the competition's selling, and *it must be better for your target audience.*

Forget about reviews and best seller rank for a minute. Ask yourself if you would buy your own product. If you're not the target audience, would you recommend the product to someone in your target audience? If you handed that person your product and the top-selling competing product, which one would they buy? If it's not yours, then you need to improve it.

One of the quickest ways to find out how to make your product better is to skim the competition's bad reviews. Find out what people don't like about that product. Make sure your product doesn't have that problem. Make sure it's really good wherever that other product is weak. Then be sure to show how it's better in the listing. That should be obvious to you, the seller, right? Let me tell you about something that isn't so obvious, and that many sellers miss.

Sellers tend to focus only on the one-, two-, and three-star reviews to identify weaknesses. But you can also learn a lot from four-star reviews, because these are written by customers who like everything about the product—except for one detail. And they'll tell you all about that detail in their review. Also read the five-star reviews that tell you what customers love about a product, and make sure your product has all those qualities. I've seen sellers "improve" a product to correct a defect in a competitor's product, but they neglect to include everything that's great about the competing product.

Read the questions on the Amazon listings, too, and the answers. Customers ask questions about what's important to them, and what's important to customers should be important to you.

When you're deciding how to improve your product, don't overdo it. Your customer has a certain expectation and while you want to exceed that expectation, you don't want to put yourself out of business. It still has to be affordable for the customer and profitable for you. And you still need a reasonable time to market. Otherwise, by the time you launch, your improvements may no longer be relevant.

One more point on making the product better: it's best if you can show that's it better, best if it can be done on the main image of the product. In case you have a better product and it's visible, it's so much easier to sell.

You can also improve your product by offering it as a bundle. This means that you include something with it that adds value. If it doesn't add value to the main product, then it's probably not a good choice because the customer won't care about it enough to choose your product over another one. If you can add another feature or function to your product that the customer wants and the competition doesn't offer, you can improve your product.

You can also improve your product by where you source it from, or by working with the current supplier to manufacture the product in a way that makes it better. Chapter 5 provides more detail on this very large topic. For now, if your product works, is easy to install and use, and it's better for your target customer than the competition's product, you will avoid one-, two-, and three-star reviews. Be sure to make the improvements obvious in the main image of your listing. I'll tell you more about this in Chapter 6.

The Fourth Star: The Product Must Be Five-Star Worthy

For this star, you have to be completely honest with yourself. After fully testing the product, would you leave it a five-star review? Is there anything at all about the product that might cause you to leave anything *but* a five-star review? Four stars isn't good enough.

Most people don't leave a review at all even if they like a product. Something about the product must compel them to leave that review. Is there anything about your product that would compel you not only to leave a review, but to leave a five-star review?

This is a matter of due diligence to safeguard your product against bad reviews and ensure great ones. Of course, you may not get it exactly right the first time. You may think your product is spectacular, but then you get a four-star review and realize that you missed one tiny detail. That's OK, but you must fix the problem in the product immediately so other customers don't have the same problem with it. The bottom line is that if your product is just OK and not amazing, you're going to be looking at a lot of four-star reviews.

Be proud of every product you sell. If you aren't proud of a product, don't sell it. Your products should be so good that you'd buy them for your sister, your mother, and your grandmother. They should be good enough that you'd be proud to buy them for your kids, if that's your target audience. This isn't just good business, it's a lot more fun. Wouldn't you rather work with happy customers than spend your time dealing with unhappy ones?

The Fifth Star: The Product Comes with Great Customer Service

I've spoken with thousands of sellers, and they all seem to get one thing right: customer service. When a customer reaches out to them for assistance, the seller does whatever they can for the customer to avoid a negative review. From what I have seen, Amazon sellers deliver top-notch customer service.

Even though you're probably already doing this, let's talk about customer service. There are two parts to this: responding to questions on your listing and responding to messages from customers. Most customers aren't aware that they can connect with the seller, but they can, and some do. They call Amazon or contact them through the site to tell them they're not happy with the product. If it's a shipping problem with an AMZ or FBA product, Amazon takes care of it, but if it's a problem with the product, the seller has to handle it.

When you get a message from an unhappy customer, you have to deal with it within 24 hours. First off, you don't want an unhappy customer. You want a happy customer who continues to buy from you. Second, you don't want to make Amazon look bad. Your customers are their customers, and you have to take care of their customers. Third, the longer you delay, the more time that customer has to leave you a bad review. The general rule of thumb when dealing with complaints is to replace or refund—do whatever makes the customer happy. Here's how I deal with the three most common scenarios:

- Customer isn't happy with the product and wants a refund: I refund the customer's payment, then I respond to their message letting them know that I've already refunded their money. I also tell them there's no need to return the product. I'm not going to resell it anyway because I don't know whether the customer used it, and I'm not selling a used product to a new customer. There's no sense in spending any more time on it or bothering the customer with a return.

- Customer isn't happy because the product arrived damaged: I ask the customer if they prefer a replacement or a refund. Then I wait for them to respond before doing anything else. Again, I tell them not to return the product.
- Customer isn't happy with the product because it isn't exactly what they wanted: If I have a product that would meet their needs, I offer them that product as a replacement. Or if there's a competitor's product that meets their needs, I offer to buy it and have it sent to them. Either way, they can keep the original product. This may seem like a lot of trouble to make a customer happy, but it's worth it to make the customer happy and avoid a potential one-star review. And I may get a five-star review in the process.

When you're communicating with the customer, don't ever refer to yourself as "we" as in "we the company." That's very impersonal and off-putting. The customer wants to know they're talking to a person or a team of people whose job is to take care of customers. You don't need to sign off with "Andy Roberts, CEO" even if you are the CEO of your business, because the customer probably wouldn't believe that anyway. But you can use your name, or just sign off with something like "Andy, Customer Service Team, Tomer's Treasures."

Every interaction you have with a customer is a chance to get a positive review, even if they had a bad experience. Customers who took the time to reach out are customers who care. They are giving you the chance to make it right. They might even turn out to be raving fans for your brand and share the experience they had with you and your company with their friends.

"Customer service starts when the customer experience fails."
—Chris Zane

The Sixth Star: The Product Must Deliver a Six-Star Customer Experience

Great customer service is the minimum customer interaction requirement, but in my opinion, it should account for only a small percentage of seller-customer engagement. The rest of your interactions should be around the customer experience. Think about it: When do most sellers engage with customers? That's right—when there's a problem. The customer complains about the product and the seller reacts to that complaint. Sure, they provide a great response—great customer service—but why would you want to limit your interactions to fixing problems?

What if, instead of just responding to a customer's negative experience, you invested time in creating a positive one? This is the difference between customer service and customer experience: where customer service is reactive, customer experience is proactive. The seller takes it upon themselves to create a memorable experience for the customer.

The other difference between customer service and customer experience is that customer service seldom compels customers to leave a review, never mind a five-star review. I'm not suggesting you send all your customers love letters or stalk them on social media. You can give customers a great experience through your product, the packaging, or something else.

Many professional Amazon sellers get the first five stars right. Yet, they still struggle to get five-star reviews. This is because shooting for five-star reviews will get you five stars occasionally, but more often it will get you four stars, three stars, or no stars at all. Customers need a reason to leave you a review, and they need something from you to leave a five-star review. The Six-Star Experience—delivering a great customer experience—is how you get five stars.

The magical thing about my Six-Star Formula is that you only have to do it right once. Then you can sit back and relax, because you'll continue to get five-star reviews on an ongoing basis without having to change up your strategy. That will drive your Amazon ranking higher than you can imagine.

So how do you do that? I'm glad you asked (I love it when you ask me questions!).

You do what 99.99 percent of sellers don't do.

Are you ready to join the 1 percent of sellers who know how to deliver a Six-Star Experience? Well, you'll have to read the next chapter.

BREAKERS

Want to see my full live lecture on The Six-Star Experience? Watch it right now on my Breakers site at tomerrabinovich.com/breakers.

CHAPTER 4

UNDERPROMISE, OVERDELIVER, AND SURPRISE

*"The key is to set realistic customer expectations,
and then not to just meet them, but to exceed them—
preferably in unexpected and helpful ways."*

—SIR RICHARD BRANSON

live in the countryside of northern Israel, near Golan Heights. There's not a lot of businesses in the area, but there is this one small burger restaurant called Route 90. A few 30-year-old friends who grew up in the area decided to buy the place a few years ago and remodeled it with a tractor theme. They put pictures of tractors on the walls and some of the seats were actually made out of tires. They're open from noon to midnight every day, and they're always packed. People who come here from Tel Aviv know about the restaurant, and it's become a favorite stop for travelers. Let me tell you about the first time I ate there.

So, I take my family to Route 90 for dinner. It's Monday, which is typically a slow night for restaurants. I'm surprised to see all the people already seated—how can a tiny burger joint be this busy on a Monday?

The hostess ushers us to a clean table and hands us the menus. They're pretty basic, single-page, but clearly written, so we know exactly what we're ordering and how much it will cost. We order quickly—the simple menu makes it easy to explain to the server without having to provide all kinds of complicated details. He's courteous, friendly, and he gets our drinks right away. Despite how crowded the place is, our burgers arrive shortly and they're delicious. They come in these special fluffy buns that the place makes, and I've never tasted anything like it! In fact, everything they do is on point: great product, easy to understand menus, much nicer than any other burger joint in the area, and great customer service too. The place nails the first five stars of my Six-Star Formula.

But that's not all. Apparently, on Mondays, something else happens at Route 90. We finish our meals, and the server brings me a pair of dice.

"If you roll double ones tonight," he says, "you get a prize. And if you roll double sixes, all your meals tonight—your entire ticket—is free."

What? I can't believe that offer. I roll the dice. I don't get a prize, but it's fun just the same. The server explains this is a Monday night tradition and double sixes always means free meals, but the prize for snake eyes changes from week to week, so you never know what you might win. It could be a discount or a free side the next time you come in, or it could be something else.

The server goes to another table packed with a family of five—three little kids and their parents. He hands the mom the dice. She rolls...and the whole place explodes. She's rolled double sixes. Free meal for the whole family! Everyone's screaming, cheering, and clapping for them. It's a joy to watch.

Here comes the server again, and he's brought my wife and I each a free black coffee along with the check. This is a trendy gesture in Arabic restaurants, but I've never seen it done anywhere else—especially at a busy burger joint. It takes time to drink the coffee, and it's the restaurant's way of saying, "We're not rushing you out to fill your seat with the next paying customer. Please, stay and enjoy your coffee."

My wife and I finish our coffees and as we're heading toward the door, the host asks us if our children would like to choose a small toy to take home. There's a collection of small cars at the counter, and each child picks one. Everyone leaves happy—we've all enjoyed a terrific meal at a friendly, welcoming place, and we have a lovely memory of our night out for dinner. I can hear the kids in the back seat of the car playing with their new toys. Tonight's a big win for my wife and I, and it's a big win for Route 90 too. They not only knocked it out of the park with stars one through five, but they also delivered big time on the Six-Star Formula by overdelivering and surprising me with a wonderful customer experience.

Did I leave a big tip? You bet. Will I be back? Absolutely.

Most restaurants stop at five stars, and it's the same with online sellers. They skip the sixth star—the one that ensures ongoing, organic, five-star reviews. They forget about the customer experience, which is all about underpromising, overdelivering, and surprising the customer with something they didn't expect.

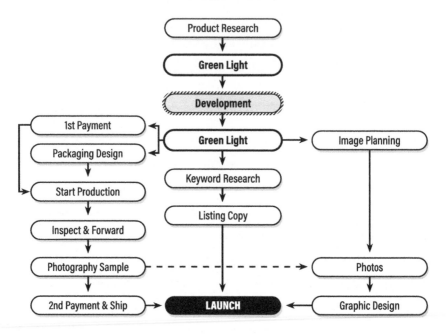

THE SIX-STAR EXPERIENCE

Figure 3: Make a plan to underpromise and overdeliver,
well before you launch a product.

Giving and Receiving

"Underpromise and overdeliver" is based on a giving and receiving theory, where if you give without expectation, you'll receive more in return. You don't give people only what they expect, and you don't give them more to make them feel obligated to respond in kind. You surprise them with a little something extra—no strings attached.

In a typical transaction, you might give me $20 for a product. I give you the product, and the transaction is complete. It's the end of the sale, our relationship, and your experience. There is little emotion involved. Contrast that with giving me $20, getting the product, and then getting something from me that you didn't expect.

Overdelivering with a surprise evokes a positive emotion in your customer. It makes them happy, and they'll want to leave you a review. Not because you asked for one but because they want to. You're sparking a feeling in them, maybe putting a smile on their face, and giving them a memorable experience. And just like the diners at the burger joint who are inspired to leave a bigger tip, your customers will be inspired to leave a great review.

Some sellers sell a product, ask for a review, and expect to get one. That doesn't feel good to the customer. They're not obligated to give you anything beyond $20. Yet, you're asking them for more? Give without expectation. Without obligation. That's how you receive ongoing, organic reviews.

Think of a business that you go to again and again. Any business: a restaurant, a barber, even a laundromat. Why do you go back? Maybe they have a good product, but that's typically not enough to earn your return business. Think about the customer experience they create for you and how that attracts you to the place. What do they do that keeps you coming back?

> **GIVE WITHOUT EXPECTATION.**
> **WITHOUT OBLIGATION.**
> **THAT'S HOW YOU RECEIVE ONGOING,**
> **ORGANIC REVIEWS.**

Deliver the Six-Star Customer Experience

In the restaurant example, the Six-Star Formula comprised the dice-rolling for a potential prize, a free coffee, and a small toy for the kids. I didn't expect any of those things when I walked into Route 90. All I expected was a clean, friendly atmosphere and a good meal at a decent price. That would have satisfied me, but I wouldn't have gone out of my way to over-tip the server, leave them an online review, or tell you about the place in this book.

Just remember that to overdeliver and surprise, you have to under-promise. That means you can't wave the surprise in the customer's face before they place an order. It's all about the surprise! Another thing to remember is to make the surprise commensurate with the product. If you bought a new car and the dealership gave you a free keychain, that wouldn't be much of a surprise, right? Make overdelivering and surprising customers part of how you do business. Include it in your launch plan, and in your budget. The Six-Star Formula isn't an afterthought—it's critical to every single launch. But only if you want five-star reviews.

What questions do you have? Ah, OK:

"Tomer, are you asking me to buy all my customers a cup of coffee?"

Not exactly. But there are four other ways that work just as well! Let's talk about them.

Packaging

The product listing is the initial "packaging." It's all a customer sees when they order your product. You could show the actual packaging on the listing, and if your packaging is especially attractive, you may want to. Alternatively, you can surprise them with it. They'll expect the product to show up in a plain box, but when they open the shipping box— woohoo! They get something completely unexpected. Something that makes them smile. The choice to show the packaging depends on the product and the package. Again, look at your competition. Are they all showing the packaging? Then you should also. If they aren't, that's something you can show to differentiate your product, or you can save it as a surprise.

One of my favorite packaging ideas comes from Scotch® brand Magic™ tape. The big selling point of this tape is that once you stick it to something, it's transparent. It seems to disappear. The company had a contest to come up with a unique way to package the tape, and the winning entry used a beveled mirror inside the box to hide the tape. The box appeared empty because the mirror gave that illusion. It was brilliant. Another neat packaging idea was a baby safety lock set that came in a box that looked like a cabinet. Think of packaging as another way to improve your product and surprise your customer. And if you have an especially cool package, put it on your listing!

Your online product packaging doesn't have to be the same as the packaging you see in retail. Products in a store must be clearly labeled on the front so when they sit on a shelf, the customer can see what's in the package without picking it up or turning it over. You don't have those restrictions with your packaging when selling online.

Here's an example. Say you get a delivery from Amazon. You open the shipping box and inside, there's a simple black cylinder. You're thinking, *What the heck did I order?* Then you notice a little keyhole in the cylinder. You open it up and there's a message:

Congratulations! You just picked your first lock!

That's right—it's the lock-picking kit you ordered. What a great surprise! You want to show all your friends the cool package, and you might want to write a review.

I actually designed this package and put all the necessary labeling on the bottom, out of sight. By the way, Amazon doesn't allow those to be sold anymore, but I've used the idea to create similar packaging.

You don't have to design the package yourself. Hire someone to do it for you. Visit my Breakers site for a list of companies that currently provide package designing services.

TOMER'S TIP:

Get Your Packaging Labels Right

To sell a product in the US, including through Amazon, you must put a label on it. The label must include certain information including a Fulfillment Network Stock Keeping Unit (FNSKU), which is the barcode that uniquely identifies the product; the name of your product; and the country where the product was made. You should also include your brand's logo and if you have a website that supports email and customer contact, include the URL.

Free Surprise Product

Include an unexpected gift with your product. The gift must be different than the product they bought, and not just more of it. People buy in quantities they want, and just giving them more isn't enough.

So what do you do? You give them a complementary product—something that goes along with the product they paid for. Say the customer purchased a set of makeup brushes. Along with the brushes, you could send a brush holder to put them in. It must be a good-quality brush holder, too, not a cheap one. Adding a cheap product—even a free cheap product—could get you bad reviews. It should be commensurate in quality with the brushes. Don't just throw the brush holder in with the brushes or the customer won't understand that it's a gift. Package it in a nice box and include a note thanking the customer for their order. Spend the few extra cents to deliver an experience. And most importantly, don't ask them for a review. You don't ask them for anything. Giving and receiving theory, right?

TOMER'S TIP: What Makes You Smile?

Think about the companies that you buy from again and again—the ones that make you feel special. What is it that they do that other companies do not? What can you do that's similar to keep customers coming back to buy from you and leave great reviews?

One company that gets the customer experience very right is Chewy.com, the online store for pet supplies. When you create an account with them, they ask a lot of questions about your pet. Some companies ask a lot of questions but never do anything with that information. How many times has a company asked you about your birthday, but never sent you a birthday card or email? Not Chewy. They send you a welcome card. They send your pet birthday cards. They make you feel like part of the Chewy family. Chewy's phone number is on every card they send and if you call it, you're not stuck on hold. You get a real person talking to you within three beeps.

Sometimes they send customers surprise gifts, even oil paintings of their pets! Can you imagine? Of course, those kinds of gifts get shared via social media and sometimes go viral. A happy customer and free advertising! What more could a seller ask for?

Running your business this way isn't just more successful, it's also a lot more fun.

Inserts

Inserts are another way to overdeliver and surprise your customers. Inserts can be a warranty, or instructions, or a thank-you note. They can be anything that adds value to the product or the customer's experience.

They cannot be a request for a review. Have you ever been to a restaurant where, as soon as you get your food, the server asks if you're enjoying your meal? You haven't even swallowed your first bite yet! That's what it's like when you ask a customer to leave you a review this soon. Only give the customer one thing in the insert, such as a warranty. If you offer them a warranty and several other things, you'll come across as too salesy. Visit my Breakers site for more on inserts and warranties.

You can also offer the customer a discount on their next purchase. A discount like 10 or 20 percent off probably won't have the effect you expect. It may not motivate the customer to make another purchase or leave a review. Unless it's an expensive product and the discount equates to a good amount of money, you have to offer a more substantial discount. And never offer a dollar amount discount; the price could change before they opt in. A small discount is not a gift to your customers; it's a gift to you.

You can use discounts to upsell customers as well. If you have a selection of pricey products and a selection of less expensive items, for example, you could include a discount for an expensive item in the insert of the cheaper one. So a customer might buy a $10 item from you and get an offer for 40 percent off a $100 item. That's a great deal for them, you make another sale, and it can improve your best seller rank (BSR). And of course, you could get a very happy customer and a five-star review out of the deal to boot.

Whether you offer a warranty or a discount on a future purchase, there must be a sense of urgency. Tell the customer they must sign up for the warranty within seven days of receiving the product or sign up for the discount within two weeks. You don't want people signing up for a warranty or trying to get a discount from you years after they've purchased a product. Then be sure to provide the warranty or discount immediately.

Now they've had two good interactions with you: the great Six-Star Formula product and a free warranty or discount.

One of my brands is a baby brand, and for those products, I include an insert for a warranty or a discount, but I also include a thank-you note that appears to come from their baby, thanking the parents for buying the product for them. It's written in a kid's-type font and it's very cute and playful, and there's nothing included that tries to sell more products or ask the parents for anything—just the note and the brand logo. Those kinds of notes can end up being posted on social media, which is great for you. Just don't expect it, and never suggest the customer do it. The point is to connect with them on an emotional level, not try to turn them into a brand ambassador for your product. If they choose to go that route, that's up to them. Just don't expect it, and never ask for it.

Finally, always include the email address for customer support on all inserts or on your packaging. No long message inviting them to contact support—just the words "customer support" and the email. Don't make a big deal out of this or it will make the customer think you have a lot of problems with the product.

Adding Humor to Speak to Your Customer

Adding humor that's tailored for your target customer can create a positive experience for your customer. For example, you can use playful language in your listing copy and on the packaging. To do this properly, you must know you customer so whatever you write resonates with them. One company that does this well is Frank Body. The company makes body scrubs and other personal care products. Instead of the usual marketing messaging on a body scrub, a Frank Body coffee scrub says, "Guess what? You'll be naked in one minute." All the products' messaging is written in the first person, as if the product is speaking to the customer. It's always playful and humorous and works well for their target market. It makes people smile.

You don't have to, and may not want to, imitate Frank Body's style, but you don't have to be super-stiff and professional either. In most cases, professional is just another word for boring. Have some fun with your product. Put some personality into it. Speak to your customer the way you think they would like to be spoken to. It's not a business meeting—they're interacting with your product in the privacy of their own home. It's OK to make them laugh.

Another example is eyeglasses company Warby Parker. When you open your rectangular box with the glasses inside, printed inside is the message: "Nice to see you." Funny and clever, right? That would make you smile. These small touches add personality to your brand and to the overall experience of the customer.

Of course, you need to know your customer to do this, to understand what they'll think is amusing versus offensive. And you also want to keep in mind the nature of the product. The tone should fit the product and the target customer.

So now you have four ways to give customers a Six-Star Experience. Which one is right for your product? The answer is up to you. You can adjust your packaging, include a free surprise gift or insert, or use humor and personality to engage customers and give them a positive experience. You can combine these methods too. There's no clear-cut answer as far as which one works best, so do whichever one makes sense for you and your product. But you will need to build the cost into your budget. Commit 5 to 10 percent of your profit to customer experience. Yes, this cuts into your margins slightly, but the payoff will more than make up for it.

Remember, you are overdelivering and surprising. This means you can't give away the surprise on your Amazon listing. But you still want your listing to be attractive and enticing. Just be sure to balance what's in your listing and what's in the package. That way, you'll attract buyers, and you'll also attract five-star reviews.

BREAKERS

There's more to learn about underpromising, overdelivering, and surprising your customer! If you haven't watched my live lecture on The Six-Star Experience, which I mentioned in Chapter 3, now is the perfect time to take a break and check it out at tomerrabinovich.com/breakers.

But before you go…remember when I said you should not ask people to leave a review too early—before they've had a chance to really enjoy your product? Well, we're at that point in the book where it's perfectly acceptable to ask for a review. Please go to tomerrabinovich.com/review-wave and let me know what you think of this book so far. Thank you.

CHAPTER 5

SOURCING AND DEVELOPMENT

"The very important thing you
should have is patience."

—JACK MA

The Canton Fair is the biggest trade show in the world. For three weeks every April and again in October, suppliers and sellers from around the world converge on Guangzhou, China's third-largest city and the country's busiest port and transportation hub. More than 60,000 booths are set up in three phases, with one-third of the booths representing electronics and industrial products set up the first week. After a few days, the booths are taken down and replaced with household and consumer goods booths, which are replaced, after a few days, with clothing, footwear, toys, cosmetics, and food product booths. There's every product you can imagine—it's a seller's paradise.

Most sellers go to traditional sourcing websites like Alibaba for products, but whenever I can, I like to research my products firsthand. Prior to 2017, I'd never been to China. That year, I joined a group of Amazon sellers that goes to the Canton Fair every year.

So here I am, on my way to Guangzhou. I have a list of products in mind, but really, I just want to see what the trade show is all about. I check into the Four Seasons, get cleaned up, and head over to the fair.

I'm walking around, looking at products and talking to factory representatives about their products and how I can get samples to my team in the Philippines. I take pictures of everything and send them to my team—they'll get the samples right away and validate them before sending the best ones to my hotel, where I can test them myself. Now I come to this one booth, and we talk, and I give them my business card, which has my brand name on it.

"Oh, we know your brand!" they say, "we actually sell one of your products." This means they're selling the same product that I'm selling.

I'm kind of surprised, but I shouldn't be. If you sell a lot of products, you're bound to run into vendors that sell the same stuff.

I'm looking at this product and it's just like mine—same quality and everything. We start talking business and I tell them I'm selling around 50,000 units a year, and I tell them how much I'm paying my supplier. On the spot, they tell me they can give it to me for a dollar less. We talk a little more, and exchange contact information.

Since then, I've been to China three more times for Canton Fair and to meet up with some of my suppliers. To be clear, I don't like going to China. I would rather stay home with my family or speak at an Amazon event. But going to the Canton Fair and visiting your suppliers in person is one of the best things you can do for your business. As a business owner, you don't always do whatever you want to do—sometimes you do what needs to be done right now so you can have the freedom you seek later. The funny thing is that every time I go to China—as much as I dislike it—something big happens. Like talking to that one vendor that first time. After I left the Canton Fair, we kept negotiating over email and I ended up with two dollars off every unit.

That one trip saved me $100,000 on my bottom line, amounting to $100,000 in pure profit *every year*. I believe that every dollar saved is a dollar earned, and that year, I earned it just by showing up at a trade show.

Sourcing products is a big, complex topic. It deserves more than a chapter—it needs a whole other book. But you have to do it, and you owe it to yourself to learn as much as you can about it. As I discovered at the Canton Fair, you may think you're getting the best deal, but that best deal could be much better—as much as $100,000 a year better.

To optimize your sales and your bottom line, you need to do the research that's necessary to find high-quality products at a fair price with an efficient time to market. This, like everything else in this business, can be outsourced at some point, but you still have to know what you're looking for. I'll give you all the highlights you need to get started. Let's begin with the money.

Return On Investment

In Chapter 2, I told you that I look for a product that meets my criteria for sales that scale. But once I find a product like that, I don't immediately start production. I've validated it in terms of revenue, but I still need to look at my return on investment.

When I say "revenue," I'm not referring to the selling price of a product or how much money I make by selling a product; I'm looking at overall monthly revenue. Whether I sell 10 products a month for $1,000 each, 100 products for $100 each, or 1,000 products for $10 each, I'll generate the same $10,000. This is what I mean by revenue. Once I've established that I can hit my revenue goals with a product, I look closer, at the ROI. I want to know how much of the revenue I'm generating is profit—money that I make over my investment.

Sellers look for, at a bare minimum, a 100 percent return on investment (ROI), with most sellers preferring a 200 to 300 percent ROI.

To figure out ROI, you have to look at a few things. COGS, or cost of goods sold, includes production plus shipping costs. In addition, you have Amazon's fees, which are 15 percent plus fulfillment plus storage, with these fees varying depending on the product and other factors. You have to consider all of those costs to see what a product costs you before you can figure out the ROI of that product.

Say I invest $4 in a product (COGS), and I sell it for $18. Let's assume the Amazon fees are $6. That leaves me with an income of $12, $8 profit, or 200 percent ROI ($8 profit / $4 COGS = 2). Doing this, I triple my money every time I sell an inventory of the product. I'll note here that the return doesn't take into account money I've spent on pay-per-click (PPC) ads, but it's still a good number, comparatively speaking, for determining ROI.

Now I have more money to invest in more stock. If I started with

2,000 units costing $8,000 (2,000 × $4 each) and sold all my stock, I now have $24,000 to buy the original order of 2,000 units and an additional 4,000 *more* units. I don't just look at this as profit but as capital to scale the business.

I'll have much more to say about the importance of ROI in Chapter 10. For now, let's talk about why you have to keep researching products after your first launch, and your second, and your third, and so on.

You Need More than One Product

Way back in Chapter 2, I showed you four ways to select a product. Remember that? There was the Low-Hanging Fruit, Apples to Apples, the Big Apple, and One Tree, Many Leaves. Use these methods to select your products and have more than one product in your pipeline at any given moment. Hopefully a lot more. That way, if the first product doesn't sell well, you will have a backup waiting. Or if you make a mistake with the first product launch, you can fix it with your second product launch.

Sales can fluctuate, and distributing your investment across several products lowers your risk over time. If one product starts to lag and the niche is getting saturated, you can liquidate your inventory (I'll talk about this more in Chapter 9), but you should never stop researching products, even if you're selling other products that are doing well.

New sellers often ask me what to do with a budget of X dollars to spend, say $50,000. I recommend starting with no more than one-third of that budget for your first product. If it goes well, you will need more money in the bank to invest in the second shipment, since you won't have enough money coming in yet from the sales of the first shipment. If the product doesn't go well, you will need to work on your second product, which requires more of that budget, and then the third product, if necessary.

New sellers should go into this business planning to launch at least three products, not at the same time, but one after the other, regardless of how successful each product is. Think of those first three products as your tuition to Amazon—once you've done your research and launched, you're in Amazon school, always learning, and paying as you go.

Most sellers quit after they fail with their first and second launches, but those launches are the experience that can set you up for success. Like comedian Steven Wright said, "Experience is something you don't get until just after you need it." Don't let this be the case for you. Use the experience that you gain with your initial launches, learn from your mistakes, and continue launching more products. Remember that product research is never-ending. Every successful business, from Apple to Amazon to Tesla, is constantly researching and launching new products.

Once you have a few potential products, you have to find a supplier, or suppliers, who can get you the products. That's where sourcing comes in. You need to find sources that deliver the best products at reasonable prices. You also need to bear in mind the time to market for each product and keep that time to a minimum while still allowing enough time for design, improvements, packaging, and shipping.

TOMER'S TIP:
The Only Time You Should Bundle Products

Bundling products is where you group complementary products together in one convenient bundle for the customer. A yoga mat with a free yoga towel. Bath bombs with a free bath mitt. A diaper bag with free baby wipes. All of these are poor examples of how to bundle products.

On Amazon, customers buy exactly what they need; they usually don't care for bundles unless it improves the overall product. For example, if you look at "baby proofing kits," you would think that an entire kit would sell better, since it comes with locks for your cabinets, straps to hold dressers in place, and outlet covers. The truth is, each of those individual products sells a lot better than the whole kit, even if buying them individually is more expensive, because customers buy what they need at a specific moment in time, knowing they'll get free shipping and two-day delivery. Basically, if you're going to bundle products, the additional products have to increase the value of the main product to the customer. They can't just be "add-ons." So if you offer a yoga ball for pregnant women, adding a free yoga strap won't work, because it doesn't add value to the yoga ball while the woman uses it. Adding nonslip yoga socks might, since they improve her balance on the yoga ball itself.

In other words, the only time to do bundles is if it improves the original use of the product. Finding a supplier who produces a nonslip yoga ball is one solution, and an example of improving the product, but you can also sell a standard yoga ball with nonslip socks as a bundle.

This method is highly effective in the Big Apple, since you can just add a small bundle to an item to make it specific for your target audience. This works with products like a yoga ball and nonslip socks and a bath bomb for kids that comes with a small toy in each bath bomb, and it also works with products like kitchen jars that come with free pantry labels, or a tumbler that comes with a straw. In each example, the customer is getting a better experience with the main product due to the bundled extra.

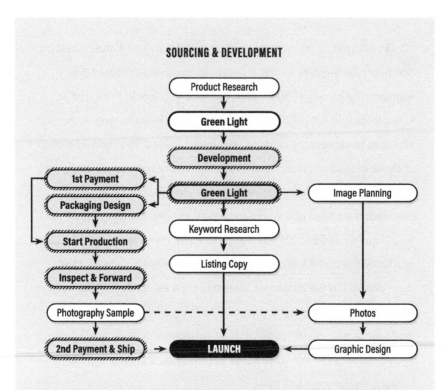

Figure 4: Once you have a potential product, you have to find a supplier who can get it for you. That's where sourcing comes in.

Suppliers

Suppliers work with a lot of people. Not just Amazon sellers, or just online sellers, but sellers all over the world, selling in all kinds of places. You don't want to come off like an inexperienced buyer trying to find your way around. When you're researching suppliers to create a new product for you, you want to sound like a seller who knows your customer and knows what your customer wants. When you reach out to a supplier, know what you're talking about.

Prepare a detailed product description. Ask the supplier specific questions like, "Can you make a product that solves this problem?" or "Can you create something that meets this criteria?" Be prepared to give them details, such as the "specs" (specifications) of the product. For help with this, look at the specs of similar products online. You might use the same or similar ones, or you may want to change them completely. If you need a product that's better than what's available, be specific about the problems you see with current products and how yours must be better. Also list all the features and/or varieties you're looking to add.

The easiest way to do this is to create a two-column list for your product: one column that explains what you want in your product and the other explaining what you don't want. You can label these however you want: yes and no, pros and cons, dos and don'ts, wants and don't wants. Your "yes" column lists everything the product must have and do, and the problems it must solve. The "no" column might include issues you've seen with similar products that you do not want in yours. For example, if you note that customers complain about a similar product being too heavy, or only being available in one color, you might note something like "not more than two pounds," or "not limited to one color."

Reach out to several suppliers with the same request and see what you get back. You can initiate conversations with suppliers by email, but switch your communication to an app such as Skype or WeChat as soon as you can. Keep in mind that if you're dealing with suppliers in China—and you often will be—traditional social media won't work, since it may be blocked.

Be efficient with your communication. Suppliers are busy, so get to the point. You have three goals, three questions to answer:

- Can the supplier get you the product?
- Can they get it to you at a price that's profitable for your business?
- Can they send you a sample or samples right away?

This is why you need to take your time and create detailed lists before you contact the supplier: You need to know what to ask for. You also need to know how much you're willing to pay to make it profitable so you can negotiate with the supplier via these initial communications. Based on their responses, you can eliminate some and zero in on the best supplier for your product. Consider these reasons to take a supplier off your list:

- They can't get you the product you need. However, if they suggest a different product that solves the problem you want your product to solve for your customer, and maybe solves it better, be open to their suggestion. They know their products best. But don't let them talk you into something that clearly doesn't meet your needs. If you've done your due diligence, you know what customers want, and it may not be what the supplier wants to sell you. Just keep an open mind, either way.
- They won't negotiate to a profitable price. You are not running a nonprofit or even a low-profit business.
- The sample doesn't pass your inspection. The sample that you get from the supplier is the best product they will ever produce for you. If it arrives damaged, don't work with the supplier. Just don't. They may tell you that this is the first time they've ever seen this happen, but move on. The supplier is handpicking his best units to ship out as samples to close deals, and if the sample fails, then so will the mass production of products. If they had a better sample, they would have sent it.

Don't contact too many suppliers, but contact enough so you have some options. If you spend time filtering for candidates, you should be able to narrow your search down to around 3 to 15 suppliers for a product. For some products, you may only find 3 suitable suppliers to start with. Once you contact them, they are going to hound you to do business with them, because you're a potential customer. All those WeChat messages take time to respond to, so limit your potential suppliers and start eliminating the ones that don't work for you.

Here's an insider tip: Before I order a single sample, I send my pros and cons lists to the potential suppliers and tell them that I have already received samples from several suppliers, and they all failed my inspection. I state that the reason they failed is because of my cons list, which is basically everything that's wrong with what I've received so far. This lets them know that I am already shopping around, and I'm a serious buyer. I try to answer every question I think they'll have upfront, in my request, so they don't have to ask it. I'm never vague, but very, very specific. In other words, I would never ask for a "small set of headphones." I would say that I want headphones within a specific size and weight range. This lets them know that I know exactly what I want and do not want, and that if they can meet my criteria, they have a good chance at getting my business.

Once you have your lists, you can start researching potential suppliers.

Alibaba

The main source for locating suppliers is the website Alibaba. You can filter by product, price range, and other information to identify a supplier that might work for you. Don't settle for the first one that pops up in your search, though. The most popular may not be the best, and with a little digging, you may find a supplier with products that have the features you're looking for, and at a better price. There are great resources online on how to filter and search effectively on Alibaba.

Trading Companies vs. Factories

Trading companies are middlemen (and women) between sellers and the factories where products are manufactured. If a supplier's website or their booth at a trade show displays many unrelated products, say, yoga mats, diaper bags, and kitchen utensils, they are likely a trading company.

I prefer to work directly with factories whenever it makes sense. Factories manufacture products, and some of them also supply sellers directly. If you visit a supplier's website or booth and they specialize in one thing, like only bamboo kitchenware or only baby toilet seats, they are probably a factory. There are benefits to working with trading companies and factories, and I recommend researching them before you decide on your preference. A trading company is a good option if you are sourcing a complex or expensive product such as electronics. They can vet the product for you and make sure they are supplying you with high-quality goods. Another reason to work with trading companies is when your product is a combination of many different pieces that will need to be made in several different factories.

Whether you work with Alibaba, a trading company, or a factory representative or owner, know that they are not the enemy. They're in business, just like you, and they have to turn a profit. Negotiate with them, but don't be unrealistic. They can cut the cost, sure, but you may be sacrificing quality in the process. Treat them the way that you want your customers to treat you. Aim for long-term, mutually beneficial, and profitable relationships. Just as Amazon wants its sellers to do well, your suppliers want you to do well too. If you grow, they grow. I've worked with factories that grew due to the extra business I gave them—some had to hire more people and buy more machines. They appreciate my business, and I appreciate the quality service and products they deliver.

Sourcing Agents

A sourcing agent is another kind of middleman/woman. Instead of you reaching out to suppliers such as trading companies, you provide the agent with your requirements and they reach out to suppliers for you. Sourcing agencies may have relationships with factories and trading companies. If you go this route, you may have several sourcing agents and you may also use Alibaba for your own research.

If you're looking for the best supplier for a new product you want to launch, you may reach out to all your sourcing agents and ask them to find the best suppliers and get samples for you, while you research suppliers on Alibaba.

Sourcing agents can be very effective. Since they have existing relationships with factories and other suppliers, they can often negotiate a better price. And they want your business, so they'll work hard to find a high-quality product that meets your criteria.

Sourcing agents have different ways of working and being paid. If I work with one, I prefer to have them make the initial connection for me and I pay them a flat fee. Some sourcing agents maintain the relationship and take a small percentage off the top of every order. Others work on a retainer. I advise against keeping them involved in the relationship. As a seller, you need to own and develop the relationship with the factory. Sourcing agents have been known to get kickbacks from factories, so they make more than what you paid them for their services. You have no way of knowing whether this is the case. You'll just have to make sure the price you pay makes sense for your business, and then plan to negotiate with the factory for future orders after you've made a few orders and built a relationship.

You can find sourcing agencies and agents online and at trade shows like the Canton Fair. Some are freelancers who advertise their services on freelancing websites, and others have their own companies with multiple agents. You can also find them on Alibaba.

If you decide to use a sourcing agent to find a supplier, you'll still want to do your own research to see if you can find a better product and better deal through other suppliers, such as factories and trading companies you work with, and Alibaba. Think of sourcing agents the same way you view sites with search engines, like Alibaba: these are all places to look for future products. I use multiple sourcing agents on every product I source, and I also research products on Alibaba. My sourcing agents know that I work with other sourcing agents, so they're motivated to find the best quality product at the best price to get my business.

Whichever suppliers you use, keep it professional. To your customers you may be a friendly little family-owned mom-and-pop shop, but to suppliers, you want to appear as if you've been at this awhile. Don't use your personal email—set up a business email. And never tell them you're just getting started—even if you are.

Order Buffer Time

The time between when an order arrives and is in stock to sell and when you place your next order is your "order buffer time." A zero-buffer time means that you are ordering around the same time an order comes in to Amazon. An order buffer of 30 means you are waiting 30 days between the time an order comes to Amazon and when you place the next one. For a new launch, I recommend starting with a buffer time equal to production time plus shipping time. So if your supplier says the production time is 30 days and you know that shipping is 15 days because you can ship the product by air, plan to place your second order 45 days after your first order comes in, which will be a total of 90 days of stock you will need to supply in your first inventory.

Note: If you're unfamiliar with shipping methods, don't worry—I'll tell you all about them in Chapter 9.

Plan to shorten the buffer time with subsequent orders, as your sales increase. A successful product will eventually have negative buffer times, where you're placing an order before the previous order even arrives. These are general guidelines, and of course, can vary depending on how quickly or slowly your sales are ramping up or down.

Ask your freight forwarder for a cost estimate to ship different quantities of your product using the various methods. You'll need this information for budgeting and to see whether it even makes sense to launch the product. For example, if the product is so large or so heavy that the shipping cost outweighs the profits, you'll want to rethink your product selection. As a seller, you have access to the Amazon FBA Calculator, a free tool that gives you an estimate of Amazon's fees to store your product for fulfillment, etc. Just plug in your Amazon Standard Identification Number (ASIN) number to get an estimate.

As I mentioned earlier, to make 100 percent ROI, you will need your total COGS cost (cost of goods sold, which is production plus shipping) to be 50 percent or less of your net income after Amazon fees. For example, if your cost to produce a product is $9 and the cost to ship is $1, your COGS is $10 (9 + 1). If you sell the product for $35 and your total Amazon fees are $10, that's $25 net income (35 – 10) and $15 profit after you deduct the COGS (25 – 10). If you then divide your $15 profit by your $10 COGS, you'll see that you get 150 ROI (15/10). This is higher than the 100 percent target, and on the safe side of profitability. Again, this target varies between products and sellers, but 100 percent ROI should be the bare minimum you are willing to consider.

Note: Want an easier way to compare offers between suppliers? My Batch spreadsheet, available on my Breakers site, makes the process super easy.

Minimum Order Quantity (MOQ), Lead Time, and Pricing

How many units of a product you order depends on how much money you have to invest. Consider your return on investment, discussed at the beginning of this chapter. A general rule of thumb is to make sure that you have 2.5 to 3 times the amount of your initial investment in reserve so you can pay for future orders.

Also, if you're starting out using the Low-Hanging Fruit method, before you start negotiating with your supplier, look at the competition again. You're not looking for competitors that have been online for a while, but those who have recently launched. You can tell how long they've been active by the reviews—how many, and the dates of the earliest reviews. Focus on the new launches with fewer than 100 reviews and see how many units they're selling per month. Use this as a guide for how many you should expect to sell per day (your daily sales target) your first month, and how many you should order. Don't order so few that you run out that first month, but don't order more than you need, either, even if the supplier won't lower the minimum order requirement or if you have to pay a little more for a smaller order. Make sure your order makes sense for your budget, for the market, and for your profitability.

In your conversation with the supplier, you need to ask about their minimum order quantity, pricing, and lead time. You need this information to see whether their minimum is more than you need, their price works for your budget and financial model, and their lead time works for your launch schedule.

For example, if their MOQ is 1,000 units and you only need 500, that isn't going to work for you. But don't come right out and ask, "What's your MOQ?" That tells them immediately that you're a novice. Instead, tell them how many units you need, and ask for the cost of that many units. Get quotes for at least three quantities—say, 200, 500, and 1,000. Once you know the cost, you may change your mind about how many you want. If the cost is lower than you expected, you may want to get more; if it's higher, you may want less (or you may want to shop around). But you can still negotiate. One thing to understand is that the true MOQ is always one—just one unit—if you're willing to pay the price for that one unit. Most suppliers can give you any quantity, but the fewer units you purchase, the higher the cost per unit.

However, a couple of things can affect a supplier's MOQ: specialization and packaging. If you want your logo embedded in the product, for example, they may need to do a MOQ of say, 500 units to make that change profitable for themselves. Or they may need to do a minimum of 1,500 to justify the packaging. Suppliers usually work with another factory for packaging, and that factory's minimum might be 1,500 units (packages). If this is the case and you only want to purchase 500 units right now but know that you'll be purchasing 1,000 more over the next couple of months, you may be able to make a deal with the supplier to get you the first 500 now, with the promise that you'll use those additional 1,000 packages for future orders. In case the MOQ is too high for you, what you want to understand is why it's so high.

New sellers may not want to worry about specialization such as embedding a logo just yet. You can start by selling off-the-shelf products while you learn the business, then decide whether you want to change up your products with logos or even create a new design, which is where patents and molds come in. We'll get to those shortly.

In this conversation, you also need to ask the supplier about the production time. Thirty days is typical, but if they give you a longer time, ask them why it takes so much longer. You might discover that they don't have one part of your product in the factory, and they have to source it from another factory. Then you can decide whether you can change that part, source more of that specific part at once, or—if it isn't worth the delay—remove it altogether to shorten the lead time.

REMEMBER THAT PRODUCTION TIME + SHIPPING TIME = LEAD TIME.

Published prices on sourcing sites like Alibaba are usually incorrect. You have to contact the supplier to get the real pricing. Making changes to the design affects the price, too, so until you speak with a supplier about MOQ, production time, and specialization, you won't know the true cost. Before you start the conversation, figure out your target price (which is probably similar to what's currently selling on Amazon)—this is the most you'll pay to make the deal profitable for you, but without sacrificing the quality of the product. How do you get there? Well, let's think about a typical conversation.

You need to get the product for five dollars, and the supplier tells you that it's seven dollars. If you tell them that you want it for five dollars, they might agree to do that for you, but expect to get an inferior product instead of the one you were expecting. The supplier has to make a profit, too, so your discount will be reflected somewhere. Instead, ask them if there is a way to get the same product for five dollars. They might say they can do it for five dollars if you order more units. Or they might be able to do it for five dollars if you change the design or the packaging. For example, you could switch from a colored box to a poly bag to save a few cents. There's always going to be a balance between quality and price, so make sure you're getting the quality you need at a price that makes sense for your business.

If there's anything at all that you don't like about their offer, discuss it. There's usually a reason behind the MOQ, the price, and the production time. Most suppliers will discuss all three of these factors, and if you fight them too much on any of them, the quality of the product may suffer. They can always give you fewer units faster for a cheaper price, but you may not like what you get. Once you've agreed on an MOQ, lead time, and price, request a sample.

The bottom line is that for your first order, you need to order the right amount of product so you aren't overstocked and you don't run out of stock. Following is a handy formula for figuring that out.

> **UNITS TO ORDER IN YOUR FIRST SHIPMENT = AVERAGE DAILY SALES TARGET × [LEAD TIME + BUFFER TIME] + UNITS TO GIVE AWAY**

We'll talk about "units to give away" in Chapter 7.

Samples

Get several samples from different suppliers, and always order a few similar products from your future competitors on Amazon for comparison.

Suppliers waive the cost of the product sample, but you, the seller, are responsible for paying for delivery—typically between $30 and $100 for express, for a quick shipment, which takes just a few days. The shipping cost varies due to the weight and size of the sample. For expensive products, the supplier may not waive the cost of the product sample, but if you decide to source with them, they'll most likely agree to reimburse you for the cost of that initial sample.

Before you ask for a sample, negotiate the price and quantity for the price that you need so you can ensure the deal is profitable. If it isn't, you don't need a sample. You're not placing an order—you're doing research.

That will take an investment of your time and money, but you don't want to throw away either on products that don't support your business's financial model.

Do not, and I repeat, *do not* order a sample and *then* try to negotiate a price. You could end up paying $50 for delivery of a $20 product that doesn't make financial sense for your business.

When you get your samples, use them. Test them rigorously. Think about what's going to happen to that product once it's in the customer's hands. If you're selling hydration packs, put the pack in a backpack and take it for a run. If you aren't a runner, give it to a runner friend and ask them to test it for you. If the hydration pack starts to leak, it's not the right product for you. Depending on the product, customers might step on it, throw it against the wall, or drop it in the bathtub. Whatever is likely to happen to the product, test it for those circumstances. It's better to uncover issues yourself, before you invest in the product, than to hear about them in a bad review.

Checklists

Checklists will help you decide whether you have the right product. I refer to my checklist before finalizing my decision:

- I start with The Six-Star Experience. The product must meet that criteria at a minimum to be considered for my launch. Let's review:
  - ▷ First star: the product must do what it's supposed to do.
  - ▷ Second star: product installation and use must be crystal clear.
  - ▷ Third star: the product must be better than the competition.
  - ▷ Fourth star: the product must be five-star worthy.
  - ▷ Fifth star: the product comes with great customer service.

- ▷ Sixth star: the product must deliver a six-star customer experience. Always underpromise, overdeliver, and surprise!

- Next, I double-check the cost to make sure it meets my current cash flow status. Now remember, I've already discussed MOQ, price, and production time with the supplier, but since that conversation, my financial status may have changed. I may have more to invest in inventory, but I may have less. I have to ask myself, "Based on my current cash flow, does this baby monitor still make sense?" A number of factors come into play here. For example, "baby monitors" is a very competitive niche, so I'll need to invest time and money in marketing (keywords, PPC). These products are also somewhat expensive, and I'll need to order a lot of them upfront so I don't sell out while doing an aggressive launch. If I have only a few thousand dollars to spend, this product won't work for me right now.

- I have to ask myself a few more questions before making a decision, starting with "Is this a trend? Am I going to sell 500 and have another 500 sitting in a warehouse?" In this case, the answer is no. People will always want baby monitors.

- Then I ask myself whether this product will be outdated soon because of better materials, technology, etc. Again, the answer here is no. In fact, in this case, new tech such as apps seem to make the product more difficult to use, which wouldn't work for my target customer.

- Do the minimum order quantity and lead time still work for me? Again, a seller's business—inventory, launch dates—is always in flux, and what may have worked for me two weeks ago may not work today. I also have to consider everything else I'm doing that might add to the lead time, such as getting an MSDS report or adding a complementary product to overdeliver and surprise.

- Does this meet my timeline? You may find the perfect product, but the timing isn't right. It may not fit your current cash flow or launch date, or you may check to see how the competition's doing and discover that the market is approaching saturation. If that's the case, you can hold off. You don't have to move forward with the supplier, but you've done the research for a later date.
- Will I be able to go deep with the product? Remember in the Apples-to-Apples method of product selection that we're building a brand. I prefer to launch products that, if they go well, I can just launch more of the same products.

Once the product "checks all the boxes," I know I have a winner.

TOMER'S TIP: Molds and Patents

I've worked with many sellers who never created a product that required a mold or a patent. Still, some sellers think the best and only way to truly differentiate their product is to have the factory create a new mold for a product or come up with a new design that they can patent.

Molds can cost anywhere from a few hundred dollars to many thousands of dollars, and you will usually be looking at a high MOQ (minimum order quantity) in your first shipment. However, molds can be a long-term strategy for launching new products.

It's the same with patents. You could be working with an industrial designer and the factory for many months to come up with a final design. That's fine, but in the meantime, continue to launch off-the-shelf products or products that you're simply branding and are different enough from the competition for a successful launch.

If you create a new design for a product, you'll want to hire a patent attorney to write a design patent for you. Then you can submit it to the appropriate patent office (in the US, this is the United States Patent and Trademark Office, or USPTO), and while you're waiting for approval, your product's status is "patent pending." During this time, expect other sellers to copy your design. From Investopedia:

> A design patent is a form of legal protection of the unique visual qualities of a manufactured item. A design patent may be granted if the product has a distinct configuration, distinct surface ornamentation or both.[3]

Bear in mind that competitors can make the slightest change in your design and the design patent is most likely no longer valid.

Utility patents are for entirely new products. Again, you have to create the product and have a patent attorney write the patent, then submit it to the patent office. Utility patents protect your product for 20 years, then they expire and others can copy your product legally.

Again, per Investopedia: "A utility patent is a patent that covers the creation of a new or improved—and useful—product, process, or machine."[4]

Once your patent is approved, you can have the copycats removed from Amazon, but this takes time. Defending a patent can be difficult, too, because you have to prove that the copycat is just like yours.

---

[3] Will Kenton, "What Is a Design Patent?" Investopedia, August 20, 2019, https://www.investo pedia.com/terms/d/design-patent.asp.

[4] Kenton, "Utility Patent."

Recall Chapter 1 and why you started your business. Do you want to spend time defending a patent, or doing something else?

Many times, you may think you need a new mold or a patent, but you don't. Consult with suppliers and sourcing agents. They may already have access to the product you're looking for or may be able to tweak the design in a way that meets your needs and doesn't require a new mold or patent. They are the experts because they do this for other sellers every single day.

If you still want to create a new mold or get a patent, speak with an attorney to get all the details before you invest a lot of time and money into this strategy.

Green Lights

Everything you've done to this point—selecting potential products; negotiating MOQs, prices, and lead times; testing samples—has been research. You may have spoken with many suppliers and have a lot of samples, but you are not committed to launching any of these products. Only when you have successfully completed every one of these steps and the product still meets your criteria, and still makes sense for your business, do you give it the Green Light.

Green-lighting happens when you give your supplier that first deposit, typically 30 percent upfront and the remaining 70 percent once the product is ready to ship. During this time, you need to work on packaging. If your packaging is complicated, you may have to do this step before you green-light the product, but most packaging is simple enough that it can be designed during the production window.

TOMER'S TIP:
Open the Product Listing on Amazon
Before Starting Production

When I was new to selling, I made a lot of mistakes—some of them quite expensive. One of the biggest was my fetal doppler mistake. Researching products, I came across an at-home heartbeat monitor for pregnant moms, or "fetal doppler." Only one seller had these machines on Amazon, and he was selling a *lot* of them. Why didn't he have any competition? I didn't know, and I didn't even take the time to find out. Instead, I lined up a supplier immediately and started production on my own fetal doppler!

Waiting for my first fetal dopplers to arrive, I set up a listing and created a sample shipment. *And was immediately prompted by Amazon that I could not sell fetal dopplers to customers in the United States.* What? How was that possible? Someone was selling them— why couldn't I? It turned out that the other seller's listing used terminology that sort of disguised the product's function, while making it clear to buyers. I had paid my supplier, and now I had product coming that I couldn't even sell. That was a costly mistake that I could have easily avoided—and will never repeat!

Before you commit to a product, or start production, or pay your supplier, make sure you can actually sell the product on Amazon. Also make sure you have all the appropriate documentation. You can do this in two easy steps:

▶ Open your product listing on Amazon. This isn't the final listing— it's just a test listing that you'll be revising before you launch.

The quickest way to do this is to refer to a competitor's listing and copy and paste their title and bullet points, without their brand name, into your listing.

▶ Then create a shipment for the product.

Completing these two steps will trigger Amazon to let you know if you are allowed to sell the product on their site, or sell it in the US, the UK, and other countries. Amazon will also let you know what documentation you need to proceed, such as a Material Safety Data Sheet (MSDS), which you should be able to get from your supplier. However, *verify this and get the documentation before moving forward*. Otherwise, you may end up with a bunch of products that you can't sell.

Now it's time to place your deposit with your supplier and the final countdown begins! You have roughly six to eight weeks until launch. You're working on your packaging and your listing. This isn't the time to slack off. It's time to make it better—the subject of the next chapter.

BREAKERS

Choosing a supplier can be tricky, but I've made it easier for you. My Batch spreadsheet allows you to compare offers from suppliers and see outcomes such as profit per day, ROI, and more. You can vary the number of units and the shipping method, too, to see how that affects the results. If you want to make smarter buying decisions, check it out at tomerrabinovich.com/breakers.

CHAPTER 6

MAKE IT BETTER

*"I have been up against tough competition
all my life. I wouldn't know how
to get along without it."*

—WALT DISNEY

W ho's your top competitor? You should know the answer to this
because you've probably looked at their Amazon listing hundreds
of times. If you haven't launched yet, you've at least looked at who
the competition might be when you *do* launch. This is the go-to product
that attracts the majority of your market. This seller dominates the niche.

That seller sleeps well at night. Their sales are fantastic, and not by
accident. That seller planned the whole thing.

Do you want to dominate your niche?

When you dominate your niche, you're ranked number one for most
major keywords and as the number one product in your subcategory. You
have that shiny best seller badge. You're making more money than everyone else in your niche too—and gaining ground with sales as a percentage
of the larger market too because "money sticks to money": the more you
sell, the more people will want to buy from you. Being in that top spot
makes you more attractive to your market, and that's where you want to
be. Affiliates will point to your product, bringing you more traffic. Think

of a product in your niche that's in the top spot right now. They've probably been there a while. Once you're established in that upper echelon of a niche market, it's difficult for someone to take your place. Difficult, but not impossible. You can get there by making your product better than the competition.

If I'm launching a product in a niche where some people are doing $10K a month, and others are doing $100K a month, I'm not shooting for $50K a month. That's not good enough. I want to be the guy making $100K a month—or more. Realistically, the pie is only so big, and you can't make it bigger, but you can get a bigger slice. In a good-size niche, being the number two or number three seller can still amount to a lot of sales, but always shoot for that number one spot. The closer you are to the middle, the shorter the road to the bottom. *Whether you're launching for the first time or you've been at it for years, your goal with every product and every new launch should always be to hit and maintain number one status.*

That's what I aim for, every single time. It might take me six months to two years to get there, but it's worth it. If I'm going to put in the time to do everything that I've told you so far—picking the right product, getting it from the best source, giving the customer a Six-Star Experience—when it comes to selling in my niche, I don't want to settle for second-best. You shouldn't settle for that either. Your goal, with every product and every launch, should be to eventually dominate your niche.

To get there, you need to have the best products, the best images, the best keywords, the best copy, and the best reviews. You don't need to be the best at all of those in all of Amazon, just better than your competitors. It takes work, but you can get there. First, let's look at why the top sellers are so comfortable in that number one, number two, or number three spot. Then we'll look at what you can do to get there too.

Why It's Hard to Compete with Top Sellers

Sellers that dominate their niche have done the work to get where they are, but if it seems like the internet conspires to keep them in that top spot...well, it does! As I've mentioned before, people are more likely to buy bestselling products. If you're online and you can't tell the difference between several products, but one has more sales, more reviews, or better reviews, you'll likely choose the more popular product. (This is an opportunity for you, by the way, that I'll get to shortly.)

So why do top sellers tend to stay in top-selling spots? Well, when you have a best seller badge and are ranked on top on every keyword, and you have the most reviews, your product gets sold more often than any other product.

Another reason is affiliate sites. These websites provide links that direct customers to products, often to products on Amazon. They don't list every product on Amazon, but they typically list the top 10 in a certain category. When a customer follows a link and makes a purchase, the affiliate gets a cut, or commission. That cut doesn't come from your profit—Amazon pays the affiliate from the percentage that you pay them. They like having affiliate sites point people to their site. The more people click on those links and buy those products, the more sales and more reviews those products receive, and the more likely they are to stay in the top 10 on Amazon, and on those affiliate sites.

For example, if you're looking for Bluetooth headphones, you might google "best Bluetooth headphones." The top results will be articles titled something like "Top 10 Best Headphones to Buy in 2022." When you click on the article, you'll see the list of headphones and maybe a review of each one, along with links to the listings on Amazon. If you click a link and purchase the product, the publisher of the article receives a small percentage of the price. Amazon doesn't mind paying affiliates because it draws customers to their site.

Affiliate links are found on websites dedicated to them, in blogs, in online newspaper columns and articles, and on social media sites like Instagram and YouTube. There can be many, many sites directing people to those products, which is another reason that once they're in a top spot, they tend to stay there. To compete with these sellers, you have to copy what they're doing, only do it better.

First, you have to find your competitors.

Identify the Competition

To identify the competition, look at products that are like yours. In the Amazon search bar, type in words and phrases that your customer would type to find your product. Don't be too general—instead of "knife set," search for the specific product you're selling, like "knife set with wooden block" or "knife set with roll bag." Words and phrases that are too broad will deliver too many products outside your market, with a wide variety of features, benefits, and prices that target people outside your market.

Let the search bar's autofill feature help you. Type in a word or two, hit the space bar, and see what other words come up. These are the most common phrases, or "long-tail keywords," that customers are searching on, so they show you what people are looking for. From among the long-tail keywords that appear, look for those that match your product. Now search on each of those long-tail phrases and look at the results. You want to identify those products that come up on the first page, are most like your product, and have similar price points (cost about the same as your product). These are your direct competitors.

When you're identifying the competition, don't look at only the best-selling products. Those sellers have probably been in the game a long time and are doing well in part due to their high reviews and the other reasons I mentioned that keep top sellers in those top spots. You also need to look at newcomers who are gaining ground—sellers who are going through what you're going through right now, figuring out how to compete, and doing really well. You might have a combination of sellers who have been around a long time with thousands of reviews, and newer sellers who have dozens or hundreds of reviews and are making good sales. Again, your focus should be on the highest sales-to-reviews ratio. Those are the sellers that are on their way to eventual niche domination.

Ideally, you should plan to dominate your niche before you launch, but if you've already launched, you can still get there. In fact, if you did everything right so far, you're already on your way to the top. You're selling the best products and getting five-star reviews. Keep doing what you're doing, and don't slack off on any of it. Getting to that number one spot takes a little more work, but basically there are just three more things you have to do. That's it, I promise! Just three more things to go from second-best to niche domination. I won't keep you in suspense: it's all in your listing.

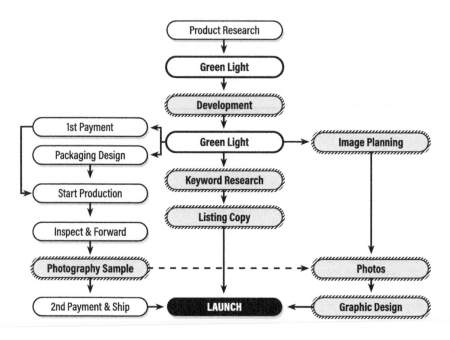

MAKE IT BETTER

Product Research → Green Light → Development → Green Light

Green Light → Image Planning

Green Light → Keyword Research → Listing Copy → LAUNCH

1st Payment → Packaging Design → Start Production → Inspect & Forward → Photography Sample → 2nd Payment & Ship → LAUNCH

Photography Sample ⇢ Photos

Image Planning → Photos → Graphic Design → LAUNCH

Figure 5: You'll have a number of tasks to complete in the Make It Better phase before you can launch your product.

Your Listing

Beyond product selection and a five-star review strategy, the secret to niche domination is all in your listing; specifically, it's in three parts of your listing:

- Copy, including the title, bullet points, and the product description or A-plus content (formerly known as EBC, or enhanced brand content) that may include copy and images and usually appears below the bullet points
- Images, which may include video
- Keywords, indexed either in the copy or the backend

Sounds simple, right? It is, yet many sellers don't give their listing the attention it requires. Then they wonder why they're languishing in the middle of their market. They don't understand why they aren't selling more.

> **WHEN A SELLER SHOWS ME THEIR LISTING AND ASKS, "IS THIS A GOOD LISTING, TOMER?" I TELL THEM, "I DON'T KNOW—I'D HAVE TO LOOK AT THE TOP COMPETITORS IN YOUR NICHE."**

Think about how people shop. They don't go to only your listing—they click on a few listings and compare them. If your product and listing look better than all the others, which one are they going to buy?

I told you it was simple. How you get there takes some work, though, because you have to convince the customer that yours really is the best. In other words, having the best product isn't enough; you have to convince the customer that it's the best, and you do that in your listing. That's how you break from the crowd, leave the competition behind, and get to that number one spot.

Work with professionals to create your listing—photographers, copywriters, and graphic designers—but set them and your listing up for success by doing all the initial research to determine what needs to go in the listing. You need to research your competitors and analyze what they're doing and then give that information to the professionals who help you create your listing.

> **TO SELL THE MOST, YOU HAVE TO BE THE BEST. NOT THE BEST IN THE WORLD. NOT EVEN THE BEST ON AMAZON. JUST BETTER THAN EVERYONE ELSE WHO SELLS THE SAME PRODUCTS AS YOU ON AMAZON.**

This isn't about making the product better. You already did that. It's about improving your customer's perception of the product. When you improved your product, you had a starting point: the product. With the customer's perception, you're starting from scratch. That's why you have to start with the competition. They've been there and done that, and you can learn a lot from them.

Copy

Copy refers to the words in your listing. It's what the customer reads when they click on your listing and the page opens to your product. Even a professional copywriter can't tell you what the best copy is for your product. But your most successful competitors can. Reviewing the copy on the bestselling competition's product sites shows you the copy that compels people to buy. You've already identified the competition, so now you need to take a closer look at their copy, their reviews, their images, and their keywords.

Start with their copy—specifically, the title. In terms of copy and keywords, the title is the most important real estate of your entire listing. Sellers often make the mistake of choosing a title based only on words that have the highest number of keyword searches, and that's a mistake. People may be searching on that keyword, but that doesn't mean they're buying the product. What words and phrases are in the competition's title? You want those words and phrases in your title too.

List the title words used by 5 to 10 competitors that are around your same price point. Look at the big ones that have been around a while and some newer ones that are doing well too. For example, say you're selling a first aid kit. Of course, you'll include the words "first aid kit" in your title. What else do you need? Well, you notice that the top-selling first aid kits include the number of pieces in their titles. "100-Piece First Aid

Kit." "250-Piece First Aid Kit." Do you think you should mention how many pieces are in your kit? Absolutely!

Continue combing through all the titles and pick out all the words that appear. Combine them into a new title, and only then try to improve it. Make it better. This is where you should start doing keyword research, to see if your competitors missed anything. Is there a word or phrase that isn't in the competition's title that should be in yours? Once you've done that, then you can look at words that are often searched on and consider adding those, but only if it makes sense. They have to reflect your particular product. If your title is exactly like everyone else's except it has that one extra word that makes it appear better to the customer, or that one word that a lot of people are typing into the search bar, you're going to attract more people to your listing. That little bit of effort can make a big difference in your sales.

There are a lot of myths about titles. Some sellers think you shouldn't use commas, dashes, brackets, or other punctuation. I don't believe this. If the top seller has commas, dashes, brackets, asterisks, and exclamation marks, then that's what's going in my title too. It's working, and that's all I care about. This is also true for repeating words and phrases: if my top competitors repeat the same words and phrases, I do too.

Next, move on to the bullet points. These are generally based off of features and benefits—what's special about your product and how it benefits the customer. For example, for a pillowcase "silky smooth texture" is a feature; "for a better night's rest" is a benefit. A benefit is usually a result of a feature; the silky-smooth texture creates a better night's rest. Expert copywriters may tell you to focus mainly on benefits, but I disagree. I say, "Look at the competition." Whatever they're doing, you should be doing too. Just like with the title, list all the bullet points from that list of your top competitors, the ones you identified earlier. Look for trends. Are they using phrases that focus on how easy it is to use the product, or the results, or maybe noting something like "satisfaction guaranteed"? You want to be saying the same thing. Also look at how the bullets are ordered. Which bullets are at the top of the list most often? You want to mimic the order in your listing.

The rest of the copy should elaborate on those bullets, but again, look at the competition's copy. They've tested their titles, their bullet points, and the rest of the copy. They've tweaked it and validated that it works. I'm not proposing you plagiarize another seller's copy; just use it as a guide to write your own, then make it better. What are they saying about their product that's also true about yours? How can you rewrite that copy to make it even more attractive to a customer and improve their perception of your product? Finally, is your product better in some way? If so, make that very obvious to your customers. Use words, images, and bullets to showcase why your product is superior and their best choice.

Once you have a rough draft of the title, bullets, and the rest of the copy, hire a professional copywriter to do the final writing for you. Freelance copywriters can be found online. Give the writer everything that you want reflected in your listing. Tell them to write something similar, only better. Give them all the specifics of your product, too, so that everything is accurate. This will make it so much easier for the copywriter since they won't have to start from scratch and wonder whether they're getting it right. They will instead take advantage of all your research and hard work to create the exact copy that you need for your listing.

Reviews

In Chapter 3, we discussed ways of being creative in terms of getting reviews. At the same time, you need to figure out how your competitors are getting reviews. First you have to identify which competitors have the highest sales-to-reviews ratio, or the most reviews per number of sales. Free tools are available that will show you the number of units each seller has sold, and the number of reviews they received over the last 30 days. Divide the number of reviews by the number of sales to get the review percentage number. For some products, such as commodities like cheap, disposable cups, the number will be low. For a more personal product like hairbrushes, the number will be high. Isolate the competing products with the highest sales-to-reviews ratio. These are the competitors whose reviews you need to read. What are people talking about in the reviews? Are they posting photos of what they did and did not like about the product? Do you see a trend?

I did this process for a set of makeup brushes that had an 8 percent ratio—8 reviews for every 100 sales. That's ridiculously high, right? The review average was 4.7, which is also very high. Then I looked for repeating phrases in the reviews. As a seller, you have access to a search bar in the reviews. One phrase came up again and again: *wrapping paper*.

What does wrapping paper have to do with makeup brushes? The first review gave it away. The customer loved how the brushes came wrapped like a nice little gift. Other reviewers mentioned the same thing. They liked how it felt like they were getting a present in the mail. People who had sent the product as a gift were thrilled knowing that the receiver would get this nicely wrapped product, like a gift. And those who bought it for themselves wrote in their reviews things like, "It felt like a gift for myself!"

By the way, nowhere in the product listing did the seller mention the lovely gift wrap, not in the copy and not in the images. This seller was overdelivering and surprising! So how can you use this idea? Well, if you sell a makeup brush kit of your own, wrap it in gift paper, but not just any gift paper—a *better* gift paper! Maybe add an emotional note on it as well so it's even more clear that it's a surprise, or a note mentioning the wrapping paper once they open the packaging. Get inspired by your competitor's ideas and build on them.

On top of reading your competitors' reviews, consider buying their products. Evaluate them for quality, features, and benefits. Look at the packaging. Figure out what's so great about the product that's earning it such a high sales-to-reviews ratio.

Images

When you shop at a store, how much does a product's packaging influence your buying decision? Do you notice the labels? Are you more likely to choose a frozen dinner or a can of soup with an attractive label over one with a plain-Jane wrapper?

Packaging is incredibly important to sales. But your online products don't rely on packaging. In fact, your customer may never see the packaging until they receive the product, open the box, and peel back the Styrofoam, paper, or other packing materials. So how do you entice customers if you don't have clever packaging? You do it with images.

Images on your listing are the equivalent of packaging. And just like the fancy boxes, bags, and labels on your favorite store-bought items, they're incredibly important, with the main image being the *most* important. When you see a great listing on Amazon, you'll notice that the copy and the images match. The bullets reflect the images and vice versa. That's how your listing should look. Even though you're hiring an individual copywriter, a photographer, and a graphic designer to design your listing, it's up to you to make sure the pieces fit.

Before you meet with a photographer, refer to the images on the listings of the competitors you identified when choosing your product. Start with your main image. This must be on a white background, and it must show your actual product with or without the packaging, depending on the product. Your main image is the most important one. Its only job is to get people to click on your listing. You need to think about the color, size, and position of it in the photo. If it's many pieces, like a first aid kit, you probably don't need to show all the pieces in this image—just the kit itself, in a nice-looking case. Most importantly, *it must look better than all the other main images out there.*

> **YOUR MAIN IMAGE IS THE MOST IMPORTANT ONE IN YOUR LISTING, AND IT MUST STAND OUT FROM YOUR COMPETITION'S MAIN IMAGES.**

Instead of looking at just one listing and its images, or looking at them one at a time, look at all the images shown on your competition's listings. You can even copy and paste them into a document, but you need to see them together. What do the different listings have in common? What are the trends? Look for the commonalities. This will tell you exactly the types of images you must include in your listing.

Your main image and all the other images on your listing must be similar but better than the competition's. For example, say you're selling a knife set. You go to multiple knife-set listings online for comparison and notice some things:

- Every listing's main image is a sharp, clean photograph of the knife set outside of the packaging.
- Some show the knives in the knife block, and some show them out of the block. The best ones have images of the knives both in and out of the block.
- Among these better listings, some of the knives are lined up next to each other so you can see how they compare in size.

One photo has a piece of fruit in it, which adds some color and pulls your eye toward it.

- Still another listing shows all the knives laid out with their quantities, dimensions, and names listed: one 12-inch bread knife; six 8-inch steak knives; one 6-inch paring knife, cheese knife, pizza knife…you get the picture.

Now, eliminate the "one-offs." If only one competitor shows a knife cutting fruit, maybe you don't need that image. Select the best example of each type, eliminating the duplicates, and put one of each type of image aside—these are the ones you need to improve for your listing. Keep doing that until you have only unique images. Think about whether these images are useful for influencing your customer's perception of your product. You might decide to improve them or discard them, but if an image appears on most or all of your competitors' listings, you probably need to have that type of image too. Now you have your basic images—the ones you need your photographer to re-create for your product. This way, the photographer now knows exactly what you want and doesn't have to guess or assume what they think are the best images for your product.

After you have those, look at your bullets (which you should have developed, again, based on the common ones among your competitors) and see what other types of images you need. Use lifestyle images that show the product in use to showcase each feature and benefit. To show the size of the product, have an image of it next to something that's familiar to the customer, for perspective. If the product comes with additional parts or bonus products, show them too. Depending on the product, you might want to have your graphic designer create an infographic to give more detailed information in an easy-to-understand visual format. You can even have "before and after" images of the results of your product, such as a collage of photos captured from Instagram posted by users of your product and tagged with your brand name. If you have other products within that brand, you can include them in your images as well, as long as you make it clear that they are not included with the individual product's purchase.

If there's something special about your product that isn't shown in these images, you should showcase that difference in the second or third image to differentiate your product to the customer. You may have bullet points that the competition doesn't have that describe your product's special features and benefits. This is your opportunity to have a better listing by adding an image that illustrates your product's superiority. For example, yoga mat listings may all proclaim "nonslip surface" in their copy, but how many actually show you the nonslip underside of the mat? Likewise, if you identify images that aren't mentioned in the copy, that's an opportunity for you to add that bullet to your copy.

Once you have all your images, look at them and ask yourself, "What am I getting?" Have you made it clear to the customer that they're getting the exact product you're selling, in the size, colors, and dimensions shown, and that it comes with the parts and pieces that are actually included? Are all the features and benefits clearly represented in the images?

Now look at them again, one at a time, and ask yourself, "Does this image improve the customer's perception of the value of my product?" If the answer is yes, then you need that image. If the value stays the same or is actually decreased, then don't use the image. And never use a bad image. Remember, aside from the main image, the job of the other images is to convert the customer—to turn them from prospect to buyer and increase your conversion rate. You want to use all of the images, but in case you don't have anything to put in the last image or two, it's better to put nothing than stock photos that will actually lower the value of your main image. More on this in a moment.

Include descriptions of the images when you submit similar ones for reference to your photographer. Then tell them that their job is to make a set of photographs that look like those, only better. Your images must be better than the competition's corresponding images. Besides showing you have a better product, showcase your features and benefits in different ways that are more appealing. Use simple text, with the same fonts and colors throughout your images. Be consistent with your branding, and keep the text to a minimum. Somehow, you have to make your images compel people to say, "This is the product I want."

Remember, your main image drives sessions and clicks; the other images, and your copy, drive conversions. They should focus on the features and benefits that you mention in your copy. Each image should represent just one feature or benefit. Trying to squeeze more into an image only serves to confuse the customer.

Review your finished listing and be honest with yourself about your first impression. Consider, "Would I buy my own product over a competitor's product?" If the answer is no, you have work to do. You must improve your listing until it's the best.

Which brings me to my last point: do not use stock photos. Hire a professional photographer, and if you have people in your photos, hire models or photography agencies that are already working with models. If possible, use the same model or models with the same or similar backgrounds and lighting so the images look genuine, and like they were photographed in one shoot. Images that don't go together look as if they were purchased off a stock site.

If you want to show your product in use and don't have models, instead of using stock photos or Photoshopping people into backgrounds (ugh, yes—some sellers actually do this), consider reaching out to influencers on Instagram who have high-quality images and ask if they would be advocates for your brand in exchange for products and a fee. Then, with their permission, use the images on your Amazon listing. Influencers with millions of followers are likely outside your price range, but those who have just a few thousand followers, and who you think would be positive representatives for your brand, are often open to these kinds of arrangements. This strategy only works if you sell products that will do well socially, and your brand will do well socially only if it's easily brandable. Which brings us to the next topic: your listing and your brand.

Remember that You're Building a Brand

Finally, remember that as a private label seller, you are building a brand. With your images, copy, and everything else in your listing, never forget the customer. You are targeting a niche and a customer, and everything the customer sees in your listing should appeal to them and reflect that brand. Think about this when you choose fonts, colors, and graphics. They might be bright or pastel colored. Your models should represent the best version of your customer. Think about the words you use in your listing too. They could be serious or playful, depending on the customer and your brand.

Focus on your customer, their wants and needs, or the problem they're trying to solve. A yoga mat for seniors that touts a nonslip surface will attract more senior customers, even though nonslip surfaces are standard among yoga mats. But building your messaging around that feature will help you capture that niche. This is marketing 101, but it's these details that will separate your listing from the rest.

In the past, Amazon didn't provide guidance for building a brand. A seller could add their logo and tagline to a listing, or apply a color palette across their products, but the platform didn't provide for any real brand establishment. That's all changed, and today you can use their Brand

Registry. First, you need to get a registered trademark for your brand in the US or Europe. The Brand Registry opens the door to many more seller benefits. You've probably seen listings that include a lot of additional content below the copywriting: images and more text, for example. That's called EBC, or enhanced brand content. You can add this to your listing only if your product is in the Brand Registry.

When you have a Brand Registry, you can open your own store in Amazon. If you go to amazon.com/gillette, for example, you'll see Gillette's store. Likewise, once you're in the Brand Registry, you can open your own virtual store and put all your branded products in it.

TOMER'S TIP:
Branding and Social Media

Products that are easier to brand tend to do better on social media than others. For example, makeup. How many makeup brands can you name? Sephora, Mac, L'Oréal, Maybelline…the list goes on. Makeup is very brandable, and easier to sell socially than many other products. It's the same with sports attire, like Nike, Adidas, North Face, and so on. If you can name a lot of brands for a product, that tells you the product is easier to brand and may do very well socially.

Shoppers trust Amazon. That's why they're on that site looking for products. But Amazon won't convert shoppers into customers for you. It's all on you to create a listing that builds that trust with words and images that are consistent and resonate with your target audience. Make your listings inviting so people want to hang out on them, read them, look at the images, and eventually, buy from you.

Videos are a sort of variation of copy and images. Before you do a video, see what the top-selling competition is doing. Do they all have videos? Then you need a video. If they don't, you may not need one when you initially launch.

Videos are more difficult and expensive to produce. For the more experienced seller, a video can be a valuable addition to your listing. Just like copy and images, quality is paramount. Hire a pro to make your video. Keep it short—under a minute—and opt for background music instead of voice-over. Focus on the features and benefits, showing them in the video and spelling them out in on-screen text over the video. If you do make a video, consider making several versions to use in your listing and your PPC ads, which we'll talk about in Chapter 8.

You can only have so many images in your listing, but video allows you to squeeze in many more. You can repeat the same features and benefits that you showcased in your images and add more in the video. Remember to repeat the same look and feel—colors, fonts, etc.—for consistency to reinforce your brand.

Take your listing copy, images—and video, if you make one—seriously and don't sacrifice quality. This is your product's packaging. Many times, it will be the difference between a sale and no sale. Get it right the first time.

Keywords

Customers typically find what they want on Amazon by typing a word or phrase, called a search *term*, into the search bar on that site. A number of products appear on the page, and the customer might click on one or more of these products. Clicking on a product opens that product's listing, and other products also appear on the page. The customer can go down a product rabbit hole, clicking on products that bring them from one page to another until they find what they're looking for and add it to their cart. The important thing to remember here is that however they end up on that product, their search started with them typing a search term into the search bar.

When a customer types a search term into the search bar, your product will only appear in the results if you've *indexed* your product with those words. If you have not, your product won't appear in the results on page 1, page 10, or even page 20. It simply *will not show up* unless you've used indexing to connect your product to those *keywords*, which is how we refer to search terms on the backend.

You can index a keyword three ways: (1) include it in your title, (2) include it in the bullet points or product description in your copy, or (3) index it manually in the backend. If you want to include a keyword phrase or *long-tail keyword* in your listing, you don't have to have every word listed in the same order that they appear in the phrase. So if your title is "Garlic Press for Kitchen," you're automatically indexed for "Kitchen Garlic Press," and you don't have to add that phrase in the backend.

Look at the keywords and phrases your competitors use and make sure you have them indexed too. Some sellers say that you should never index a word or phrase twice, but I disagree. If the top sellers have "Garlic Press" twice in their title, do the same in your listing. Amazon uses an algorithm to figure out how relevant your listing is to search terms. It doesn't scan your images, so all it has to reference is the title and the bullets. Make the most of them—especially the title. Look at your top competitors' titles.

If you're already indexed for a specific word or phrase, you don't have to add them in the backend and really, there's no reason to. But if you want to add more searchable words or phrases, you have to add them. Why would you want to do this? Because sometimes your product has a feature that may not seem valuable to most customers, yet some customers are looking for the feature specifically. So you don't want to broadcast it as a feature in your title or bullets, but you still want your product to appear in the results when customers search on that term. You might also index keywords that aren't associated with your product. For example, say you're selling a stainless-steel garlic press. But you know that a lot of people buy plastic garlic presses. You might index the word plastic anyway. That way, when a customer searches on the phrase "plastic garlic press" your product will appear, and a certain number of customers—once they see your garlic press—will prefer it and click on it. You may even go so far as to index the keyword phrase "lemon squeezer" because a customer looking for that item may see your garlic press and decide to purchase it instead, or in addition to a lemon squeezer. Keep in mind that, in this example, you're indexing the keywords "plastic" and "lemon squeezer" but you are not including them in your listing, which would be inaccurate and misleading to the customer.

Here's another good example: silicone utensils. A customer may know they want cooking utensils that don't scratch their nonstick cookware, but they don't know the name of the material these utensils are made of, so they type "plastic cooking utensils" into the search bar. Unless you have "plastic" indexed, they will never find your silicone utensils. Make sense?

A great way to discover search terms that get used a lot is to look at the specific terms that the top competitors are ranked on. Those are the keywords that you need to index for your product too. If you type in a search term and the top sellers don't appear, those are not the keywords you need.

Currently, you're limited to a certain number of characters in the back-end, but you will probably not need to use that many. Use only those that are relevant and not in your listing, and then add misspellings. For instance, you might want to add the word "garlick" or "garlik" to your garlic press listing. You can also add words in other languages. Use online tools like those noted on my Breakers site to find the most commonly misspelled words relevant to your product and use online translators to find the spelling of your product in Spanish and other languages.

Congratulations on getting this far in the book. I know you wanted to go straight to the product launch chapter, but you hung in there, and now you know why all these other chapters came first. Following my recommendations will improve your launch success! Now that you have the best product and best listing among all your competitors, your launch is going to be so much easier. Now let's talk about how you launch to win.

BREAKERS

You'll want to check out my lecture called "Make It Better" at tomerrabinovich.com/breakers for more on improving your product and listing.

CHAPTER 7

LAUNCH TO WIN

"It always seems impossible until it's done."

—NELSON MANDELA

Years ago, when I was working as a magician, I had a wonderful girlfriend who I loved and trusted. I always showed her how I did my tricks. Knowing what was going on "behind the curtain," she was never surprised by my performances. While I never surprised *her*, she loved surprising *me*. One day, when my birthday was approaching, I sensed that she had something special planned. I saw this as a chance to do something unexpected. Maybe I could surprise her for a change!

On the evening of my birthday, she took me to a fine restaurant. It was a difficult place to get into, so she must have made reservations far in advance. While she was in the restroom, I spoke with the waitress and told her about my plan.

"Are you crazy?" she said. "Why didn't you call us ahead of time?"

"It's my birthday, and my girlfriend wouldn't even tell me where she was taking me. I had no idea we were coming here," I said.

The waitress smiled, then she was off to the kitchen. My girlfriend came back to the table and somehow, I managed to make it through dinner, though I was incredibly nervous. I didn't know if the special dessert I requested would be ready on time. I didn't know if anything else would go according to plan either. I held my cloth napkin tightly in my sweating hands while the waitress picked up our plates.

"Can you bring us dessert menus?" I asked, and she nodded.

All the while, my girlfriend just smiled at me, completely oblivious to what was coming. Suddenly, I stood up, and holding her gaze, I dropped to one knee and presented a ring.

"Will you marry me?" I asked.

As soon as I said the words, I knew that I had surprised her in a good way—the right way. Another woman might want a big flashy proposal with a lot of people around, but my girlfriend would want something intimate like this. She was shocked but happy too. And for once, she was surprised. A photographer appeared to capture the special event, and the waitress brought us dessert.

That proposal could not have been more perfect. Not if I had taken months to plan it, or found out which restaurant we were going to, or called them ahead of time. I had to trust it would all work out. If my girlfriend hadn't gone to the restroom and the waitress hadn't come by, or if the restaurant couldn't make the special dessert my girlfriend liked so much, or there was no photographer available, the event may not have been as splendid. That was the risk I had to take, though. I had laid the groundwork with a solid relationship with this wonderful woman, so I was fairly certain she'd say yes. I had to leave everything else to chance.

Nothing will ever compare to the day I proposed to Shani, not even a new product launch. But a product launch is, in a way, like a proposal. It's the day you've worked up to, where you find out if all your research around product selection is going to pay off. In a proposal, it's when you discover whether *you're* the right product. In a proposal *and* a product launch, it's also the day you realize that, even if you did make some mistakes, as long as you are, or you have, the right product, everything will work out. If you *are* the right product, she says yes. Shani did, and she's now my wife. Likewise, if you launch the right product, you will have a successful launch.

Now that you've chosen the right product, why not try to get everything else, or at least the most important parts of your launch, right? Anyone can launch a product, but it takes planning and the right execution to *launch to win*—the previous six chapters worth of planning, to be exact. The more you invest in your product and your listing, the easier your launch will be. Aim to have all of your ducks in a row.

For a successful launch, your three main goals are as follows:

- Stay on budget.
- Rank for important keywords.
- Get reviews.

Real ROI

Sellers think of return on investment as an equation based on the cost of a product and the selling price; basically, the price the customer pays minus the cost to the seller (which is the profit), divided by the cost to the seller, times 100. In Chapter 5, I used the example of investing $4 in a product and selling it for $18, for an $8 profit (after $6 Amazon fees), or 200 percent ROI (8/4 = 2). That's an oversimplified description of return on investment, because there are other costs to the seller beyond what they pay the supplier for the product. All the other costs—PPC ads, social media ads, product giveaways, etc.—should also figure into the ROI equation, to give you what I call the Real ROI. If you shoot for a 100 percent return on investment, you can expect to make a Real ROI of roughly 50 percent after you run out of your first stock. This is due to all the additional costs involved in launching and advertising your product.

For example, I might invest $9 for production and $1 for shipping a new product ($10 COGS), and shipping 1,000 units of the product to Amazon. That's a $10,000 investment. Let's assume I sell the product for $35 and the Amazon fees are $10, so I'm left with $25 for every unit sold. The $25 Amazon income minus the $10 COGS leaves me with $15 profit per unit, which is 150 percent ROI ($15 profit divided by $10 COGS).

During the launch, I'll be pushing hard on PPC and giveaway units for a heavily discounted price or for free. Using the same example of the 1,000 units, I might give away 100 of those units for free, so I'm paying my COGS + Amazon fees on those 100 units. On top of that, I won't make any profit with PPC, and may even lose some money overall to push my organic ranking as much as possible during the launch. That could eat up another 30 percent of the entire stock, sold through PPC, at zero profit.

I track these costs, and you should too. Know where your money's going and know how much leeway you have to spend on advertising, beyond the listing, while still meeting your ROI goals. I'll get into PPC in detail in the next chapter, but I want you to be thinking about it now in terms of budgeting for your launch. This information also ensures that your profit expectations are in line with reality. It avoids the thinking that the difference between your cost and the price the customer pays is pure profit and empowers you to take better control over your finances, including cash flow management.

TOMER'S TIP:
Click Share and Conversion Share

Many experts suggest looking at search volume to determine whether you should select product X or product Y as your next product. In other words, choose the product with the highest search volume. I disagree, and I'll even go so far as to say that search volume doesn't even matter until you launch. I'll say it again:

Search volume doesn't matter until you launch.

The way that I see it, comparing search volume between products is like comparing different BSR ranges; that process shows you certain products, but it eliminates a lot more products from the possibilities. You could be missing out on a lot of great product opportunities with markets that aren't saturated. Remember from Chapter 2, as long as there's revenue, the market is not saturated, and you can compete by offering a better product than what's out there.

It's as simple as that. Search volume only matters when you build your listing and launch your product. During product research, don't worry about search volume or keywords at all—figure all of that out when you create your listing.

More on Keywords

I've told you a lot about keywords, and I'm going to tell you more in this chapter and the next one, because keywords have a dramatic effect on sales. You want to get them right from the start—before you launch.

Keyword Ranking

When you launch a new product, you should do so with the intent of appearing on page one of the results when someone searches for your product. As you learned in the last chapter, this is where keywords come into play. There's something else about keywords that I didn't tell you, which is very important—especially when you launch a product. The more sales you get due to a customer searching with search terms that you've indexed as keywords, the better chance you have of appearing on page one. This is called "keyword ranking." Your goal is to use words that leads to sales, improving your keyword ranking—and in turn, leading to even more sales. Keyword ranking is similar to BSR in that it's based on sales. Whether you make sales from indexed keywords for your listing or those that you use in your PPC, they count toward your keyword ranking.

Targeting Keywords

Targeting keywords refers to putting exact, relevant phrases in your listing and in your PPC, and also running giveaways for those same keywords. The most important factor when targeting keywords is to choose those that will get you sales, and get you ranked, and have staying power. Think of this as "fake it till you make it," with the caveat that you must make it to the end. The two most critical factors in targeting keywords are easy to remember:

- The words must be specific and clearly related to the product.
- They must convert to sales.

If you have a well-targeted keyword, your product will end up on the first page when someone types it in. This is not always the most obvious keyword, and it's never a generic one. Here's an example that should make targeted keywords clear for you.

Say you are selling a double dog leash, which is a leash with one end for your hand, but the leash splits into two lengths for two dogs. You might think the keyword phrase "dog leash" would be best, right? Wrong. That's too generic, and you will never end up on the first page. You will be buried on page 30, after 29 pages of single dog leashes. You need to target customers who are looking for a specific dog leash—one they can use for their two dogs. To find out the best keywords in this example, you know what I'm going to say: Look at your competitors. Look for the ones with the most and best reviews. What keywords are they using? That's what you should be using too. Maybe it's "double dog leash," or "dog leash for two," or "two dog leash." Do your homework and find out. Look for keywords that have at least 1,000 searches a month. Don't settle for less—it will hurt your launch.

Keyword Conversion

You want keywords that a lot of people search on and that return results with your product on page one, and you also want keywords that convert to sales. When choosing targeted keywords, look at the conversion rates of the top three sellers. You get this information from Brand Analytics. If they cumulatively account for 50 percent or more of conversions (market share, basically), then most likely, if a customer clicks on a listing based on that keyword search, there is a 50/50 chance they'll buy the product. I think of these as "ready to buy" keywords, because there's a 50 percent chance that a customer who types them and clicks on a listing will buy. So if I can get on that first page with the right keywords, I have a very good chance of making a sale. This is also an opportunity for PPC—by simply adding a PPC ad that shows up on page one for that keyword, I will likely have a high conversion rate.

Choosing a keyword phrase that generates sales, for example, "dog leash for two large dogs," also improves my ranking for "dog leash for large dogs" and even "dog leash." And by using this method, fewer sales are required to improve my ranking for "dog leash for two large dogs."

Amazon's Brand Analytics, a tool available to sellers with an Amazon Brand Registry, has many features; one in particular offers insight on whether your keywords will convert to sales. When you enter a search term or an ASIN into Brand Analytics, you get a list of search terms. You also get the search frequency rank, click share, and conversion share of each search term for the top three products that were clicked within the period of time you've selected.

Giveaways, Discounts, Deals, Coupons, and Rebates

Reaching out to prospective customers during a product launch is easy when you have an email list or many brand followers on social media. If you don't have those contacts or that ready-made audience, you can use giveaways, discount sites, deal sites, coupon codes, and rebates to boost your ranking.

Some sellers feel that sales and reviews generated by these types of sites don't carry the same weight with Amazon as their organic counterparts, so they've moved away from using them. They can work, but I do not recommend them as a long-term strategy. Still, you should understand how to use them and decide for yourself whether you want to incorporate them into your launch.

Discount or deal sites drive customers to your listing and offer your product for a discounted price. A seller might put their products on one of these sites at a substantial discount, driving customers to their Amazon listings. The promise from the deal site is that they will help sellers raise their sales as well as reviews. However, many sellers believe that Amazon is aware of those reviews and their sources, and they weigh those reviews differently. In some cases, the listing may even be temporarily blocked from receiving reviews.

Because of this, you don't want to get reviews from those sites— Amazon sees these sales and the reviews as coming from very low-quality customers. Quality customers, on the other hand, are customers that found you organically, such as by searching by keyword. Even higher quality customers are people who have bought from you in the past. Sellers sometimes worry that if a customer buys a product from them and leaves a review, then buys another product and leaves another review, that Amazon will remove the review, thinking the reviewer is being paid to write reviews. But if it's a valid sale, Amazon doesn't seem to care—they are only concerned with "illegitimate" reviews, such as those generated by people buying regularly from deal sites.

Using coupon codes entails emailing these codes to customers or posting them on coupon code websites. The codes give customers a discount on the product price. More recently, rebate sites have gained in popularity. They allow you to offer customers a partial refund of their money in the form of a gift card or a direct payment. The seller deposits money into the rebate site's wallet and when someone purchases your product through their site, they rebate the customer from the money in that wallet.

Plan Your Giveaways

Giveaways can help you rank for keywords during your product launch. Service sites, such as the ones listed on my Breakers site, typically charge a flat monthly fee or a per-unit fee.

Many sellers that do giveaways offer them as full-price rebates. The general idea is that the customer buys the product on Amazon for the full price, and the seller reimburses them for their purchase, either via PayPal, a gift card, or with a check in the mail.

Rebate services help your ranking, but do not rely on them for reviews. Customers who take advantage of them are generally "low-quality" customers who all buy the same unrelated products on Amazon, and the site flags them as such. The best reviews come from real customers who bought your product because they searched for it and wanted it—not because they're getting it for free. This is why that Six-Star Experience is so important. Those are the people you want to impress, and the people whose reviews matter the most.

Budget for Giveaways

If you do giveaways, consider them in your budget and track the cost—paying for the full price of the product plus the Amazon fees can get expensive. Figure out what you can afford to give away and still hit a 100 percent ROI, or 50 percent Real ROI. Remember, you can use my free Batch spreadsheet to figure this out. Some sellers plan their giveaways after they launch, but I like to get the numbers worked out ahead of time so I can do them early for a more impactful product launch.

How Many Units to Give Away

There are tools that show you how many units you should give away per keyword to rank on page one of the results, but I believe the main factor in their calculation is search volume. This does not necessarily equate to conversions. We don't know for sure, because Amazon has never released that information, but it's what I believe based on my own observations. I don't want to give away units based on keywords that don't generate sales, because that will not sustain my BSR. It will help my ranking initially, but to maintain that spot, I need to generate organic sales.

In the past, sellers would do a giveaway blast, giving away something like 300 to 500 units in a short period of time—in a day, or even in a couple of hours. That gave them a high ranking, and they stayed there for a long time. That method no longer works. Amazon knows what sellers are doing and when you try to manipulate the system, it adjusts. You may rank high for a short time with that method, but soon after the blast is over, your ranking will plummet. Amazon rewards sellers with long-term, consistent marketing and sales methods that promote growth, and punishes those who try to trick the system. So I do not recommend those high-volume giveaway blasts.

First, consult your budget to figure out how many units you can afford to give away. Then select your keywords. Use Brand Analytics to check the search frequency rank (SFR) of your keywords and shoot for the lowest SFR (highest search volume), while accurately describing your product. Brand Analytics shows you the top three selling products for every keyword that's clicked on. Also, make sure those three top products combined have more than 50 percent conversions. If people searching on a keyword click on a product but only a small percentage of them buy the product, that's not a good keyword for your product.

For giveaways, target long-tail keywords, not short-tail keywords. If you're giving away a double electric breast pump, don't use the two-word short-tail keyword "breast pump." Use the long-tail keyword "double electric breast pump," which is more specific and likely to have more reviews. The same product with a generic keyword phrase like "breast pump" will have fewer reviews and lower ranking. For your second long-tail keyword, try to use words that don't appear in your first one. So don't use the long-tail keyword "mothers double electric breast pump." Use something else, like "mothers pump for breastfeeding."

Getting your product ranked on those long-tail keywords also gets them ranked on the short-tail ones, so you want to get as much bang for your buck as you can. In this example, along with getting ranked for the long-tail keywords, you're also getting ranked for "breast pump," "mothers pump," and "breastfeeding."

Let's say you decide to give away 100 units. Start off by giving away just a few units each day. So you may be giving away five units per keyword for five minutes a day. Do this for seven days, to give away about 100 units (five units × three keywords × seven days = 105). During this time, track your organic rank. Where are you ranked for each keyword, and on which page does your product appear in the search results? One day, you might be the sixth listing on page five, and the next day, you're the tenth listing on page two. That's good—you're moving up! The goal is to keep moving up until you hit the number one spot on the first page, or at least appear on the top half of page one.

The results of this method may surprise you. Sometimes giving away just a few units a day for two or three days will put you on page one. Other times, you might give away units for several days and still have a low ranking. If you aren't steadily moving up, you can try a couple of things. Either change the keywords and see if that makes a difference or double the quantity of giveaway units. I start with just a few units and track the progress. I want to show Amazon slow, steady growth. That's how you get ranked. You stay ranked by targeting the right keywords, so even though you are gaining your initial ranking artificially, you sustain that ranking organically.

Google, Facebook, Instagram, Pinterest, and TikTok

One of my favorite questions for the past few years to ask advanced sellers was "How do you think Amazon expects us to launch new products?"

The usual answer was "I don't know," since it seems that everything we do these days is against Amazon's TOS (terms of service). Giving away your products for free is not effective when trying to build a real brand long term. The truth is, all Amazon wants is to get more outside traffic and increase their sales. For most products, just running PPC ads won't get us where we want to be, and we need an extra boost, or in other words, outside traffic. Some sellers split the traffic, so the Amazon ads are only for Amazon, while the outside traffic is only sent to their own website. Instead, I suggest sending both inside *and* outside traffic directly to Amazon. Amazon will reward you with better ranking when you attract high-quality traffic.

Also consider preselling your products to your audience before launching, which can be highly effective. Sharing the products you're working on with your audience and showing them what's happening behind the scenes keeps them on the edge of their seats and ready to buy once you launch your product.

You should be on the platform where your customers are, but you don't have to be on all of them. Selling makeup products can work well on

Instagram and TikTok, while selling products for seniors can do wonders on Facebook. I used to sell refrigerator water filters, and while you can't really build a passionate audience around that product, my team has leveraged Google Ads to help us launch and rank new products. Before you bought this book, you might have seen it in a Facebook group, heard me talk about it as a guest on a podcast, became aware of it through my email list or one of my industry friend's email lists, or maybe an Amazon seller friend recommended it. Those are the different ways I intend to launch this book, besides running Amazon ads on it. In Chapter 6, we've talked about being better than your competitors. When it comes to launching your product and knowing where your customers are, you should look at the biggest brands in your space to see what they're doing. Sign up for their newsletters, visit their websites, and join their VIP programs. All of these actions will get the ideas flowing to see what will actually work for your brand.

Building that audience is not easy and you won't see immediate rewards from it, but it's 100 percent worth building.

LAUNCH TO WIN

```
                    ┌──────────────────┐
                    │  Product Research │
                    └──────────────────┘
                             │
                             ▼
                    ┌──────────────────┐
                    │   Green Light     │
                    └──────────────────┘
                             │
                             ▼
                    ┌──────────────────┐
                    │   Development     │
                    └──────────────────┘
                             │
  ┌──────────────┐          ▼                    ┌──────────────────┐
  │  1st Payment  │◄──────────────────┐          │  Image Planning   │
  └──────────────┘     │   Green Light ├─────────►└──────────────────┘
  ┌──────────────┐◄────┘                                   │
  │ Packaging Design│            │                         │
  └──────────────┘              ▼                          │
  ┌──────────────┐      ┌──────────────────┐               │
  │Start Production│     │ Keyword Research │               │
  └──────────────┘      └──────────────────┘               │
         │                       │                          ▼
  ┌──────────────┐      ┌──────────────────┐      ┌──────────────────┐
  │Inspect & Forward│    │  Listing Copy    │      │      Photos       │
  └──────────────┘      └──────────────────┘      └──────────────────┘
         │                       │
  ┌──────────────┐ - - - - - - - - - - - - - ► 
  │Photography Sample│            │
  └──────────────┘               ▼
  ┌──────────────┐      ┌──────────────────┐      ┌──────────────────┐
  │2nd Payment & Ship│─►│      LAUNCH       │◄────│  Graphic Design   │
  └──────────────┘      └──────────────────┘      └──────────────────┘
```

Figure 6: After all your hard work, the big day is finally here—launch time.

Launch Time

So far, I have given you a lot of background information that will help your launch succeed. Heading into the actual launch, be prepared to take care of the following, in this order:

1. Closed listing
2. Pay-per-click ads
3. Open listing
4. Initial reviews
5. Honeymoon period

6. Second shipment

7. Existing product relaunch

Let's tackle each one.

Closed Listing

At this stage, your keywords, copy, and images are in place, and you have inventory at Amazon. Bear in mind that when stock gets checked in at Amazon, it's in receiving mode, and not yet sellable. They release a certain number of units at a time and if you open the listing too soon, they could sell out. You don't want to be out of stock that early in the game, so wait until at least a few dozen units are available before moving forward. We'll get to reviews in a minute, but while your listing is still closed, have a few potential customers lined up—it's best if these are people who actually want the product. Ask them to buy your product and leave an honest review after they've tested it. I'll tell you over and over again not to manipulate the system, but you need a few reviews to get things rolling.

Pay-Per-Click Ads

I wrote a whole chapter on pay-per-click (PPC) ads, which is coming right up, but I want to mention it here because it's best to plan your PPC campaigns before you launch.

You might think having your listing on top of the first page of search results is the best position for your PPC ad. This isn't always true.

For short-tail keywords, too many people will click on the first listings and most of them won't buy. They'll click through more listings searching for an exact match—the product whose title, images, copywriting (bullets, product description, specs, etc.), and reviews describe the perfect product for their needs. So I want my product to appear a little later—say on page two, three, or four. I don't want them to click on my page unless there's a good chance they're going to buy. This way, I'm paying for conversions—sales and potentially ranking, reviews, and more organic sales—instead of sessions that deliver nothing. For the keywords "yoga mat," I don't want to pay what it costs to be on the first page, at least initially, so I bid lower. Let me explain:

I want my PPC ads to convert to sales. Otherwise, what am I paying for? A new listing isn't going to have a lot of reviews, so it's less likely to convert to a sale than a listing with a lot of reviews. Think of your product as having a life cycle. Initially, the listing for that product attracts customers slowly, and as you get more sales, you also get reviews and a better ranking. Once your product has many reviews and can compete with the leaders in your niche, it makes sense to pay for PPC ads that appear in the first page of search results. Your reviews and ranking will attract clicks and conversions. Until then, you are throwing your money away. At the early stages of the life cycle, you're better off appearing on page two or page three. That way, people who get to your listing haven't found what they're looking for on page one and they are more likely to click on your product and buy it. Of course, eventually I would love for my PPC ad to show up on page one—but only when it's positioned to generate a lot of sales.

There is one exception, and that's video ads. Video ads get clicks, so if you're running one for a new listing that doesn't have a lot of reviews, get it on the first page of the results for your keywords. People will click and they may buy. Video and audio ads are the future, and it's in your best interest to learn about them. The bonus here is that people can view them without clicking on your listing. So you aren't paying for every click that doesn't convert.

With long-tail keywords, my listing is more specific, so a customer's click is more likely to result in a sale. If I use the keywords "girl's pink yoga mat," I want to be the first listing on the first page of results, so I bid higher.

You'll want to read Chapter 8 for all the details on how PPC works, but for now, let's walk through the rest of the checklist.

Open Listing

As soon as you open your listing, check to make sure that everything you set up (or think you set up, because it can be a *lot*) is actually working. Check to see whether your PPC campaigns and keywords are getting impressions. Do this by testing the indexing of your keywords. There are tools for this, or you can just type the keywords and the ASIN into the search bar, for example, "water bottle B08Y5AP886." If your product appears in the results, it's indexed for those keywords. Checking your indexed keywords is especially important if you run PPC ads. If they aren't indexed, your ads won't show up (and you won't get impressions).

Next, make sure your product is in the correct main category and subcategory, and that the price is correct. You may have started setting up your listing months ago and something changed around the product description, but you forgot to update it in your listing.

If you are going to start with a lower price, now is the time to check that. I often start with a slightly lower price, maybe 10 to 20 percent lower than what I have in my financial plan. This is temporary, because I don't want price to influence a customer's buying decision when I don't even have any reviews. Start with a competitive price, but make sure you don't go too low so your product doesn't come off as too cheap.

Initial Reviews

Once you've checked to make sure everything on your open listing is accurate and working properly, reviews and keyword ranking are your top priorities. If you followed my Six-Star Experience formula, this won't be a problem for you. You'll start getting organic reviews early.

Another thing you can do is sign up for the Amazon Vine Program. For a small fee, Vine Reviewers receive your product for free and leave an honest review. You can use the program until you have a certain number of reviews, and it's a great way to kickstart the process. My only warning about the program is that you will get honest reviews, so if you aren't confident in your product, you may not want what could be negative initial reviews. But since you've gotten this far in my book, you should know by now that you should be selling only high-quality products and delivering a Six-Star Experience.

You might also have friends and family willing to buy your product and leave you a good review. This is a quick and easy way to get those first few five-star reviews on your listing, as long as you don't abuse it. Don't ask 50 people to buy your product and leave a review. And never promise someone something in return for a review. For example, I've seen sellers post their products on social media, asking their friends to buy the product and leave a review, and the seller will reimburse them in exchange for that review. This is a big no-no; it's against the of service. Again, Amazon does not like their site being manipulated. You can, however, offer to rebate them if they buy your product, and then, afterward, ask them for a review. The difference may seem subtle, but it matters. In the first example, you're offering a free product for a five-star review, basically. In the second example, you're offering the product for free, and later asking for a review, so the offer of a free product isn't contingent on a good review. Just like you should have confidence in your product before using the Vine Review program, you should also feel confident about the reviews you might receive from friends and other people you can reach via social media.

If you don't have an online following or a contact list, start building one. This will help you build an audience for your brand by introducing customers who like your current products to new ones. You can also ask your followers and list subscribers for reviews, but again, do not promise them anything in return. Finally, never say something like, "If you like my product, leave a review, and if you don't, let me know." This is encouraging people to leave only good reviews while discouraging them from leaving reviews that might expose a problem with your product.

In all your dealings, be honest, authentic, and transparent. If you have any questions around what's OK and not OK, imagine that Jeff Bezos is looking over your shoulder as you write that email or create that social media post. Would he be smiling or shaking his head? There's your answer.

Honeymoon Period

Like I mentioned earlier, Amazon rewards consistent growth. Your goal is to work with their algorithm to make that happen, and not to manipulate it to cheat the system. The first 30 to 60 days that your listing is open is referred to by many sellers as the "honeymoon period." No one's proven that this period actually exists, but to experienced sellers, it seems like Amazon fuels new listings with a little extra gas for a successful launch. You want to take advantage of that time to get some traction, which means sales, reviews, and a high ranking. This is another reason that it's critical to have all your prelaunch work done before you open a listing. Sure, you can optimize your site anytime, but fully optimizing it ahead of the honeymoon period is like building the best rocket possible so that when Amazon gives you that initial fuel injection, your rocket really blasts off.

Many sellers miss out on this opportunity. Their product's in stock, their listing is open, and they start seeing sales. They get excited, thinking it's going to blast off. But they haven't worked out the PPC campaigns, and some of their images aren't that great. They haven't tested their keywords either. So all those impressions and conversions they could be getting don't happen, and by the time they figure this out, the honeymoon's over. They've squandered that window of opportunity to really get it right.

Be ready and follow your launch plan aggressively during the honeymoon period. While you're evaluating and validating the success of your launch, the number one question you need to answer is "Am I ordering a second shipment, or do I liquidate this product?"

Second Shipment

In Chapter 5, we talked about setting a goal for how many units you want to sell each day. After you open a listing, track your sales. If you've done everything right, they should increase steadily, so you'll know when you're within a few days of hitting that goal. At that point, order a second shipment. Don't delay putting in that second order. If you're not sure how much stock to order, order too few units rather than too many. You don't have to place a full order every time, and sometimes it makes more sense to order only half as many units until you get a better feel for ongoing demand. You'll have to pay a bit more per unit, but you're less likely to get stuck with product that takes longer to sell than you anticipated. You also don't want to tie up all your cash in one product, because you're probably planning other launches and will need to have cash flow to support them.

I'll tell you much more about ordering in Chapter 9, but the bottom line is order early enough to avoid running out of stock, but don't feel pressured to order too much for fear of running out.

For example, say you have an order of 3,000 units sitting at Amazon, and you start selling. You know that you need to sell an average of 30 units per day, or about 900 per month. At first, you're selling 20 or 25 a day, but as soon as you start selling 30 a day, you have to start thinking about talking to your supplier. You might order the same number of units, or you may decide to order more, but you should check on availability. You're not placing an order yet—just getting information. Ask them when they can start production and how long it will take to produce the units, and don't forget to add in shipping time and the time it takes Amazon to make them available. Don't wait to do this. It will take a few days, or even a week, to get this information, and in the meantime monitor your sales to see if you're staying steady at 30 per day or selling more or fewer units. Read the reviews. Use this time to decide whether you should order a second shipment or stop selling the product. If you're not sure, you can place another order so you don't run out, but you don't have to order more than you ordered the first time. You may actually want to order less, and continue to monitor sales and reviews while you decide whether you want to place a third order, which you can do at any time. The key point to remember is that it's better to order exactly what you need or fewer than you might need, and order them sooner than you need them. You can always order more. If you have an order in and decide you need more, your supplier may be able to add them to the current shipment, or you may have to wait for the next one. You don't want to run out, but you also don't want a bunch of product that you can't sell.

A common mistake is waiting too long to order. A seller might think their sales aren't going to continue, and they don't want to make another investment. But the sales do continue, they run out, and all that momentum they developed with their sales, and ranking, and reviews, disappears. Don't make that mistake.

Existing Product Relaunch

Sometimes a launch doesn't go well. You have to figure out the problem and then decide whether it's worth fixing and relaunching the product, or if you should abandon it. Maybe the product was selling well but you ran out of stock, and now that you have it available, it isn't selling so well. Maybe sales were increasing and now they've plateaued, or even decreased.

The first thing you need to do is figure out where you are in the market. Look at your top competitors, those with the same price point as your product. Identify those with about the same number of reviews and review rating as your product. Compare their sales to yours. Let's say you have 1,000 reviews and you're doing $2,000 in sales a month. You think you can do more, but the only way to verify that is by comparing your sales to the competition. If they have, say, 300 reviews, yet they're doing $30,000 in sales a month, that's a clear sign that you could be doing a lot better. The bottom line is that if they're selling more than you are, they're doing something right, you're doing something wrong, or both.

On the other hand, if your competitors with about the same price point, number of reviews, and rating are also doing about the same as you are in sales, the market is probably saturated. There is more supply than demand. Another reason this happens is when one seller is dominating the niche. That leaves little demand for everyone else. In this case, there isn't much you can do. But you need to know whether either of these two situations is true before you make a decision about relaunching.

Next, look at how many units you have left to sell. Relaunching a product may require an investment in improving your listing and offering giveaways. If you have only, say, 200 units in stock, and you give away 100 units for your relaunch, you will have to order more units before you open your listing. Is the investment worth it to you? You may be better off liquidating your stock and putting that money into a different product.

Sometimes relaunching makes sense. If you have a few thousand units in stock and your sales aren't awful, you may be able to improve your listing, spend some money on giveaways and PPC ads, and sell enough units to make it worth your while. This will also buy you some time to track sales and see if you want to continue with the product.

If you decide to relaunch, you need to do two things. First, redo your listing. Start all over again with new images, a new title, new bullets, and new keywords. You may even want to change the subcategory of the product. Revisit the competition and make sure everything about your listing is better than theirs. Second, run giveaways such as rebates, etc. for the product. It's important that you take these two actions on the same day. This sends the message to Amazon that you changed the listing and it's working. Amazon will give you the benefit of the doubt and your product will get a boost—it may even appear on the first page of search results. If the ranking doesn't improve, your relaunch will fail.

Sometimes you shouldn't relaunch a product. Your product may be doing only $10,000 a month, yet your competition is doing $50,000, so you know you can do better. You don't want to take down your listing and lose sales, ranking, and reviews. Instead, improve your listing one feature at a time. For example, replace the main image and monitor sales. Give it a week, and if sales decrease dramatically, change it back. If they decrease just a little bit, wait a few more days and continue to track your sales. If they stay the same or increase, improve one other thing. Sound familiar? It should—you are basically following my advice in Chapter 6. Make incremental improvements, see how they affect sales, and continue making improvements to get to your $50,000-a-month target.

You can also try launching a variation of your product. If you're low on stock, order a variation of it and update your listing. This way, you won't lose reviews, and you may get a boost in sales. Your ranking will start from scratch, but the reviews should provide a nice boost. If you decide to do this, pause the PPC for the old variation and start PPC for the new variation. Again, look at your competition and add a variation similar to one of their variations. For example, if most of your competitors offer five colors of a product and you offer the product in only two colors, add the three colors you're missing.

You might think that you don't need to get more reviews, but as mentioned earlier in the book, getting five-star reviews on an ongoing basis helps you rank better. Remember that as well when relaunching your product.

Research doesn't stop just because you have a product that's selling. You have to continuously monitor the market, your place in the market, and your competition. Be aware of where you stand. Otherwise, you may be caught off-guard and unable to correct quickly. Your competitors are looking at you and deciding whether to improve their products and their listings, so you need to be looking at them.

A relaunch is just like your initial launch, only better. Look at every detail of your listing and figure out how to improve it. This may entail moving your product to a different category, lowering the price, and creating new images and new copy. Revisit your keywords and test new ones. The difference between a relaunch and traditional listing optimization is that with optimization, you make small, incremental changes and track the effects. You give each change a few days to work and see how it impacts your sessions, conversions, reviews, and rankings.

In contrast, relaunching your product is all-at-once, and it's dramatic. You literally want to shake up the system—you want to show Amazon that you know your listing has problems and you're determined to fix it.

Launching a product takes money, time, and patience. Do it well the first time. Then give it a chance to succeed. Make subtle changes to improve your listing, monitor the effect, and above all, be patient. It can take a while to work out all the kinks and hit your units-per-day goal, and to make your listing the top-ranked one in your niche. And even if you have to relaunch or liquidate, don't look at that as a failure. Being successful on Amazon takes commitment, and you can't be discouraged by setbacks. You will have them—we all do. But if you're persistent and work out each issue, you will have a winning launch. At the end of the day, it's a numbers game. Never stop researching and launching new products.

You will have failures. No matter how good your product seems, or how well you launch, you will have an occasional bust where the product doesn't do well, and you will have to liquidate your stock. You will have products that do so-so. And you will have winners. This is the case for all sellers who stick with it. Even top sellers have failures. But they don't give up. They continue to find and launch new products.

BREAKERS

Want to know more about launching to win? Check out my free lecture "Launch to Win" at tomerrabinovich.com/breakers.

CHAPTER 8

PAY PER CLICK

"Stopping advertising to save money is like stopping your watch to save time."

—HENRY FORD

C hapters 2 through 7 showed you how to go from researching and selecting products to launching them. These next three chapters show you what to take care of once your product is launched: PPC, inventory management, and key performance indicators (KPIs). Get these three things right, and you win. We'll talk about winning, too, in the last chapters. For now, let's dive into pay per click, or what everyone refers to as simply "PPC."

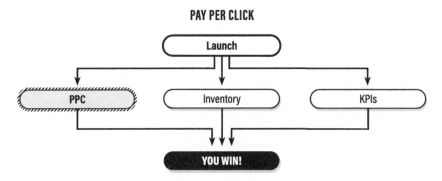

Figure 7: Pay per click is one of three areas that you need to focus on to go from product launch to winning.

This chapter started out being the longest one in the book. Then I edited it, and it ended up being the shortest. PPC is a big topic, and there are entire books written on the subject. The problem with writing about PPC is that it changes and will continue to change. And I don't want you to think you have to be an expert to use it. You need to know the basics, sure, but then you are better off hiring someone to do it for you. However, if you don't have someone on your team who knows PPC and manages it for you, then you absolutely do have to become an expert, or at least well versed in it enough to do it well. It's that important.

If you think PPC experts are hard to come by, just go to an Amazon sellers conference. Everyone and their brother claims to be an expert. The trick is getting the right person for your business—someone who understands it or is willing to learn, and who can explain their PPC strategy to you so you can decide whether it's the strategy you want to follow, and figure out whether it's actually working.

If you're already familiar with PPC, feel free to skip this section. I'm going to give you the basics only, then it's up to you to either hire someone to manage it for you or learn all the details on your own. I won't give you all the terminology either—it's extensive, and growing every day. This chapter is intended to be general guidance for managing PPC on a macro rather than a micro level, and you should take it upon yourself to use it and learn it in more detail.

YOU MUST HAVE SOMEONE ON
YOUR TEAM WHO UNDERSTANDS PPC.
IF YOU DON'T HAVE ANYONE,
THAT SOMEONE IS YOU.

Pay Per Click Defined

A pay per click, or PPC, ad is exactly that: an advertisement on Amazon or other retail platform that the seller pays for every time a customer clicks on it. When you search for a product and an image and a listing title pops up along with the word "sponsored," you're looking at a PPC ad. The positions on the page vary—you can have them placed at the top of the page, the bottom of the page, or in the middle.

When a customer sees the ad, that's an "impression." If they click on it, that's a "session," which we talked about earlier. With PPC, you're paying for every click. The click-through rate (CTR) is the number of click-throughs as a percentage of impressions. If 50 people see your ad and 5 click on it, you have a 10 percent click-through rate. If this sounds familiar, it's because we talked about it in Chapter 6. We also talked about the conversion rate (CVR), which is the percentage of people who clicked on your ad and made a purchase.

So, what makes your sponsored product appear in a search? It depends on how you set it up. You can use keyword or product targeting. Before we get into that, let's start with the language of PPC.

The Language of PPC

You'll want to learn the terminology of PPC so you can understand how it works and communicate better with your PPC expert. Following is just a sample—check out my Breakers site for many more.

Advertising Cost of Sale

Advertising cost of sale (ACoS) is what you spend to make a sale. In simple terms, a 10 percent ACoS means that for every 10 cents you spend, you make $1 worth of sales. The lower the ACoS, the more profit you've made.

Sellers have a target ACoS for their PPC ads, often a break-even amount, so that the cost of the sale is equal to the profit, after all the other expenses including inventory cost and fees to Amazon are figured in.

If I sell a product for $21, my COGS (cost of goods sold) is $7, and the Amazon fees are $7, I'm making $7 profit per unit. My breakeven ACoS is 33 percent (7/21). In other words, if I spend 33 percent of the selling price ($7 of $21) on PPC, then I've made my break-even ACoS. Why would a seller want to break even? Because it helps your organic sales—those that you don't get through PPC. Your ads improve impressions, sessions, and conversions, and conversions improve rankings and reviews. And I don't need to tell you what improved rankings and reviews do.

With pricier products, sellers typically target an ACoS below their break-even point; they are able to make a higher percentage profit compared to the cost of the ad. For the average product, though, a break-even ACoS is a typical target. Keep in mind that if the price of your product or shipping increases/decreases for whatever reason, that will alter your break-even ACoS as well.

Total Advertising Cost of Sale

Total advertising cost of sale (TACoS) is similar to ACoS, except that it includes all sales, not only those generated through advertising. To figure out your TACoS, divide how much you spent on advertising by your total sales. For example, if you've made $50,000 in total revenue and spent $5,000 on PPC, and ACoS is 30 percent, your TACoS is 10 percent (5,000/50,000).

Campaigns and Ad Groups

The way you structure your PPC campaigns is important. Campaigns are like the trunk of your tree, the ad groups are like the branches, and the search terms are the fruit. Campaigns are PPC ad projects, and ad groups are subsets of campaigns. On Amazon, your PPC ad controls differ at the campaign and ad group levels. There are certain things you can do only on the campaign level, such as setting a daily budget for each campaign, which is the average amount of money you're willing to spend on ads each day.

By the way, Amazon's current maximum campaign budget is $21 million—they will not allow a seller to spend more than that on PPC ads in any one day. Your campaign budget pays for bids. Sellers bid on how much they are willing to pay for a click. If I bid $1 on a click, that means I am willing to pay up to $1 every time someone clicks on my PPC ad.

> **AMAZON WILL NOT ALLOW YOU TO BUDGET MORE THAN $21 MILLION FOR A CAMPAIGN IN ONE DAY (DON'T ASK ME HOW I KNOW THIS!).**

PPC and Me

If I gave you $2 for every $1 you spent on PPC, how many dollars would you spend? That's the kind of opportunity PPC offers the Amazon seller—*if* they know what they're doing.

Most sellers make the same mistakes I did when I first started selling on Amazon, especially when it comes to PPC. When I started out, I did just about everything myself. Sure, I had a local photographer shoot my products for the images and I used a few copywriters for product descriptions. But I assumed that I could manage all the backend stuff on my own, including the PPC. But then I started learning how PPC actually worked. The more I learned, the more I realized how much I didn't know. And I had this awful feeling that not knowing was costing me a lot of money. At the end of the day, PPC is your biggest spend after inventory cost—and it's worth every penny. You have to get it right.

Before that, I'd open a few campaigns and hope for the best. I'd adjust the bids on my keywords to optimize my campaigns by trying to get to my target ACoS and wait a day or a week, then I'd adjust them again. But I had no idea what I was doing. I wasted a year managing PPC that way. Then I decided to outsource it. I hired a freelance team and paid them a few hundred dollars a month to take over my campaigns. The problem was, they wouldn't show me what was going on behind the scenes. They'd make an adjustment, and my sales might go up, or they might go down. I'd ask why they went up or down, and I didn't really understand their answers. They had a strategy, but they couldn't explain it to me, so I never really knew what was going on. They responded to my questions with short answers. With no communication and without understanding their strategy, how could I know if they were even doing a good job? And how could I make my own decisions about PPC?

I finally let them go and decided to take another stab at it myself. This time, I tried using tools to automate the whole process. I tried many different tools. Most of them seemed to work the same way: I'd plug in my goals—targeted costs, budgets, etc.—and the tool adjusted the bids for me. But again, just like when I was doing it manually, and just like when

I was paying somebody else to do it, I still didn't really understand it. For example, if your product reviews go from five stars to 4.5 stars and your conversion rate drops, the automatic tools don't adjust accordingly, so you might end up bidding much higher than you're actually converting, and it's taking the tools too long to adjust. Yet, the software wasn't aware of the change, and just like the freelancers, it couldn't explain why.

I felt like I wasn't in control, and I did not like that feeling. I knew I needed to learn more about PPC, but I didn't want to spend all my time on it. So instead of becoming a pay-per-click expert, I did the next best thing. I hired someone to learn everything they could about PPC. The big difference between this person and the earlier experience I had with outsourcing was that I hired this person onto my in-house team, and I didn't hire a PPC expert. I wanted someone who wouldn't bring their preconceived ideas about how to do PPC with them to my campaigns. I wanted them to learn from scratch, and keep learning, because the rules around PPC are always changing. This person's whole job is taking care of my PPC and telling me what they're doing and why they're doing it. They have a strategy that they can explain to me, and when they make a change, they can tell me why they did it and show me the results. They plan ahead, so they know what to do ahead of Prime Day, for example, and at other times of the year such as holidays and Q4 (Christmas shopping time) that might create sales spikes.

I know a lot more about the topic now than when I started, but I'll never know everything. Amazon is always coming out with new features and new places to advertise. The changes and the options are endless. PPC is so complex, it's a whole profession. And you can hire a PPC expert, but you're still going to need to know what they're doing and why they're doing it.

That's been my experience, but it doesn't mean that whatever you're doing for PPC is wrong. There's no one way to do it right. You might have an agency that's doing a fantastic job and you're happy with the level of communication. Or you may have found a tool that works really well. Either situation is entirely possible, and I don't want to give you the impression that you have to hire someone onto your team and demand they become a PPC expert. There's more than one way to solve the PPC puzzle, but it's important that you do solve it. PPC can literally make or break you as an Amazon seller.

PPC, and the best ways to implement it, will change over time. But the basics will likely remain. There will always be target keywords. There will always be brand pages, such as amazon.com/Disney. There will always be placements, where you get your ad in front of the right people—your target market. Amazon may add more layers to the process and give sellers more ways to better market their products, but it's not likely that keywords, brand pages, or placements will ever go away.

Campaign Strategy

Consult with 10 PPC "experts," and you'll get 10 different campaign strategies. But they will likely all agree on the fundamentals:

- Make it scalable.
- Manage it in-house (or if you choose to outsource it, at least have a good grasp of it in-house).
- Follow the 80/20 rule.
- Make it bulletproof.

Whichever strategy you use, make sure it incorporates these fundamentals. Mine does, and following is a brief explanation of why I do it that way.

Make It Scalable

A complex campaign structure will be hard to manage and very difficult to grow, and you will not be able to see the results of your strategy, or the impact changes to that strategy have on overall performance.

Your campaign structure, whether designed with or without a PPC tool, should be simple so that as your business grows, you can grow your PPC. You have to be able to find all the information quickly and easily. You also need to be able to add products to existing campaigns and open new campaigns easily. In addition, it shouldn't take long to optimize it by you or your team. A good campaign structure allows you to implement your strategy, monitor the results, and review the overall performance.

Manage It In-House

Managing PPC in-house was the best solution for me. I needed someone who was willing to learn it and explain it to me enough so that together, we could devise a strategy. I needed someone who could take my general instructions, implement them, and show me the results.

You can hire an outside agency for PPC, which will save you time because it's completely hands-off. You just trust the agency to do a good job. The risk is that you are giving up insight into how PPC works, instead of developing a team member who, over time, can become an expert. And don't expect an agency to explain all the ins and outs of PPC to you. You will learn very little about PPC or how they're applying it to your business.

The other risk is that if you decide to stop using an agency, you're starting over from scratch. You may be able to continue some of their process, but you won't understand it fully. On top of that, they could have their own proprietary software, spreadsheets, and macros that you don't know how to use, or can even access. An agency could also drop you if they get a big customer and no longer have time for their smaller clients. The same risks come with hiring a freelancer to do the work. Your employee might quit at some point, but having the processes documented in-house will help in the future in case you bring in someone to replace your current employee. There is no guarantee that a freelancer will document their strategy or process for you.

I know people who run agencies that do PPC, and they're very good at what they do. If I hired them, I would still want an in-house person who understands PPC, keeps up with the changes, and can explain the PPC process they are using for my campaigns to me.

Another option is PPC software. Some software allows you to set a goal and the software makes all the decisions for you, while other software helps you make decisions and then you guide it to the results you want. But similar to working with an agency, PPC software is not a "set it and forget it" solution—you need to know what the software is doing in your account. If you need to lower sales because you're running out of stock/ push sales for a slow-selling product, you have to know how to do that. You also need the visibility required to make sure you aren't burning cash (making bad decisions that cost you money). So as tempting as completely automated software may be, I do not recommend investing in anything that makes all the decisions for you without showing you those decisions and why they return the results you're looking for.

I believe that the best combination when it comes to managing your PPC at scale is to have someone in-house managing it on their own, or with either an agency or software, and monitoring them closely so you understand it as well—at least at a high level. There's a lot of PPC software out there, and you can find additional resources on my Breakers site.

However you manage PPC, my bottom-line advice is to make the effort to understand it. Make sure that you have someone in place who stays on top of the changing PPC technology, features, and trends. Make sure that if your PPC person takes a vacation or goes away completely, your campaigns will run undisturbed until they return, or until you can hire and train a replacement.

Follow the 80/20 Rule

The Pareto principle or 80/20 rule states that 80 percent of consequences come from 20 percent of the causes. Applying this to online selling, and especially PPC, I focus on the critical 20 percent of campaign tasks and activities that have the most impact on my business.

Some sellers get caught up in other facets of the business such as accounting, photography, and all the details of PPC, which can become a full-time job. Pay per click and all that it entails is never-ending—it can take up all your time and focus. I prefer to focus on the most critical 20 percent of the business, including the most critical areas of PPC. Even though I stay involved with quality control, I hand off much of that other work—including the day-to-day management of my PPC ads—to others and let those people do their jobs so I can focus on mine: making sales and growing the business.

Make It Bulletproof

Finally, I you want your PPC to be bulletproof. This means making sure you aren't bleeding money by spending on keywords that don't convert. You can target thousands of keywords, but odds are you'll get 80 percent of your sales from 20 percent of your keywords, or even more likely, 95 percent of your sales from 5 percent of your keywords. So you must get those keywords right. This is why I take more time than many other sellers, typically, to have my listing optimized. The better your product and listing than the competitors', the easier it is to leverage PPC.

BREAKERS

Visit my Breakers site at tomerrabinovich.com/breakers for resources including software, agencies, and services that can help you with PPC.

CHAPTER 9

INVENTORY MANAGEMENT

"I never ran out of stock."

—NO AMAZON SELLER EVER

his was going to be a very short chapter. Here's what I had:

- Don't run out of stock.
- Don't have too much stock.
- The end

If you can follow those simple rules, congratulations—you've mastered inventory management! Unfortunately, inventory management isn't quite that simple in practice.

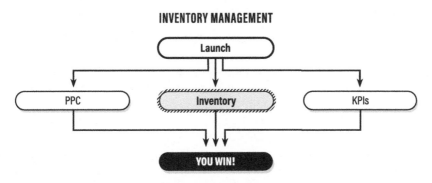

Figure 8: Inventory management is a critical task in your journey from product launch to winning.

On the bright side, it's been around forever. Think about it: nobody was talking about PPC, ranking, keywords, or BSR when we were kids, right? But inventory management has been around as long as businesses have been in business. Every business with physical products has inventory, and every business owner has to manage it.

Because it's been around so long, there's a lot of information out there about how to do inventory management right. Unlike certain other topics, we don't have to reinvent the wheel because the same rules that held true a hundred years ago—don't run out of stock and don't have too much stock—are still true today.

Inventory management online, and specifically on Amazon, as complicated as it might seem, is a heck of a lot simpler than, say, managing the inventory in a bunch of retail stores where customers are coming in and out all day buying and returning items, asking for more products or for refunds. Everything can be managed online. Even so, we Amazon sellers manage to screw it up. I'm almost embarrassed to tell you about my first inventory experience, but you need to hear it so you know what not to do.

Here I am, your typical noob Amazon seller, all excited to launch my first product. I take all the money I have, $3,000, and order 500 units. (By the way, blowing my entire budget on the first order was probably my first major mistake, but I digress.) Anyway, I have my product and it starts selling. And it keeps selling. I'm seeing my inventory go down and down and down, and I don't know what to do. Do I order more? What if it stops selling? *What do I do?* So I wait, and wait, and wait…and then I start freaking out because I'm so low on stock, so I order 1,500 more units. But I waited too long, so now I'm out of stock. Not for just a day or a week, either—I'm out of stock for a whole month! Oh no!

Rule #1: *Don't run out of stock.*

Finally, my second shipment is received by Amazon. I keep refreshing my page to see if it's available to sell. It's still in receiving mode. Refresh, refresh, refresh. The anxiety is killing me.

Refresh, refresh, refresh…it's live!

I'm selling like crazy. And again, I wait, and wait, and wait to place another order. I guess I'm a slow learner, or I was back then, because of course, I run out of stock again. And again, just before that happens, I place another order—for 2,500 units! It's a lot more than I need, but now I'm terrified of running out. Well, the good news is that I don't run out of stock again. And before my inventory gets low, I don't order just 500 units, or 1,000, or even 2,500. I order 8,000 units!

About this same time, I'm getting ready to launch another product, but guess what? All my money's tied up in inventory for my first product, so I have a cash flow problem.

That brings us to rule #2: *Don't have too much stock.*

You have to admit, when it comes to making mistakes, I was very efficient. I didn't drag them out over multiple product launches—I made them all at once.

I could have talked to my supplier and discovered that I didn't have to order that many units. I could have ordered fewer, and even though I would have paid more per unit, I still would have come out ahead. But I was inexperienced. I had so many options, but I wasn't aware of any of them.

When you launch a product and it's selling well, you have just three major concerns. First, optimize the product and listing, which we covered in Chapter 6. Second, have your PPC dialed in so it's aggressive enough to maximize sales without losing money. Your third big concern is inventory management.

Inventory management is possibly the biggest product killer when selling on Amazon. Running out of stock hurts your rankings and unless you correct the situation immediately, it's all downhill from there. If you're out of stock for a month or two, many times it's game over. Recovery will be difficult to impossible.

The other side of this is the fear of running out of stock, which can lead to other bad inventory management decisions. Remember when COVID-19 began, and people hoarded toilet paper? Don't be that person walking down the aisle with a whole cart full of toilet tissue.

Inventory management affects your cash flow, and it also costs you money. Amazon has long-term storage fees. They don't want your stock sitting on their shelves and after a few short months, those fees kick in, killing your profits. The best-case scenario is having exactly enough stock at Amazon so it's always available, but it's on the shelf for the least amount of time. In a perfect world, if for example you sell 50 units a day, you only bring 50 units a day to Amazon, it sells out, and the next day you bring in another 50 units, but that's not possible. You have to get as close to that as you can without risking running out of stock.

Inventory
Performance Index

The inventory performance index or IPI score was introduced by Amazon in 2018. This is a score between zero and one thousand, and it's based on your entire store, which is all of your products. You need to be at a certain number to bring in as much stock as you want.

In the past, Amazon gave you limited "shelf space." Now, as long as you have a certain IPI score, you get more storage space from Amazon as long as you're "in the green," versus in the red with your score. Amazon hasn't revealed how that score is calculated, but they do give us some clues as to what lowers your score.

Stranded inventory has a negative effect on your IPI score. This is inventory that isn't sellable, for a variety of reasons. You might have a lot of reviews that say the product is defective. The easiest way to get rid of stranded inventory is to dispose of the units, and Amazon offers free or low-cost liquidation services. Problem solved.

A second factor that impacts your score is running out of stock, and a third factor is having too much stock. A fourth issue is not selling stock fast enough, which is similar to having too much stock on the shelf. Amazon doesn't want stock on the shelf longer than 90 days. They want you to have the least amount of stock possible without running out.

Aside from the effect on your IPI score, too much inventory ties up your cash, and you're paying for that shelf space. Amazon charges a monthly storage fee that tends to go up every year. In Q4, those fees can be four times the usual amount, due to the holiday rush in online shopping. Sellers prepare for the increased sales by stocking up, but Amazon has only so much space. You can help Amazon—which you want to do, because they're helping you a lot—by storing just enough product in their warehouses. Remember, too, that storing inventory for longer than six months comes with long-term storage fees.

More recently, due to COVID and the surge in online retail, Amazon began limiting new product quantities. The company isn't doing this to punish sellers—they want you to have an aggressive launch. There simply isn't enough room. They are always trying to be efficient and optimize their business to maintain the customer's expectation and enhance their experience, so you can help them do that by managing your inventory. COVID changed the rules, and you can no longer trust that it will be OK to ship two to three months' worth of stock to Amazon ahead of time; you have to be more flexible with how you plan your inventory, while being much more aware of your numbers.

Ordering

Because you don't want to run out or have stock sitting on the shelf, you have to order smaller amounts, and order them more often. Say you sell 3,000 units per month (100 units per day). If it takes 11,000 units to fill a shipping container, a seller might ship 11,000 units every three months just to fill up that container. But you don't need 11,000 units right away. The better option is to have them ship, say, 3,600 units per month. This covers you for the month with 20 percent extra units, so you don't run out waiting for the next shipment. You pay the supplier just 30 percent up front for the 11,000 units and pay the 70 percent balance when the units leave the port each month. That 30 percent, by the way, is necessary for the factory to pay for the parts and labor needed to start production.

When you ship products to Amazon, you request shipping labels, which they send to you in a PDF file. Those go to your supplier. If you have 1,000 units in 10 boxes of 100 each, you have to get 10 labels.

Though you want your stock shipped to Amazon, ideally, you may have to order more stock due to a supplier's minimum, or to get a better price, than makes sense to have sitting on Amazon's shelves. If that's the case, you can have some stock shipped to a third-party warehouse. Some suppliers will also hold on to your inventory for a month. Ask them. Keep in mind that every time the supplier makes a shipment, you have to pay the 70 percent balance for that inventory. Again, this helps with your cash flow because until that shipment goes out, you can use that money for other things.

The typical seller strategy is to have a positive buffer time to ensure the product is selling before they place a new order. I prefer a negative buffer strategy, which I mentioned in Chapter 5. Let me tell you how this works, and why I do it this way.

Let's say production time is 30 days and shipping is 30 days. So, when I place an order, it's in stock 60 days later. I want to place an order every month, so as soon as production ends on one order, another one begins. I don't know how well the order being shipped will sell, but I'm already having more product made. This may seem counterintuitive until you look at the outcome: Seller A orders 3,000 units all at once, has them shipped all at once, gets them in stock, and starts selling. I order 3,000 units, but ship 1,000 units the first month, 1,000 units the second month, and 1,000 units the third month. It's still 3,000 units, so there is no more risk involved than if I had ordered all 3,000 at once.

Another benefit to having multiple shipments is that you are not storing all your stock in one place. You have some at Amazon, some shipping, and some being created at the factory. This way, if something goes wrong—like a shipment being held up—you already have stock at Amazon and more coming shortly.

Most sellers don't use this strategy because they don't want to put in 10 or 12 orders a year for every product, or they don't want to pay a little more per unit for the smaller quantities, or they don't want to pay for multiple shipments. Checking in inventory might take a bit longer, too, with multiple shipments to deal with. It's still the better way to go, because all of those issues are offset by benefits like increased cash flow. I'm not paying for 3,000 units all at once, so I can use that money for other things, like new product launches. The bigger benefit is having fewer units sitting on the shelf, and no units sitting on the shelf for more than 60 days.

Another reason to break up your shipments like this is to lower risk. Your one big shipment could get delayed, either in customs or somewhere else. All the money you put into it is tied up until you get the product online, and you're about to run out of product. If you have deliveries coming every month, even if one is delayed, the worst-case scenario is having to wait for the next one that's already in production and shipping in 30 days. With money tied up in one big shipment, you don't have the cash to place another order, so you're in limbo. If you do have a spike in sales, you can always order two months' worth of units at once too.

BASIC CASH FLOW PLANNING
Starting Cash = $15,000

#	EXAMPLE 1			EXAMPLE 2		
	Expenses	Income	Total Cash	Expenses	Income	Total Cash
1	$3,000	$0	$12,000	$3,000	$0	$12,000
2		$0	$12,000		$0	$12,000
3		$0	$12,000		$0	$12,000
4	$7,000	$2,000	**$5,000**	$2,333	$2,000	**$9,667**
5		$2,000	$7,000		$2,000	$11,667
6		$2,000	$9,000		$2,000	$13,667
7		$2,000	$11,000		$2,000	$15,667
8		$2,000	$13,000	$2,333	$2,000	$15,334
9		$2,000	$15,000		$2,000	$17,334
10		$2,000	$17,000		$2,000	$19,334
11		$2,000	$19,000		$2,000	$21,334
12		$2,000	$21,000	$2,334	$2,000	$21,000

Figure 9: Inventory management doesn't just prevent you from overstocking or running out of stock—it also affects your cash flow.

Figure 9 illustrates an example of how inventory management affects cash flow. The first column, numbered 1 through 12, represents the 12 months of the year, or 12 consecutive months to place orders. Next are three columns depicting example 1 and then three more columns depicting example 2. In each example, the seller has $15,000 cash in hand.

In example 1, the seller pays the 30 percent deposit of a $10,000 order, or $3,000 in week 1. Thirty days later, in week 4, the product is ready to ship, and the seller pays the 70 percent balance of $7,000. The seller is, in this example, making $2,000 a week income on those units.

In example 2, the seller also pays the 30 percent deposit in week 1, but instead of paying the 70 percent balance of $7,000 in week 4, they pay just one-third of that amount for one-third the number of units. The second and third installments of one-third of the balance are made in weeks 8 and 12. The seller in this example is also making $2,000 a week income from those units. Compare the cash flow amounts in the red rectangle and the green rectangle, and you can see how much more money you have on hand every week by spreading out shipments.

I mention this because sellers often hesitate to order because they're not sure what the demand is going to look like next week or next month. They postpone ordering until they're so low on inventory and the demand has ramped up so much that they have to order a full order and more. Now they have a lot of cash tied up in that one order. Another reason that sellers postpone their second shipment is because they want to get a discount from the supplier for a larger quantity. In most cases, you can negotiate with the supplier. Even if they won't give you a good deal, you may still be better off paying a little more and ordering less inventory to keep that cash available.

What if you hit your daily sales target (which we discussed in Chapter 5) before your buffer time? For instance, you set a 30-day buffer to sell 10 units per day. On day 15, you sell 10 units, on day 16 you sell 12, and on day 17 you sell 11. If this happens, place another order. Be prepared to place an order as soon as you hit your daily sales target, but don't think you have to place an order for a larger amount. Weigh the benefits and the risks around maintaining stock and cash flow.

Forecasting and Reordering

Ten to fifteen days before you place your next order, contact the supplier to negotiate terms and supply time. Again, calculate the time from order to inventory and ready to sell based on production time, shipping, and buffer time. For your first shipment, you estimated how many units you thought you would sell based on competitors' sales, but now you have an idea of how much you'll sell based on your own current sales. Look at one-week sales and four-week sales, and consider special events like holidays, when sales spike. Also consider the Chinese New Year. For several weeks around the end of January, people in China don't work, and you will not be getting any product from that country. You have to plan ahead so you don't run out of product.

Once you have the quantities and timing worked out with your supplier, contact your freight forwarder. They will need to communicate with your supplier to arrange for pickup. Stay organized with your production, shipping, and selling timetables. Use a calendar with your expected date to hit your sales target marked as Day 0, and then figure out what needs to happen in the days and weeks leading up to that date.

When to Order the Second Stock

If you've decided to reorder, think about how many units you need. If you started with an order of 1,000 units, for example, and you reach your target in 10 days, you might want to order 1,500 units for your second stock. Let your supplier know right away and pay the 30 percent deposit. If the production time is 30 days, then contact your freight forwarder two weeks later to negotiate the price and get a lead time from them on how long it will take to get to Amazon and set up shipping. Your freight forwarder will know if any delays are expected. Then, if it's the first time this particular supplier and freight forwarder have worked together on a shipment for you, connect them. Once the production is complete, pay the supplier the 70 percent balance for the product and contact your freight forwarder to let them know the product is ready. From there, you don't have to do anything except wait for it to arrive at Amazon and get checked into inventory.

Again, keep a list or a calendar to keep track of dates and activities. In time, you'll begin to see trends and be able to forecast production times well ahead of time. If you can forecast six or nine months, or even an entire year ahead of your needs, you may be able to get better prices from your supplier because that helps them plan their resources. Helping your supplier sets you apart from other sellers. If something happens and your needs change, suppliers understand that you're in a B2C (business-to-customer) business and despite your best efforts, sales can be unpredictable. They won't typically hold it against you if you have to change your forecast. If you develop a solid relationship with a supplier and can accurately predict your production needs, you may be able to get special terms as low as 10 percent upfront and 90 percent due 30 days after the product is checked into Amazon. To get a deal like this, you have to have built a close and trusting relationship with your supplier. You may have to travel to the factory in China and meet with the owner. If they see that you are a professional seller who's serious about making money and can help them make money, too, they will want to work out a deal that benefits you both.

Think of your relationship with your supplier as a partnership. There may be times when, instead of asking for better terms like 10 percent up front and 90 percent later, that you offer to pay them 100 percent of the cost up front in exchange for a discount on the cost. The supplier may need the cash flow and it's more important to them to get that money up front than to make more profit on the sale. Just as Amazon helps sellers be better sellers, sellers should help their suppliers be better suppliers. In the end, everybody wins.

Building these relationships can pay off in other ways. Before the Chinese New Year, your supplier may have a lot of sellers needing production, but they only have the capacity for a few orders. If you have been helping them out and others have not, which seller's order is most likely to be fulfilled?

Liquidation

If you aren't hitting your target sales but you still have a good product, you can optimize your listing and relaunch. If you aren't hitting your sales targets, you need to decide if you should relaunch or liquidate. That decision might depend on what's going on in the markets. If I have 200 good reviews but I'm only selling one or two units a day, I look at the competition. Maybe they also have about 200 good reviews—and like me, they're only selling one or two units a day. This tells me that I'm in a saturated niche and there isn't enough demand to support all the sellers of the product. In this case, it's impossible for me to make any money.

In another scenario, I have 200 good reviews, but another seller has 1,000 reviews and they're selling a lot more units. Their product isn't better than mine—it has a higher ranking and more reviews, so it's attracting more buyers. In this case, I can either bow out, or stay in and try to boost my reviews to compete with the top seller. I look at how much money I have to invest in the product and decide if it's worth it to try, or if my money would be better spent on another product launch. Sometimes I stay in and have a very successful product; other times I decide to invest my money elsewhere.

Another reason to liquidate is when a product just isn't selling well. This can happen when customers don't like the product or don't understand how to use it. If you're getting two-star reviews, you have to improve the product and relaunch, or let it go. Letting go of a product you've put time and money into is hard, but this is why you shouldn't get emotionally attached. No matter how much you love a product, if customers don't love it, the product won't sell, and it won't make you any money. Remember that this is a business, not a hobby, and you're in it to make money and have a better lifestyle. If you can't reach your goals with a product, you have to get rid of it.

Liquidating stock is a difficult topic for many Amazon sellers because no method is profitable. You can put your stock on a site such as liquidation.com, but you might only get $1 for a product that cost you $10. A better option is to sell out your stock on Amazon at cost or slightly below. Let's say you're stuck with 1,000 units and you paid $5 per unit. You have $5,000 tied to that inventory. You can opt to simply destroy it—ask Amazon to get rid of it for you—but you may have to pay a fee for that also. Sometimes Amazon offers that service for free. The worst-case scenario is that you're out $5,000. You can also drop the price and increase your PPC bids to sell out the stock and recoup some of that money. Getting $3,000 for $5,000 worth of stock is better than getting nothing for it, even though you're still losing money. Keep track of how long the stock stays at Amazon—after six months you have to pay long-term storage fees, and at that point you're better off destroying the inventory. Long-term inventory has a potentially adverse effect on your IPI score, which can justify destroying or liquidating.

If you have to get rid of inventory, don't let it get you down or sour you on selling. Every seller has to do it at some time. There are millions of other products out there waiting to be discovered, and the sooner you get rid of a bad product, the sooner you can find your next winner. No matter how good a seller is at product selection, launching, and PPC, failures happen and there's nothing you can do but move on. Despite how much you know about selling, it's still a numbers game to an extent, and the more launches you have, the better you'll become at selecting products, and the fewer failures you'll experience as a percentage of all your launches.

My first launch was spectacular. It went so well that I thought that selling on Amazon was a lot easier than I thought, or that I was some kind of genius. Then I launched four more times and failed with all of them. That was a wake-up call for me, and the experience forced me to rethink everything I thought I knew. That's what got me to this place, where the successes outnumber the failures by a very long shot.

What makes me sad is seeing sellers have a failure and give up. This happens more often than you can imagine. Those who quit never have success as Amazon sellers, while those who stick with it tend to have success, after success, after success. If they see another failure, they fail fast and move on to the next success.

Do you know who else does that? Amazon. Google. Big companies that aren't afraid to try something new, and succeed or fail, then try something else. If they didn't, they would never have gotten where they are today. You have to think the same way—like a professional seller who knows that the occasional failure is just another step toward the next big win.

Shipping

Once your order is produced, the supplier ships it. It's your job to tell them how to ship it. You can choose Ex works (EXW), free on board (FOB), or delivered duty paid (DDP) shipping. There are more shipping options, but these are the most common.

With EXW, the supplier (or factory) boxes the inventory and sets it outside to be picked up. It's the seller's responsibility to have it picked up by a shipper. With FOB shipping, the supplier brings it to the closest port and the seller arranges the shipping from there. With DDP shipping, the supplier handles the transportation from factory to Amazon or another warehouse that you've designated. The supplier works with a freight forwarder to do this, which is a professional shipping company that specializes in getting freight from one location to another.

I do not recommend DDP shipping, because this puts your supplier in the middle of a function that is not their specialty. Shipping isn't their main concern, and if there are delays, you can't talk to the shipper—you have to go through your supplier. Take control of this step and work with the freight forwarder directly. As for choosing between EXW or FOB, I typically go with whatever the supplier prefers. They will either have a process for getting your stock to the dock, or they'll ask you to have it picked up.

Freight Forwarders

Try several freight forwarders and choose ones that are honest with you, communicate well, and give you a good price. For the most part, freight forwarders do not negotiate, so the price they quote you is the price you pay. If you use just one without shopping around, you will never know if they're overcharging you. Speak with the freight forwarder about their services and whether they offer insurance in case your inventory is lost. Make sure they are 100 percent transparent with you about everything they do and what happens with your freight. Find out when they expect your stock to arrive at Amazon and what their process is for notifying you if a shipment is delayed.

Even if you find a good one and use only that one, you will not necessarily get a good deal every time. I prefer to use three freight forwarders. For some deliveries, I call each one to get a quote, and they all know I'm working with other companies, so they give me a good price to get my business. Once you find a couple or more freight forwarders that you can rely on, build a relationship with them. Your business depends on them doing what they say they will do, within the time frame they tell you and for the price they quote you. Getting several quotes adds to your buffer time, so plan ahead. Get quotes within a week or two of the actual shipping date, because the cost could change. The closer to the actual shipping date, the more exact the quote.

Shipping Methods

You can ship several different ways, and the faster the shipping, the higher the cost. With air express, your inventory will be at Amazon in just a few days. With regular air shipment, your inventory will probably be checked into Amazon in two to three weeks. Prior to COVID-19, express sea shipment and regular sea shipment, depending on the port you shipped from, could take about 25 to 40 days, and sometimes longer. Regular sea shipments took as long as 60 days. Since COVID-19, these numbers have almost doubled. Avoid shipping by air, as that eats into your profits. Plan ahead so that a sea shipment of some kind meets your timeline. Your freight forwarder can ship by any of these methods.

If you're not sure which shipping method to use, do the math. If I'm at risk of running out of stock and I can choose between a 15-day air delivery and a 30-day sea delivery, I figure out how much money I stand to gain or lose in that 15-day gap. If it's $1,000 a day, or $15,000, and that outweighs the difference in shipping cost, I'll ship by air.

I always consider the size and cost of the item too. For a small, lightweight product that's relatively expensive, such as Bluetooth headphones, it might make more sense to ship by air because the cost to ship is low and the potential loss from running out of units is great. I wouldn't ship extremely heavy items, such as dumbbells, by air, because the cost to ship would outweigh the benefit of having them available to sell.

Speak with your freight forwarder to find out how the cost is calculated. It may be by size or weight, but they will know, and that information will help you decide which method to use. Get a quote from them before you decide to launch a product. It will be an estimate, being so far out from your launch date, but it will help you decide if launching the product makes sense. This information will also help you plan your budget. See my Breakers site to download my Batch spreadsheet, which can help you figure out that piece.

To give you a quote, the freight forwarder will need an address; if you're having your product shipped to Amazon, you need to get that address ahead of time. The company has warehouses on the East and West Coasts of the United States, so the quote will vary depending on which warehouse the delivery goes to. When you create the shipment in Amazon, you'll find out exactly which warehouse it needs to go to, and you can then let your freight forwarder know.

3PLs

Prior to COVID, I shipped almost everything directly to Amazon. The only exceptions were during Q4, when storage costs were at a premium due to the holidays. Since COVID, sellers have had to learn about 3PLs, third-party logistics companies. Again, you don't want to have all your products in one place due to the uncertainty around shipping. Besides, Amazon doesn't want to be a storage facility for people who can't efficiently manage their inventory. They just want to distribute products. Your goal should be to store as little as possible at Amazon without running out. You also don't want to store a lot of product at your 3PL, though, for the reasons I've already explained.

When you use a 3PL, figure in the extra time and cost to have the stock transported from the 3PL to Amazon. As I mentioned earlier, 3PLs are generally costlier and they delay getting your products in inventory for selling, but these days they make a lot of sense.

Every big seller uses a 3PL, and some of the bigger sellers have their own 3PL, space in an existing facility or their own facility. New sellers should research 3PLs and have one lined up when they start ordering inventory, preferably close to where Amazon is requesting them to ship their products to.

HTS Codes

Another thing to consider that can add a cost to shipping is the Harmonized Tariff Schedule (HTS) code. This is a globally recognized code that's unique for each product type. Towels have a code. Yoga mats have a code. The code determines the tariff that you have to pay to export products from China to the US. Your freight forwarder can tell you how much the tariff is for your HTS-coded product. Products can often be classified by two different codes, with one code carrying a lower tariff than the other. Ask your freight forwarder for their advice on which HTS code to use for the lowest tariff. The caveat is that US customs can decide to assign another, more expensive code, so be prepared to pay the highest-tariffed HTS code, but assign the lowest-priced one that makes sense for the product.

Inspections and Audits

Before your products leave China, have them inspected. You can pay your freight forwarder to do this or pay a third-party inspector. Do this for every shipment to ensure there are no quantity or quality problems with the merchandise. Different types of inspections exist; an acceptable quality limit (AQL) inspection is common.

Have the factory where the products are made audited, too, to verify there are no quality or ethical problems. Again, you can talk to your freight forwarder about this or hire an auditor in China.

> **MAKE SURE THE FACTORY IS FOLLOWING ETHICAL PRACTICES AND THAT THE PRODUCT IS THE SAME QUALITY AS WHAT YOU SAW IN THE SAMPLE.**

This may cost you a couple hundred dollars, but you need to be sure you don't have factory or product problems before your inventory leaves the factory—not through bad reviews from angry customers on Amazon.

BREAKERS

For additional information and resources to help manage inventory, such as my Forecast tool, visit my Breakers site at tomerrabinovich. com/breakers.

CHAPTER 10

KEY PERFORMANCE INDICATORS

"Lack of direction, not lack of time, is the problem. We all have 24-hour days."

—ZIG ZIGLAR

Sellers should identify and track certain KPIs, or key performance indicators. Those who do often maintain a narrow focus on KPIs, though. They look at the micro rather than the macro view.

Say their sales went down yesterday, or this week, so they need to do something. But they don't know why their sales went down, and they don't really know what to do to correct the problem. Maybe they need to be more aggressive with PPC or change their pricing. Often, they act on impulse instead of figuring out what's really going on and taking the appropriate steps to fix it. They don't have the data points they need to understand the cause of the sales going down, so they can't make an informed decision.

For example, let's say their sales went down by 20 percent week over week for the past three weeks. Maybe the market also went down 20 percent every week during that period. Maybe fewer people searched for their product during that time. Maybe sales declined similarly at the same time last year. A holiday may be approaching, and people could be spending their money on other things.

You have to know your market share in two ways: in terms of revenue and in terms of sales—specifically, number of units sold. You want to be number one in your market for both revenue and sales. But there's more to it than that.

Units Sold per Day, Profit, and ROI

Return on investment (ROI) is an important factor in any business, but in Amazon selling, it takes a back seat to other factors. Enjoy this little exercise on units sold per day, ROI, profit, ranking, and market share. It may change how you consider ROI in your decision-making forever.

Let's say your landed cost for a product unit is $5, you make a $5 profit on each unit, and you sell 100 units per day. That's a 100 percent

ROI because you're getting $1,000 in revenue and $500 of that is profit. Sounds great, right?

- **Option 1:** $5 profit, sell 100 units, $500 profit = 100 percent ROI

Here's another option. You sell 200 units of the same product at a lower ROI, just 80 percent, and make $800 a day.

- **Option 2:** $4 profit, sell 200 units, $800 profit = 80 percent ROI

Which option would you prefer?

I've done this exercise dozens of times with my training groups, with mixed results. Some people chose option #1 for the higher ROI, while others chose option #2.

I always choose option #2 because when it comes to KPIs, I have three goals:

- Maximize profit
- Maximize ranking
- Maximize market share

No matter what changes I make to my listing, my PPC, or any other decision—like choosing between option #1 and option #2—I am always trying to achieve those goals. Option #2 achieves all three: more profit, more ranking (because I sell more units), and more market share (a higher percentage of sales among the competition).

Even though the ROI is less in option #2, 80 percent versus option #1's 100 percent, I still prefer option #2 because it moves me to closer to my goals. The only time I might reconsider this option is if I had a cash flow problem, because my returns will come more slowly. But as long as I am managing my cash flow properly, this option makes much more sense.

Ah, you didn't really think it was that easy, did you?

There is a third option.

- **Option 1:** $5 profit, sell 100 units, $500 profit = 100 percent ROI
- **Option 3:** $2.50 profit, sell 200 units, $500 profit = 50 percent ROI

In option #3, you sell twice as many units, make the same profit, but now your ROI is only 50 percent instead of 100 percent. *Based on what you now know, which option would you choose?*

If you chose option #3, congratulations. You get it. You understand why ROI is not as important as other factors because it does not do…*what?*

That's right, it does not maximize profits, *and* ranking, *and* market share like option #3, with its lower ROI. With option #3, I'm selling more units and getting a better ranking. Those 100 additional sales are 100 units that my competitors are not getting, so I'm also gaining market share.

There is a limit to how far you can take this approach. Let's take a look at another option, option #4.

- **Option 3:** $2.50 profit, sell 200 units, $500 profit = 50 percent ROI
- **Option 4:** $1 profit, 500 units, $500 profit = 20 percent ROI

There is a limit to how low you should go with ROI. In option #4, at 20 percent ROI, you are taking on too much risk for your profit. You have to sell too many units and if you have a problem or make a mistake, you will not make a good profit and could even lose money. A shipment could be delayed, and if you run out of stock, you can't sell enough units to make a profit. Also, your profit margin is so slim—just $1 per unit—that any additional costs incurred, such as customs fees that you didn't expect, could cut deeply into your profits.

For an item where the COGS is $5, I believe the sweet spot is 50 percent or higher ROI. For a more expensive item, say $50 COGS per unit, where I have a high profit margin, I might shoot for an even lower ROI, less than 50 percent.

This is why sellers shouldn't focus solely on revenue. They should also look at number of units sold per day and seek to maximize both. I'm not just looking at how much profit I'm going to make today or next week, but how much I can make in six months or a year. Maximizing my number of units sold will sustain my sales so I can continue to get the biggest share of the market, not only today but for many, many days to come.

Remember, Amazon's BSR is based on units sold. It doesn't matter how high or how low your profit margin is—all it cares about is how many units of a product you sell. The lower BSR attracts more buyers. It gives you more opportunity for more reviews. That should be the goal, and that is why you have to track those KPIs: profit, ranking, and market share.

You should also maximize your keyword ranking. And you should do all of this without exceeding 50 percent ROI. If I'm making 80 percent ROI, I look at ways to change up my PPC or my pricing to get the ROI lower—and grab more market share—while still making the same profit.

When you understand the numbers, it becomes a sort of game, and you want to win the game. You want to be number one. Understanding the numbers, the most critical KPIs, shows you how to play so you can win.

If you're still scratching your head (because I admit, this is counterintuitive to everything we've been taught about sales), here's another example: if I had a coffee shop on Main Street, I would rather sell 100 cups of coffee at a $400 profit than 200 cups of coffee at the same profit, $400. Selling on Amazon is different because it's all about number of sales, while being in a very competitive marketplace. That is what Amazon cares about, so it's what you need to care about too. You want to sell as many cups of coffee as possible within reasonable risk. As long as you aren't going to run out of beans, or coffee cups, or hot water, you should sell as many cups of coffee as you can. You should get as many reviews as you can and try to get that best seller badge. That's the game that Amazon plays. It's the game that I play, and I play to win.

The solution to finding the right balance between units sold and ROI doesn't always require you to lower your price. You can be more aggressive on PPC, which costs money, lowering your ROI, and sell more units. You should determine the change you want to make and try it. Test it. You could lower your price and sell more, or you could raise it and sell more. You won't know until you test it.

Be Obsessed with the Competition

Know when a new seller enters the market and when one leaves. Know what their listings look like and track their sales. Otherwise, you could try to boost your sales by changing one image on your listing, and if your sales go up, you'll assume that image did the trick. But what if, that same day, your top competitor ran out of stock? You have to know these things.

Your sales might go down and you change an image, and they go down even more. Maybe a seller just introduced a better product. You can't sit on your hands—you have to act. You need to improve your product or find a better one so you can compete.

Once you start seeing real money, say $20,000 to $50,000 a month, competitors will notice you and they'll start copying what you're doing. Some will improve on what you're doing. When this happens, step up your game. Improve your listing, find better bullets, get better images. You might need to improve your product. Look at what they're doing and make it better, do it better. This is all part of the game of getting more sales. Again, it's the game that Amazon plays too: better products drive more sales for you and for Amazon.

Some sellers complain about the game: "Oh, the competitor copied me." Well, maybe they did. But they are also pushing you to be better, and you can improve the product and in turn, push them to be better. Complaining doesn't make sales—having the best product, listing, and sales strategy makes sales.

A top seller knows their competition. They can name, off the top of their head, their top five competitors for every product they sell. They might even be able to tell you the competition's supplier and how much they pay per unit. They aren't casually aware of the competition—they are *obsessed*. They know the market, where they fit in that market, and where the top competitors fit too.

What Do I Do Next?

Let's say you and your best friend, Ashton, just joined a gym. You walk in and there's this guy lifting weights who's in fantastic shape. He looks like he's been working out every day for years, because he has. What are the odds that you and Ashton are going to look like that guy after your first workout? But you stay for an hour and get in a good workout. You do this every day for a week. The second week, your friend Ashton decides he's never going to look like that fit guy at the gym, so he gives up. Now you're on your own. You keep going, and after a month, you're seeing an improvement. You feel stronger too. After three months, you're catching up to that guy, and after six months, he's asking you for training tips. You don't stop there, though—you look for the next guy who's in better shape than you are, and now that's your target. You're going to beat him. It might take a month, or six months, or a year, but as long as you continue to improve, and improve faster than he is improving, you'll get there. Of course, genetics play a part at the gym. As an Amazon seller, you don't have those limitations. As long as you have a strong mindset, you can beat anybody. Meanwhile, Ashton is back at home watching television and eating potato chips. He will never be where you are because he gave up.

The key is to keep improving. Look at who's ahead of you and who's creeping up behind. Review their product, their reviews, their copy, title, keywords, bullet points, and images. Look at their numbers too. If a competitor is outselling you, yet their listing seems inferior to yours, look more closely. They are doing something different, and you need to identify it.

Don't be haphazard about this. Keep track of your competitors—their prices, number of reviews, review averages, sales, and reviews-to-sales ratios. You can put this in a spreadsheet and update it once a month. Or bookmark the competition's listings and check them once a month. Pay attention to what everyone else is doing, and if you need to, take action to stay ahead of them.

TOMER'S TIP:
How Do I Know If I Can Do Better?

You should always be seeking ways to improve your listing. Analyze your listing versus your competitors' listings. Compare and contrast them. If someone with a similar product, price point, and star rating— yet fewer reviews than you—has a lower BSR (meaning they are selling more than you), they are doing something different. They're doing something *better*. It may be their images or their keywords. Figure that out. If there are five competitors with fewer reviews than you have on your product, yet they're all selling more product, you have a lot of improving to do. If no one with fewer reviews is selling more than you, look at the competitor with about the same number of reviews that's outselling you. Look at their listing and their keywords. What are they doing that you could be doing better?

If you make a change, do it in increments. Then check to see its effect. You can also use Amazon Experiments or other tools to test different titles, images, and so on to see which ones perform the best. I prefer to make just one thing different at a time, then wait to see the effect. After a week, I might make another change, but I never make more than one change to a listing within a week's time. I look at the click-through rate (CTR) and the conversion rate (CVR). The CTR is the percentage of impressions (my listing being seen) that resulted in a customer clicking on my listing. The CVR is the percentage of clicks that resulted in a purchase. Changing a main image or a title typically affects CTR, and less often, CVR. This makes sense because the main image may entice a customer to click on your listing, but they'll look at all your images, read the copy, and check out the reviews before making a purchase. If you want to change the other images, change them all at once and then wait a week to see the effect. Check back weekly and compare your original click-throughs and conversions with the latest numbers.

The price affects both conversion and click-through rates. I experiment with my pricing to find the price that keeps me ahead of the competition and delivers the highest profit per day (if you don't remember what profit per day or PPD means, go back to Chapter 5, where I explain it). Sellers change their pricing to compete with other sellers, to increase sales, or to increase profit margins. Sometimes if a seller is running low on inventory, they might raise their prices to slow sales until they get another shipment so they don't run out. The funny thing is that the higher price sometimes leads to more sessions and more sales! So unless you experiment, it's difficult to know exactly which price will yield the highest PPD.

I don't want to give the impression that you constantly change your listing. If it's working well, you may not need to change it at all for months. But if you're falling behind your competitors, figure out what you can do to improve it.

◆ ◆ ◆

Your listing is incredibly important, but at its core, it's marketing. It's not your product. If you're trying to decide whether to expend more effort on your product or your listing, product should win out every time. A great product doesn't require a lot of advertising to sell, but a bad product needs a lot of marketing to sell at all. It's like the difference between Tesla and McDonald's:

Do you know how much Tesla is spending on commercial advertising? *Zero!*

Do you know how much McDonald's spends on advertising a year, just in the US?

Over $1.5 billion a year.[5]

McDonald's must continue to advertise to stay in business. There's a reason for this…I'll leave it to you to figure out.

---

[5] Statista Research Department, "McDonald's Corporation Advertising Spending in the United States from 2009 to 2019 (in Billion U.S. Dollars)," Statista, September 20, 2021, https://www.statista.com/statistics/192159/us-ad-spending-of-mcdonalds/.

BREAKERS

If you missed my "Make It Better" lecture mentioned in Chapter 6, take a break now and check it out at tomerrabinovich.com/breakers.

CHAPTER 11

BALANCE THE SCALE

"Whatever good things we build
end up building us."

—JIM ROHN

After graduating from college, I worked for a company that helps small businesses. Entrepreneurs came through the doors every day looking for advice. One day, I was sitting in my office when I noticed the smell of pizza wafting in through the door. I went to the lobby, and there was a guy there with two huge pizza trays.

"Hi, I'm Andy, and this is what I do," he said. "I make really good pizza, and I want to start a pizza business."

I tried a slice, and it was one of the most delicious pizzas I'd ever tasted: crisp, delicious crust, gooey cheese, amazing tomato sauce…everything about it was perfect. I was excited to help Andy out, confident that he'd succeed. He had great pizza and he was passionate about starting a business. What could go wrong?

Andy did end up opening a pizza place, but within a few months, it closed. How could this happen?

Andy made great pizza, but great pizza doesn't make a great business. You need more than a product. You need structure. You need systems and processes. You might have to hire people to help you run the business.

I spoke with Andy about why his business failed, and he told me that launching a great business was a lot harder than making great pizza.

Sellers often build their businesses organically, just like Andy did. They sell products, set up their PPC, get their sourcing and inventory figured out, and everything else I talked about so far. Then they build a business around all those activities. That's kind of like throwing a bunch of ingredients in a pan and hoping you end up with a pizza. Andy knew what he wanted his pizza to look like from the start—he just didn't know what he wanted his pizza business to look like. Until he figured that out, he'd be making one pizza at a time, like he did for his family and friends. He couldn't scale his business. He couldn't make a hundred pizzas for a pizza banquet. He couldn't increase his profits by lowering his costs. He couldn't take a vacation. He couldn't even take a day off because he had to make pizza all day, every day. This is the life of the typical seller who doesn't have a real business. They're the boss, but they're also the sole employee. They have a job.

I want you to stop for a second and think back to why you started selling on Amazon in the first place. Chances are, it was about freedom. Time freedom, financial freedom—freedom to do what you want, when you want to do it. Go back to that time and ask yourself if those things are still important to you. If they are, make a new plan to get them. Set a deadline for yourself. It may be today, next week, or two years from now. Then look at everything you're doing now that you don't want to be doing by that deadline. Make a plan to stop doing those things. You'll build your business faster and with fewer problems that way.

If you've read this far, you have the recipe and you can make pizza all day. You can't hang out in the kitchen all day, though—you have to open an actual business. Start thinking of yourself as "business owner" before you sell your first pizza—or product on Amazon.

People with full-time careers often start selling as a side business, expecting to make a few hundred dollars a month. Suddenly, their income from sales outgrows their salary. They usually quit their job to focus on being an Amazon seller. You would think that their sales would explode with all that time to focus on selling, but that's not always what happens. When I started selling on Amazon while having a full-time job, I was very efficient with my time. With a nine-to-five job, I only had a few hours in the morning, evening, and on weekends to run my own business, so I stuck to a schedule and accomplished a lot in those hours.

After I quit my job, I had all the time in the world. Activities that I used to accomplish in two hours now seemed to take all day because I had too much time and no real schedule. This is a common problem with people who begin working for themselves from home. With no one looking over your shoulder or holding you accountable, it's easy to waste time. Within a few months, I realized that I had to organize my time better and stick to a schedule.

You can get to a point where you don't have to stick to a schedule, but you first have to do the work. You get there by building a business that meets your ultimate life goals.

In Chapter 1, I talked about why anyone would want to be an Amazon seller—why you do it, why I do it. Getting your business structure right is how you satisfy whatever goals you had for becoming an Amazon seller in the first place. A simple way to think about this is to start with your "why," "what," "how," and "when."

A Simple Assignment

I want you to get a piece of paper or a notebook and a pen, because you can't put this part off. Start this exercise now and you can finish after you read this chapter. If you don't, you'll put it aside and might not get back to it.

Do you have some paper and a pen? Great. Draw a line down the middle from top to bottom and another line across the middle from left to right. Now, in each of those four boxes, write "why," "what," "how," and "when." As you read the rest of this chapter, start filling in those boxes with your own thoughts—your own "why," "what," "how," and "when." It doesn't have to be neat or complete, but write something. I'll tell you what to do with this assignment at the end of the chapter.

Why Do You Want to Be an Amazon Seller?

Sellers want to work less and make more money. Those two goals are their biggest "why." They don't want to be employees with a boss telling them what to do. They don't want someone else dictating when they come to work and when they leave, or how many vacation days they get every year. They don't want someone else deciding how much money they make either.

Some sellers have other goals. They want to build a brand and a business, and putting in a lot of hours to do that is their passion. It's less work and more a labor of love.

This may come as a shock, but I'm not emotionally attached to my products, my brands, or my business. I care about my customers enough to give them great products and service, but the business itself is not what drives me. *I'm passionate about the freedom that this business gives me.* The time and money provided by selling on Amazon is my "why." It's why I'm excited to get out of bed in the morning and get to work. Running the business gives me time with my family. It pays for travel. It allows me to buy nice things. This is what I get from my business. It's my number one "why."

My second "why" is helping others. I get a lot of satisfaction from helping other sellers and seeing that their success. The cool thing is that the more I help sellers succeed, the more I succeed, in business and personally. Selling products is great, but I get greater satisfaction seeing sellers take action based on my methods and end up winning. It makes me happy when I see those I've consulted for getting a seven- or an eight-figure exit without needing to worry about money ever again.

Knowing your "why" helps you figure out the kind of business structure you need to build. It determines whether you hire employees or do it all on your own. Your business structure dictates how many products you launch, how many you sell, how much money you make, and how much free time you have. Then you can make decisions that help you achieve those goals. Your goals may change over time, but it's very important that you know right from the start why you want to sell products online. Why you want to start this business. Why you find the prospect of becoming an Amazon seller so damned appealing.

So, why are *you* doing this? What's your motivation for being an Amazon seller? Are you passionate about building a brand? Are you driven by a desire to be a business owner? Is this something you can see yourself doing for many years? What do you want out of it?

What Do You Want to Do in the Business?

The next question to ask yourself is "What do I want to do?" Once you've built your business, what do you want to be doing in that business on a day-to-day basis? How much time do you want to spend on it, and how involved do you want to be in the strategy, the decisions, and in the daily activity?

You might want to be hands-on, doing all the work yourself, or you may want to do nothing at all. Both answers are possible outcomes, and the likelihood of achieving them is much higher if you figure out what you want to do early in the process, when you're first starting the business.

How Are You Going to Run It?

The day-to-day operations of any company are as varied as the business owners who create them. I'll get into a lot more detail about the systems, people, and processes that make your company run, but for now, think about the tools you know and those you might want to learn. Think about how your business will run every day, and how you can build it in a way that allows you to satisfy your "why" and reach your goals.

Most sellers don't think about this when they start; they save their files on their computer and leave their PIs (proforma invoices) from suppliers in their email inbox. They don't treat what they're doing as a business. I want you to think about yourself as a bigger seller already and consider how you would behave differently. For example, if you're currently doing $10,000 a month and imagine yourself doing $100,000 a month, what would you be doing differently? Get a new laptop? Have a proper workstation? Become more organized? Sort and save all your files on the cloud? From my experience, you will need those things to get there, and not the other way around. You need to give yourself the chance to succeed.

I'm happy to be the one to break this to you: you are a business owner. Learn as one, act as one, lead as one. Don't expect your business growth to improve who you are—it doesn't work that way. You must improve who you are to scale your business.

When Do You Want to Fulfill Your "Why"?

When do you want to reach your goals and fulfill your "why"? If you have a goal of making a certain amount of money each month, set a date to get there. If you have a goal of working just two hours a day, four days a week, set a date for that too.

They say that running a business is a marathon, not a sprint. Well, I disagree. I usually work in sprints, while my business is running a marathon. When something comes up in my business that demands my attention, I commit a lot of time to it to get it done right. Once I do that, I can relax and let the people, processes, and systems take over so I can spend time on other things in my life. Initially, I had to put in a lot of time to get to a place where I can do this. Now, my business can run with just a few hours of my time each week, but when I see something that I want to add or improve, I jump back in for another sprint.

You might want to take longer than I did to get your business running because you have other commitments. That's fine. Or you may want to go all in for two years and then sell your business—also OK, and I'll talk more about that later in this book.

I'm sure you can see the importance of answering the "why," "what," "how," and "when" questions. But you're eager to get through this chapter, too, so you're not going to answer them right now. After this chapter, you'll want to read the next one, though, and you will never answer these questions. Most entrepreneurs never do. Six months later, they're still not sure where they're going or how they're going to get there. So take a moment, get out a notebook or grab a piece of paper off your printer, and start jotting down some ideas. Keep it handy and add to it as you continue reading this book. By the end of the last chapter, have all these questions answered.

Don't write it on your computer, or you'll forget about it. Tape the paper on your wall or lay it on your desk—somewhere that you'll see it every day. There's an old saying that goes something like, "If you don't have a goal, you're already there." So if you want to stay exactly where you are, you can skip this activity. I suspect you would like to change something about your life, or you wouldn't be reading this in the first place, so take some time and start writing.

Think about your goals and their purpose. If you say something like, "I want to make a million dollars a month," that's fine, but having a million dollars won't make you happy. It's what a million dollars does for you—frees you from financial worry, allows you to buy a second home in the mountains or on a lake, pays for a trip around the world for your entire extended family. So don't focus solely on the money. Think deeply about what you really, really want to do with this life you've been given.

Did you write something? Cool. You can revise it tomorrow, and every day until you're satisfied. It's going to help you create the right structure for your business.

Four Business Structures

Many business structures exist. I'm going to tell you about the three that I've had, and a fourth one that's popular with other sellers. Any one of these can work for you depending on your goals. I call these structures "The Driver," "The Driving Instructor," "The Chauffeur," and "The Autopilot."

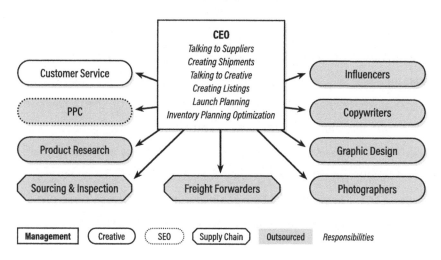

THE DRIVER

Figure 11: *As a Driver, you drive your company for better or for worse.*
You make all the decisions and take all the actions.
You might also be the bottleneck. In this example, the nonshaded
box indicates just one employee: Customer Service.

The Driver

Every seller and most businesses start here. As a Driver, you drive your own company for better or for worse. You make all the decisions and take all the actions. You might outsource some tasks to people on the backend, such as copywriting, graphics, photography, bookkeeping, freight forwarding, and inspecting. You might have an agency or a freelancer who takes care of your PPC, and even a part-time customer service agent, but you are the business owner, the boss, and the sole full-time employee. Everyone reports to you, and none of them talk to each other.

You are The Driver, and you're also the bottleneck. Nothing happens without you directing it, managing it, and making all the decisions. You do most of the work too. Many Driver businesses collapse because, like the pizza business, The Driver has a great pizza recipe, but they don't know how to run a company. Drivers have no safety net. They can't take time off or get sick, and if something happens to them, the business goes away.

Some sellers have no aspirations to ever get out of The Driver's seat. They don't like being responsible for employees and the paperwork and salaries that come with employees. They don't like managing people, and don't like working with teams. The Driver likes to be in charge, but some of them never reach their goals and give up. Others burn out and either sell their business or shut it down after a few years.

Successful Drivers are disciplined, systemized, and organized. They can do everything themselves, from creating shipments and PPC, to product selection, finding a supplier, and even taking care of customer service.

Some prefer to work few hours and keep their businesses small, while others work a lot and build seven- and eight-figure online seller businesses. If you want to stay small, The Driver is a good business structure for your goals. If you want to work very hard, ramp up quickly, and sell your business in a few years, The Driver can also be a good structure for you.

Sellers who don't know their goals and haven't figured out what kind of business structure they need to reach those goals tend to maintain the Driver structure for too long. Their business grows and gets more complicated, and they get overworked. Their business grows so fast, they don't have time to pivot to a model that scales. And now they're so busy, they don't have time to hire anyone or train them.

Alice, one of my coaching students, does all the work herself. She's also on her third Amazon business after selling the first two for multiple seven figures. She "builds and sells" because she doesn't want to manage employees, preferring to run the business on her own until she knows it's getting too big for her to manage alone. Then she sells. Alice is a classic Driver who's figured out how to make the structure work for her goals.

Many sellers don't know how to get out of The Driver's seat. If they decided from the start that that's their place, there's nothing wrong with that. But if the "whys" and their goals are unachievable as a Driver, they need to think about the kind of structure they really need and aim for that right from the start.

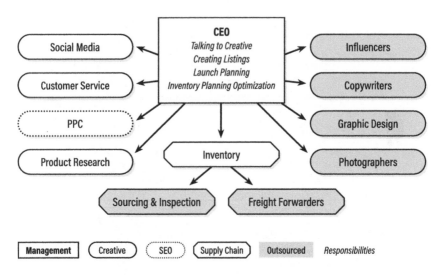

THE DRIVING INSTRUCTOR

CEO
Talking to Creative
Creating Listings
Launch Planning
Inventory Planning Optimization

Social Media

Customer Service

PPC

Product Research

Influencers

Copywriters

Graphic Design

Photographers

Inventory

Sourcing & Inspection

Freight Forwarders

Management | Creative | SEO | Supply Chain | Outsourced | *Responsibilities*

Figure 12: *As a Driving Instructor, you're still in charge, but you aren't doing all the work. In this example, the nonshaded boxes indicate five employees: Social Media, Customer Service, PPC, Product Research, and Inventory.*

The Driving Instructor

When you first learned to drive, you had an instructor. Your mom, dad, or a professional driving instructor told you when to hit the gas and when to brake, when to use your turn signal and when to pull over. The Driving Instructor business structure is one where you're in charge, but you're not doing all the work. You have employees, and you instruct them on what to do, when to do it, and how to do it.

Drivers often slowly become Driving Instructors. They hire a part-time person for social media, then they hire someone else to do product research. They might hire someone else, part-time or full-time, for PPC, and someone to work with suppliers and freight forwarders. These people report to The Driving Instructor, but just like freelancers who work for

The Driver, they don't talk to each other or work together as a team. They rely heavily on The Driving Instructor for direction.

Being an instructor may seem like a step up from Driver, but it can be much worse. Even though you have people in place to take some of the work off your plate, the time it takes to train them and give them day-to-day direction might be longer than if you did the work yourself.

The Driving Instructor structure works well if you're between structures, such as moving from Driver to Chauffeur or Autopilot. Otherwise, it's not good for the business owner or the employees. The seller is still constantly involved and unable to take a break. They're still the bottleneck in the business, and they can't scale. Company growth is limited by the seller/owner's bandwidth. The employees are simply following directions, which isn't fulfilling for them because they don't get to make any decisions or own any outcomes. With no skin in the game, there is nothing for them to take pride in—it's just a job. However, if you're training them with the intent of transforming the business into a structure that's more beneficial to employees and you communicate that to them, they may be more engaged and willing to accept the job, knowing the bright future that awaits them.

Another problem with this structure is that, at first, you don't need full-time people for some jobs. If you hire people part-time, they're going to be looking for other work. Even the full-time ones will need time off now and then, so you'll have to fill in for them. Someone could quit, and now you have to do their job until you can hire someone else.

Being responsible for so many people can cause a seller to burn out. That's what happened to me. I didn't build the business strategically; instead, when there was a problem or work to do that I didn't have time for, I'd hire someone to do it. Need some copy written? Hire a copywriter. Help with my PPC? Bring in a PPC expert. Customers taking too much of my time? Hire a part-time customer support person. And everyone reported to me! I was like the little Dutch boy trying to plug all the holes in the dyke, and I was running out of fingers.

This patchwork approach actually created more work because now I had to manage all these people. Here I was, running a seven-figure business. I should have been on top of the world. Instead, managing everyone brought me to my lowest point in the business. Mentally and physically, the work was bearing down on me, and I knew something had to change. I could either hire someone to run the business for me (the Chauffeur model, which we'll get to in a moment), or I could let everyone go, and go back to the Driver model of doing everything myself while I figured out how to build my team the right way.

I chose the second option. I let everyone go—fired them, essentially—and started over.

The first lesson I learned from this experience, other than "Don't build a team this way," was that the first couple of hires you make are critical. They have to be people who are in it for the long haul, want to grow with your business, and have the potential and the desire to manage other people. Eventually, your initial hires might manage a dozen people.

Going back to what I said earlier:

IMAGINE WHERE YOU WANT TO BE AND START RUNNING YOUR BUSINESS LIKE THAT NOW.

I saw my business growing much bigger, but it couldn't grow if I didn't design it like a real business. Not with ad hoc hires, but with a real structure and the right people in place. That doesn't mean I had to hire experienced managers. There are people out there who can be managers but have never had the opportunity. I knew I could train them, and I told them this during our interviews. They would start out doing customer service per my instruction, optimize the position, and then help me hire and train someone to replace them so they could move on to another position. In the meantime, I could evaluate them and decide if they would be good managers. Some of these people became my top managers in the business and enabled me to grow it in a way that wouldn't have been possible with my earlier business structure.

You want to hire people who can share your vision, and who complement you and your skills. If you're superanalytical, you'll want someone who's creative, for example. I'll elaborate on hiring in Chapter 12 because there's more to know about bringing in the right people, and you want to get it right the first time.

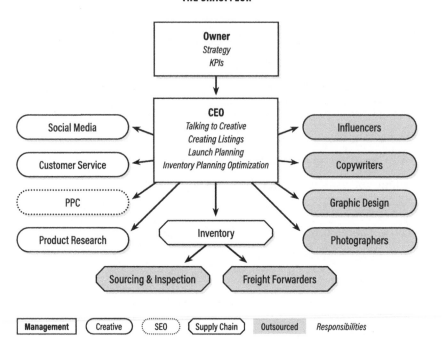

THE CHAUFFEUR

Owner
Strategy
KPIs

CEO
Talking to Creative
Creating Listings
Launch Planning
Inventory Planning Optimization

Social Media

Customer Service

PPC

Product Research

Inventory

Sourcing & Inspection

Freight Forwarders

Influencers

Copywriters

Graphic Design

Photographers

Management | Creative | SEO | Supply Chain | Outsourced | *Responsibilities*

Figure 13: *In the Chauffeur model, you hire a person or an agency and allow them to make the best decisions to accomplish your goals. In this example, the nonshaded boxes indicate five employees: Social Media, Customer Service, PPC, Product Research, and Inventory, plus one outside hire for a CEO.*

The Chauffeur

The Chauffer is similar to The Driving Instructor, except that instead of being the only one in charge, you hire a Chauffeur. You're still the owner, but this person either takes your place as the CEO or they come on as the COO or operations manager. They help you manage the company so you can take your foot off the gas and the business still runs. This doesn't have to be one person; it can also be an A–Z agency that takes control of your business and runs it for you.

When you hire a Chauffeur, you tell them your goals for the business, or where you want to go. Then you have to give them a lot of leeway to get there. They make decisions they believe will take the business in the right direction, and though you as the owner can step in any time and veto their decisions, you mostly leave it to them to run everything.

Some sellers really like this structure because it allows them to step back from their business and enjoy all the perks with none of the work. People who opt for this structure usually retire. The problem with this option is that even though you've stepped back from the boss position, you're still responsible for the company's success or failure. You interviewed the person, hired them, and explained to them what you wanted them to accomplish. Whether they do well or not, it's still your business and you have to live with the outcomes of their decisions. Think long and hard about whether you are willing to trust someone to do what's in the best interest of your business, and don't rush into hiring someone.

I have seen sellers go this route and regret it because their Chauffeur couldn't do the job. Maybe they didn't understand the products or the brand. Or they don't get along with your employees. By the time you figure out they're not the right person, you're dependent on them, so now it's hard to let them go. If you do, you're right back to being The Driving Instructor again.

If you opt for this model, I strongly advise you to hire someone you've known for a few years, and know well, or go with someone who comes with a strong recommendation from someone you've known for a while and fully trust. You and The Chauffeur must be aligned on goals and where you want to take the company in the next three to five years. They must want it as badly as you do and be willing to commit the time and effort required to get there.

The Chauffeur isn't my preferred structure, because I like to be involved and I don't want to retire anytime soon. But for many sellers, it's the perfect solution for meeting their goals. If you can't find the right person or agency to hire, you may have to put more work into the business so you can run it on Autopilot. This is my preferred structure, and it works so well, I devoted the next two chapters to it.

BREAKERS

Want more information on choosing and building the right structure for your business? Check out my online lecture "Balance the Scale" on my Breakers site at tomerrabinovich.com/breakers.

CHAPTER 12

THE AUTOPILOT BUSINESS MODEL: PEOPLE

"Managers watch over our numbers,
our time and our results.
Leaders watch over us."

—SIMON SINEK

was coaching a five-person mastermind group of sellers who were all successful, each doing over $1 million a year. Aaron, the newest member of the group, was doing around $200K a month. Aaron was financially successful, had launched a lot of products, and wanted to launch more. The problem was that he was still a Driver. Yes, this Amazon seller, doing $2.4 million a year, was running his whole business all by himself. Every day, he was creating shipments, doing customer support, and monitoring bids for his PPC campaigns. During our first meeting, Aaron talked about his goals. He wanted my advice on a new product.

"Hey Tomer," he said, "I'm thinking of launching this new product…"

I interrupted him before he could finish. "Aaron," I said, "forget about launching products—you need to launch some employees."

"Well," said Aaron, "first I need to build these systems, and set up these tasks, and maybe write some SOPs [standard operating procedures]. Once I get that all set up, I'll hire someone to take over some of my tasks."

Aaron's plan wasn't unusual. A lot of sellers feel like they have to be experts at every task in their business before they hire someone. That's not necessary at all, and in fact, it defeats the purpose of bringing on someone who might not only be better at the job, but who will be more excited to do the job if you give them some leeway around how it's actually done.

The new person doesn't care how organized you are—they want a job. They want something to do. They want to help you and enlist their own intelligence and skills to do that. If you've hired well, they are fully capable of doing the job—probably better than you could do it. Don't underestimate people. They can surprise you with how much they know and are capable of doing when you give them a chance. We sellers seem to think we have to do everything because we know everything, but that's not the case. Let them do it, and free yourself to do other things. Again, think like a business owner, not an employee.

This chapter is near and dear to my heart. It's the part of my business I started too late. Knowing what I know now, I should have been building systems, creating processes, and thinking about the kind of people I should hire far sooner than I did. I caused myself a lot of headaches by starting so late with all of this. In my defense, I had a lot of success with my first product launch, so I didn't think I needed to do anything differently. No one has successful product launches one after the other without help. Eventually, you hit a wall. You can break through that wall with the right pieces in place.

Where are you right now in your business structure? Are you a Driver or a Driving Instructor? Have you hired a Chauffeur? Would you like to scale your business without spending more time on it, provide more leadership yet hand off more responsibilities to others? Wherever you are, if you want to scale, you have to remove the bottlenecks. The most common bottleneck is you, and you can clear that by hiring other people to do some of the work. Other bottlenecks include a lack of proper systems and processes for completing tasks and activities. Every business has these, and every business could do better by improving efficiency with the right people, systems, and processes.

This is about skipping those headaches, ramping up faster, and having a better chance of achieving all those "why," "what," "how," and "when" goals you set for yourself in the last chapter. It's about working smarter to remove the bottlenecks that stifle growth.

The Autopilot

The fourth business structure is The Autopilot. With this option, you're in The Driver's seat, but you don't have to do much. You hit a few buttons from time to time, but you've preprogrammed the business to go where you want it to go. You have people, systems, and processes in place to ensure you reach your goals within your desired time frame. Every now and then you have to make a decision, but you could run the business around your schedule, so you could leave for two weeks, and no one would notice that you were gone. The business would run at top performance without you there. Now, you have time for other projects or personal goals. When was the last time you took a few days off without working in your business? If that has never happened, what are you actively doing to change that?

The Autopilot model is what I wanted. It satisfied all my "whys"—why I started selling on Amazon in the first place. Once I realized this, I looked for information on how to create this kind of business, but there was nothing available. I had to figure it out myself.

Other sellers have gone the same route of building a business that virtually runs itself. Some have taken it to the extreme where they aren't involved at all. I struck a balance where I still have control over my business, but I could also take a break for a few days or, when needed, even longer. This gave me peace of mind and fulfilled my "whys."

I began as a Driver, became a Driving Instructor, fired my team, and rebuilt my business on The Autopilot model. This doesn't mean that you have to. There is no one right way to get where you want to go. How you build your company is all about your goals, your "whys." It's about how you want to spend your time every day, where you want to go with your business, and what you want to achieve. It's about what you want your life to look like. Any one of these four structures works for some people.

Think of this as building a machine. You need people to run it, software to automate it, and processes to ensure consistency. If you have a regular job at a regular company, you know what I'm talking about. You'd be surprised how many people come from a corporate environment, surrounded by people, systems, and processes, and somehow forget all of that when they start their own company. Build your machine slowly, while you're launching products. If you try to get all of this right before you launch, creating the business could become the bottleneck. Move forward, build your business, make some mistakes, have some successes, and keep going. Learn and build. One thing that helped me was to think of my business more as a startup, and less as a corporation. When I was bringing people in, that's what I told them, that everything was still getting built and that they were here to help me build it.

Like everything else about selling, there is no one way to do this. If you know a successful seller, don't think you have to copy everything they're doing to be successful. That may not work for you and your goals. What I'm doing may not work for you either. Use my advice as a guide and bend it to suit yourself and your business. Over the next few chapters, you will understand how I've structured my team this way while running a successful business at the same time.

People

After doing over 1,000 one-on-one calls with Amazon sellers over the years, one of the most common problems I've seen is that sellers don't want to hire people, or they have tried to hire people and it didn't work out. This happens for multiple reasons, but I'm here to tell you that once you hire the right people and they start taking things off your plate while you grow your business, you'll get addicted to that feeling and want to keep hiring until all that extra work you've been doing is being handled by other people you trust.

Your time is valuable, and as the true cliché says, "You need to be working *on* the business, not in it." Hire people to work in your business and free up your time for the most important tasks, those that take a lot of quiet time, thinking and strategizing.

Shift your thinking from "I'm a worker" to "I'm a business owner." Get out of the cubicle and into the executive suite. If it helps, change your work environment at home or in your rented workspace. Get a bigger desk, a nicer chair. These are symbolic changes, and they won't make you a better business owner, but they may help you think differently about your business and your role.

Then build your team.

Freelancers and Agencies

Your first "hires" will be freelancers and/or agencies. These aren't employees; they send you an invoice either before or after they do the job, and you pay them an agreed-upon amount or rate. For your Amazon listing, you'll probably outsource a lot of the work to freelance copywriters, photographers, and graphic designers. You'll pay suppliers and factories for production and freight forwarders for shipping. These people are all experts in their fields.

Part-Time and Full-Time Employees

If you want to build an Autopilot business structure, you have to hire people who can make decisions and run your business when you're not around. Unlike freelancers and agencies, employees don't see you as a client, but as an employer. They may (but not always) be more invested in helping your business grow.

When you hired people for photography and copywriting, you probably sought out creatives—people with ideas who knew how to implement them. I claim that there are two types of people and you're usually one or the other: analytical or creative. You may lean more toward creativity, or you may be more analytical. Whichever type of person you are, I recommend that the first employee you hire is the opposite type. This can be difficult because when you interview someone and you are very similar to each other, you might tend to go with that person. You think alike and work alike. But if the person is just like you, how will they help your business? You need people who think differently from you and have different skillsets. The strongest partnerships comprise two people on opposite ends of the spectrum—creative and analytical—who have found a way to work together.

As I mentioned earlier, when I first started selling on Amazon and began hiring people, I brought on one person at a time to solve a particular problem. This patchwork style of hiring worked for a while, until it didn't. I had to start over with the end in mind, hiring people strategically to create the business structure I wanted, the Autopilot model. Unfortunately, I had to let everyone on my team go to do that. This was one of many painful lessons I learned about hiring people, and about firing them. It's easier to hire people for multiple tasks than to try and hire people for individual ones. We tend to think we are the smartest and we are the only ones who can do a certain task in our business. The truth is, running an Amazon business is not rocket science, and people are smarter than you think.

When you bring on employees, you can hire experts, people with intermediate skills, or people with no experience at all. You are not limited to the local talent pool either. People who speak the same language and share similar cultures are easier to work with, especially for your high-level roles. Hiring from first-world countries costs more, while bringing on people from developing countries is much cheaper.

Hire Early, Hire Well

By hiring, I mean bringing on an employee to work within your business. This is different than contract workers or freelancers. They might start as part-time, but in a few weeks or a few months you should be able to move them to full-time. Don't wait to reach a certain level of revenue before you start hiring. Many sellers think they need to hit $50K or $100K a month before they need help. This is backward thinking. If you don't hire people, you may never get to $50K. Doing everything on your own slows growth and limits potential. If you want to grow, hire people as soon as you can afford to pay them.

YOU DON'T GROW TO HIRE; YOU HIRE TO GROW.

Before you make that first hire, look at your skillset. I'm very analytical and organized. I love systems and processes—building them and seeing how efficient they make my business. I'm very patient. I can focus on a problem for a very long time and design a solution. I can spend a lot of time teaching another person how a system works, or how to follow a process. I want things done a certain way, and I'm willing to work very hard to make working in my business as easy as possible for my team. Knowing this about myself, I tend to hire people with no experience. This way, they do everything the way that I want it done, and not in a way they learned somewhere else. I still hired experienced freelancers and agencies for certain activities—people whose specialty was photography, for example. But for my own in-house team, I hired complete newbies.

This isn't the perfect hiring process for everyone. If you don't know how you want things done or you don't have the patience to train people, you'll want to hire people with experience.

Your first hire should be good at something you don't do well, or don't like doing. I needed help with PPC, but I was fairly good at it and I enjoyed it; customer service, on the other hand, was not my favorite way to spend time. So I hired someone to take on customers while I learned more about PPC.

Let me tell you about a seller I coached. Alicia's business had stalled because she just didn't have the bandwidth to grow. She needed to hire and train people, but when I talked to her about it, she pushed back. She didn't want to train anyone. She didn't like training people, even though she could have trained someone in the Philippines to do exactly what she was doing and pay them a fraction of the upside she had to gain. I told her that instead of hiring that person first, she needed to hire someone who was very sharp, a fast learner, who could shadow her and watch everything she did, document it, and teach it to other employees. That person would then be her operations manager, building up the rest of the team and teaching them what's needed. This way, Alicia wouldn't have to do anything that she wasn't already doing. She could just share her screen with this new hire while she worked, answer their questions, then hire people for the trainer to train. Alicia ended up hiring the first person locally and that same employee quickly became a manager, who employed a few people from overseas to work under them.

Finding the Right Candidate

If you're outsourcing work to expert freelancers, you can find candidates through your sellers' network of people. Ask around and see who other people are using. Do an internet search and check their credentials, their reviews, and examples of their work. Ask if you can speak with some of their customers. Make sure they are adept at the skillset you need for them to do the job.

Your in-house team can include people from around the globe because they will be working remotely. Advertise online for the type of person you want. Say that you're hiring for part-time at first, maybe two hours a day in customer service, with the potential to work full-time and grow with the company. Tell them the starting pay too. Then ask them to tell you, in two to five sentences, why you should hire them instead of anyone else.

You can hire people in any country, but I try to find people in my own time zone, or in a time zone that coincides with the times I'm online. I'm in Israel and prefer to work during the day, and so people in the Philippines, five hours ahead of me, are ideal employees. If I log in early in the morning to work, they're online too. I don't work late in the day, and they're asleep then anyway.

Before you hire someone, ask yourself these questions:

"Do I want to hire someone local?" If you want someone coming to your office or home office every day, or once a week, you need to interview people close-by. If that doesn't matter to you, then you can hire a remote worker.

"If I hire someone remotely, do I care about which time zone they're in?" If you and the people you hire need to sync up at certain times of the day, you'll need to make sure those times work for both of you. Maybe that means choosing someone in the same time zone, but not necessarily. If you prefer working during the day and your employee likes working evenings and they're a couple of hours ahead of you, that could work out for both of you. Find out their time zone, their hours of availability, and their preferred working hours.

"What's my ideal day-to-day experience, and who should I hire to help make that happen?" Be picky about who you hire. And if you don't enjoy hiring, hire just one person and put them in charge of hiring. You might hire one person locally to hire and manage all your remote people, for example.

Don't think you can hire the wrong person and "make it work." You'll regret it and will probably have to fire them eventually. I strongly believe in the saying, "Hire slow, fire fast." This is your business, and the people you hire can make or break it.

There are other considerations such as cost and even language differences, but there are also many, many options. To get clarity around your next steps, look at your current team, and if you have no team, your current situation of doing everything yourself. If your goal is to run a scalable business based on the Autopilot model, where do you see your team in a year? Is this the team that will make your goals a reality, or does something need to change? Do you need more people? Different people? Be honest with yourself about this. Really think about it. Make the right decisions now so that, a year from now, you won't be shaking your head and wondering where you went wrong.

I'm an expert on a lot of things, but I will admit that hiring isn't one of them. I'm not an expert. I just know what I want and have been able to hire great people by focusing on what works best for my business. You may go about it in a completely different way, but here are the main characteristics that I look for in every new hire:

- **Teachable:** I've found that teachable people are also very good at teaching others, and they will need that skill to move up in my business. You can gauge their teachability by giving them small assignments, feedback, and follow-up assignments to see if they are applying your feedback or ignoring it.
- **Honest:** I ask people professional and sometimes technical questions to see if they'll be honest with me about what they know and don't know. During the interview, I might ask them how much they know about PPC, or about inventory management. I'm less

concerned with what they know, and more concerned about their honesty. If they're teachable, they can learn what they don't know. But if they're dishonest, we're going to have problems. I also might ask them why they left their last job, or why they think they'll be a good fit for this position. I want to know if they're going to be telling me what they think I want to hear or telling me the truth. Also, I don't want to see them ranting about their last position or speaking badly about their old boss, because that might be how they'll speak about me in the future.

- **Management material:** I prefer people who have managed people in the past, but this isn't a requirement. Some people are natural managers, or they can learn. I want to build my company from the ground up, and that means hiring people who can grow with my business. They should be able to take on more tasks and prove that they are people who should be promoted into managerial positions. My people end up in management situations before I promote them, managing people or projects. By the time I promote them, they've proven to me that they're up for the job.

- **Openness:** I look for people who aren't afraid to disagree with me or tell me if something I'm doing in the business is wrong based on their knowledge and experience. I want people who think differently than I do, who can bring something new to the business. I'm open with them from day one, telling them that I want them to become managers at some point in my business. I want them to be ready to go on this journey with me, knowing that not everything is perfect and it will always be a "work in progress" because we will always be learning and growing throughout the process.

- **Willing to accept the job as a test:** I did not invent the notion of hiring slowly and firing quickly, but I believe in it. The person

I hire needs to be willing to do a test run. This can be some basic tasks I ask them to do before I hire them, followed by a two- to twelve-week test period starting on day one. The test is for both sides: I want to make sure they're a good fit for my business, but at the same time I want to make sure that I'm good for them as well. I don't want an employee who's unhappy and just here for the paycheck. I want a team that feels they're a part of something bigger, and that what they do matters. I give people every chance to succeed, but if they aren't working out, I let them go. Because of all the effort I put into hiring and training them, this seldom happens. When it does, I pay them for their work to date and end the relationship.

Promoting People into Management

Sellers always want to know who they should hire next. I ask them, "Before you hire another person, is there anyone you should promote?"

When I interview people, I don't tell them that I want them to do, say, customer service. I tell them that I want a full-time person to help me expand my business. They may start in customer service, but if that's as far as they want to go, I don't want them in my business. I want people who can be managers. I want people who can manage projects, or people, or both. If they don't have that potential, they won't be driven to help build the business.

I give people tasks until it's too much for them to handle. Then I ask them what part of the job they want to delegate to someone else. I also show them some of the tasks I'm doing that I would like to delegate. They choose which new tasks to take on and which ones to give up. We talk about the training they'll need and the time commitment to accomplish the old tasks and the new ones, because I don't want them to be overwhelmed.

Then we hire someone new to take on the tasks they want to give up, they train the new person, and I train them on the tasks I'm handing off.

I used to hire differently. Say I needed a new copywriter. I would tell one of my people, "Get me five copywriters, and I'll make the final decision." She would search hiring websites and bring me five résumés, cover letters, and whatever else was available on the candidates. I would interview them and make a decision. Eventually, I realized a serious flaw in this process: I could have easily found five candidates on a hiring website myself in just a few minutes, so why was I tasking this woman, a team member I was looking to promote at some point, with this activity? This was a missed opportunity to capitalize on the value she could bring to the hiring process, while allowing her a chance to flex some managerial muscle. So I changed my process. I asked her to bring me the résumés, but I wanted her to interview each candidate and apply what she knew about the position and the person to decide who she thought would be the best hire. I would also interview them, then she and I would put our heads together to discuss our impressions and opinions. This worked much better, and it's how I always hire now. I still make the final decision, but it's a more informed decision. I also have a team member with some hiring experience who's going to be excited to work with this person she's helped bring onto the team.

Compare that with bringing someone in on your own and saying, "This is your employee. Train them." I want them to like the new person. I want them to work hand-in-hand with that person every day. They need to choose someone they like, a person who can learn and is also excited about the job. They will pick that person for you. Once they pick the person and hire them, they're in charge of that person. They're responsible for training them, tracking their hours, and making sure they get paid. They are that person's manager.

When someone moves into management, they get a pay raise, usually of about 25 percent. This is a big raise, but if they've stuck around, done good work, and are now managing at least one other person, it's money well spent. I also give them time off when they need it, within reason. Everyone needs vacation time, and everyone gets sick from time to time. I also give them an extra month's pay around the holidays. Even if I hire them in the fall, I still give them that extra pay. I never mention it during the interviews because I like to make it a surprise.

I've found this method promotes a lot of loyalty and commitment among my employees. People like the predictability, they like being valued, and they like being promoted. They like having a say in who is hired and who they manage. They like being part of a business that treats people well.

So what do my managers do? Well, it doesn't look like they do much, because their employees handle all of the day-to-day stuff. They actually work the least, while earning the most, because they have the most responsibility in the company. When you think about it, they've actually almost completely replaced me from handling this business, which has enabled me to free myself from it and focus more on strategy and on the future of my brands.

Delegating Tasks

When I hired my first team, I thought I needed an SOP—standard operating procedure—for everything. I wrote down exactly how I wanted everything done. I even made training videos for some tasks. I thought I could just give people these PDFs and videos and that was it.

I discovered that people are smart. They can figure out how to do things on their own if you give them some training and tools. They'll be a lot more excited to do the job, too, if they have a hand in defining it. So now I make a short video and allow the person to write their own SOP, based on what they learn from the video. They send me their SOP and I make slight tweaks where it needs improvement, and I send it back to them and they revise it to satisfy my tweaks and comments. After the SOP is done, if needed, I ask them to create another video explaining it, then doing the task once. By making them write the SOP, they are forced to learn it. If they just read something I wrote, they may not even understand it. This method also saves me a lot of time because I don't have to write SOPs anymore.

They start doing the actual tasks slowly, in steps. For example, I would ask a customer service person to review the last 30 or so customer emails and see how I responded to them. Then I would ask them to write an SOP on how to handle each type of scenario. If a customer receives a damaged product, for example—what's the best way to handle that? I might have them shadow me or a manager to see how they handle the work, then I might shadow them for a while. The point is, I don't assign tasks until the person is comfortable taking them on, and I'm comfortable handing them off.

If the new person is taking on tasks that I'm not the best at, I have an expert in my business train them. If I need someone to learn a task that no one in my business knows how to do, I hire an agency or freelancer from outside the company for a certain number of hours, and the new person shadows them and writes an SOP describing the process for completing the task. Sometimes training someone on a new task is as easy as finding a YouTube video. Online selling processes change all the time, and people are eager to show their expertise by creating videos about them. So your training session could be no more than sending a link to a three-minute video to someone on your team and asking them to watch it and then write an SOP for the process.

My People

After I fired my initial team, I realized that I wanted to create a company that could run on Autopilot. With that in mind, I changed how I built it, hiring people who weren't just solving problems for me but who could eventually run the business. I created departments for each division of the business: SEO, inventory, creative, product research, and customer experience.

I mentioned earlier that the people you hire will tend to be more analytical or more creative and that your first hire should be whatever you are not. In other words, if you're an analytical person, bring on a creative and vice versa. This person will become your right-hand man (or woman), and getting this hire right can make or break your business. Get it right. I've seen a lot of business partners start an Amazon selling business, and the strongest teams are those whose members complement each other's skillsets. Having a partner who is just like you leaves out a critical piece of the leadership puzzle, whereas starting with both analytical and creative talent completes it.

AUTOPILOT

```
                          ┌─────────────────┐
                          │      CEO         │
                          │  Green Lights    │
                          └─────────────────┘
                           ╱               ╲
              ┌──────────────────┐  Strategy  ┌──────────────────┐
              │ Operations Manager│ →  KPIs  ← │ Marketing Manager │
              └──────────────────┘            └──────────────────┘
```

SEO	Inventory	Customer Experience	Creative	Social Media
Keyword Research	Sup Research	Customer Support	Listings & Copy	Social Posts & Ads
PPC	Reordering	Reviews	Images & Videos	Product Launches
Comp Research	Shipping	Comp Research	Product Research	

Sourcing & Inspection ←

Photographers ←   Influencers

Freight Forwarders ←

Graphic Design ←

Outside Warehouse ←

Copywriters ←

| **Management** | (Creative) | ⋯ SEO ⋯ | (Supply Chain) | Outsourced | *Responsibilities* |

Figure 14: My preferred business structure, the Autopilot model, puts people, systems, and processes in place to ensure you reach your goals within your desired time frame while allowing you the freedom to spend your time outside of the business. In this example, the nonshaded boxes indicate seven employees: Operations Manager, Marketing Manager, SEO, Inventory, Customer Experience, Creative, and Social Media.

Beyond that first hire, you should have both creative and analytical people on your team, and I hire that way intentionally. It's reflected in my organizational chart shown in Figure 14.

On the creative side, I have a marketing manager overseeing a three-person team, plus freelancers who fall under the creative side:

- A customer experience person who's responsible for managing customer-related issues, everything from handling negative reviews to gaining five-star reviews (via The Six-Star Experience approach discussed in Chapter 3). She handles all customer interactions and also helps out with competitor research to optimize our packaging, inserts, and anything else that impacts the customer experience.
- A creative person who's in charge of listings. This person manages all the professional photographers, graphic designers, videographers, and copywriters and makes sure our images and copy speak to our target customer. This same person is also in charge of product research.
- A social media person who manages our messaging on social platforms like Facebook and Instagram and works with social media influencers. This person is also heavily involved in new product launches.

On the analytical side, the operations manager has two people on staff:

- An SEO person to take care of the search engine optimization; PPC; and keyword, reviews, rankings, and competitor research in terms of new competitors entering the niche.
- An inventory manager who takes care of the supplier research for existing and new products, ordering and reordering, and shipping. He talks to the suppliers, sourcing agents, inspectors, and freight forwarders, and manages the outside warehouse inventory.

I take care of my own finances, but I have an accountant and book-keeper that I speak with occasionally whenever I have questions about certain things, like taxes.

I have seven employees total, but I only trained two of them, the managers. They started at the bottom and when I promoted them, they trained the people they helped hire. These managers are also in charge of human resources, hiring, salaries, strategy, KPIs (key performance indicators), and other items specific to their departments.

Partnerships vs. Sole Proprietorship

I work well with other people, as long as I'm in charge. This doesn't mean I micromanage my people, but ultimately, I have to have the right to make final decisions. In the past when I worked in positions where I partnered with others, I always felt like I was working harder and doing more than the other person. They may have felt the same. But I'm happier being the sole owner.

I have seen partnerships that work well. The most successful ones comprise people who complement one another's talents. One partner is typically more analytical, while the other is creative, so the relationship is mutually beneficial.

Another example of a strong partnership is when two people who know one another really well—and have known one another for years—join forces. These may be best friends, previous business partners, or partners in marriage.

However, money changes people. The person you know now who seems as if they would make an excellent business partner could behave unexpectedly when money enters the relationship. I've seen businesses crumble over partnerships gone bad.

Employee Experience

> **THE CUSTOMER EXPERIENCE IS IMPORTANT, AND EVERYONE IN BUSINESS TALKS ABOUT IT. I TALK ABOUT IT IN THIS BOOK. BUT THE EMPLOYEE EXPERIENCE IS EVEN MORE IMPORTANT.**

Happy employees make happy customers. Value your people, appreciate what they do for you and your business, overdeliver and surprise them every now and then. Give them a Six-Star Experience. They will do the same for your customers, and the bigger bonus is that you will love being an Amazon business owner even more. My employees are not working *for* me—they don't even work *with* me. I actually work for them. The way I see my current role in the business is that I'm here to support my team with whatever they need. One day it might be clarity with their tasks, another it might be brainstorming on a new product launch, and another it might be figuring out a two-week vacation they're taking with their family so they can go with confidence that their work will continue uninterrupted, and they'll have a good situation to come back to after that time off.

◆ ◆ ◆

Before I created the Autopilot structure, all of my employees reported to me and I was the bottleneck of my own business. One goal of the Autopilot structure was to remove that bottleneck—another goal was to encourage my employees to talk to each other. As you can see in Figure 15, having people involved in the different areas of product launch at the same time, and not going to me for every decision, opened the door to more communication and collaboration between everyone. With this Autopilot structure, everybody works together on every product launch.

You can't assume your employees will talk to each other, but if you build your company a certain way, they will have to communicate and work together. This approach is better for your employees, better for your product launches, and better for your business.

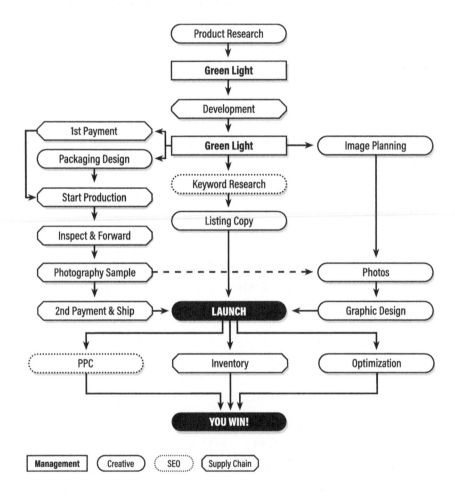

Figure 15: Build your Autopilot business structure in a way that facilitates, emphasizes, and encourages communication between your employees.

BREAKERS

If you haven't watched my lecture "Balance the Scale," now is the perfect time to check it out at tomerrabinovich.com/breakers.

CHAPTER 13

THE AUTOPILOT BUSINESS MODEL: SYSTEMS AND PROCESSES

*"You have to be brutally honest
with yourself and understand your
strengths and weaknesses."*

—JESSICA ALBA

You can't do everything yourself and scale the business. Your people can't do everything and help you scale the business without systems and processes.

I'm an analytical person, so once I started building systems and processes, I couldn't stop. It was fun, and I was good at it. But I was spending so much time on it, I neglected my products. I should have been doing both: building my company, adding structure, hiring people, and launching, launching, launching. If you don't launch products, you'll reach a plateau, and the business will stop growing. If you keep launching products without the infrastructure to support that growth, you will burn out. It's a balance.

Systems and processes can be grouped into five categories:

- **Organization:** How you organize your files. You will amass digital files for documentation, images, photographs, invoices, and other materials, and the sooner you come up with a system of organization, the easier it will be to retrieve these documents when you need them.
- **Information:** Textual information about your business, such as the contact information of your suppliers, SOPs (standard operating procedures), reusable email templates for responding to customer requests, and the physical address of your home or other location for receiving samples.
- **Communication:** How to communicate with your internal team. You might use WeChat and email to communicate with your supplier, but you'll want an internal system like Slack for day-to-day conversations with your employees.

- **Decisions and Green Lights:** This is a system for deciding whether to green-light a product for launch, to start with 1,000 or 2,000 units, expanding to Amazon Canada or Amazon UK, and all the other decisions you'll have to make in your business. Once you come up with logical decision practices, you will want to document them for the next time they're needed and tweak them as you learn more.
- **Goals, tasks, and calendars:** You will have daily, weekly, monthly, quarterly, and annual tasks for the business, plus project tasks specific to every new product launch.

These five categories touch all five of my departments, or the functions of the business:

- SEO and PPC
- Inventory management
- Customer experience
- Product development and creative
- Social media and launching

Organization

Organize everything to do with your business early and put it in one place. You can use Google Drive or another cloud-based, shared space for this, but it needs to have order and your people need access to it. Whatever you choose to use, it needs to be organized in a way that you can easily find any information you need. To start with, you will simply open the five folders: SEO and PPC, Inventory Management, Customer Experience, Product Development and Creative, and Social Media and Launching.

As an example, in the Product Development folder you might have a New Products folder with all of the new products you're currently working on. Once you give a Green Light to a product and are ready to move forward to production, you will move that product folder to the Live Products folder under Inventory Management. In each product folder, you keep files like images (current and past images), barcode, packaging, videos, etc.

You might think having a cloud-based location for your business is obvious, but you'd be surprised to find how many sellers run their businesses from their laptops and never back up anything. Their entire business relies on their hard drive. What happens when that hard drive fails? Or when they want to start building a team?

Don't laugh. It happens. I learned the hard way about hard drives and cloud-based organization, files, and folders. On my way to a speaking event in the US, I flew from Israel, changed planes in the UK, and landed in Austin, Texas. At London's Heathrow Airport, I had to check my carry-ons, including my laptop, through security. In the US, my final destination, I opened my bag. The laptop wasn't there.

Where is it? It has to be here! I remember packing it!

I had flown with a friend, Ari, and he thought I was joking. How could I fly across the world to speak at an event and not have my laptop? I thought back on the last time I'd seen it. I'd usually work on my laptop during the flight, but my friend and I had talked the entire flight, and I hadn't opened my bag. My laptop was sitting in security at Heathrow Airport.

I rushed to the Apple store and quickly put together a new presentation, but it wasn't as good as the one I had spent weeks on, the one stored on my laptop thousands of miles away. And as soon as I returned to Israel, I re-created everything in a cloud account.

I got my laptop back eventually, months later. By then I had created a whole new system online and the files and folders were useless.

Well, folders in drives are easy, but what do we do with all of the textual information? And how can we easily find a specific file or folder we are looking for? Let's talk about it!

Information

I want you to stop and think about how many times you look for a piece of information in your email inbox, on your computer, on the cloud, etc. This can be anything from a supplier's contact details to that graphic designer who did some work for you a year ago. It can be a great template your customer experience person created that would be perfect for another customer interaction right now—or even something as simple as your home address so your employees don't have to ask you where to have suppliers ship samples. You can have all of this information in one place, and there are different tools that support this. There are free solutions like Google Sites, which is basically an internal website for you and your team, with different pages where you can have text, images, videos, and more—all in one place. You might be saving SOPs in PDF format to make them look nice or putting them in a Google document (I hate those!), while instead you can just have a page for each SOP, and a home for all of the information in your business.

The goal is to create a sort of Wiki for your company data that's organized and searchable. You might be storing some of this data in Google sheets or Google documents, but those formats aren't easily searchable from one place like having everything on Google Sites (or any other tool you use). Building this out takes the longest, but again, you want to look it at like a process and not something you need to do before you hire someone. You can build a basic layout and then structure it together with your new team members.

Communication

Many sellers use Skype and WhatsApp for all their internal communications. These solutions have their place in business. I use WhatsApp in my personal life, but I don't' mix my personal and business communications. I like to use Skype for interviews and WeChat for speaking with suppliers. For conversations with my employees, I need something with many separate channels, like folders, which allow for easy organization.

Slack is a great communication tool for business. You create rooms called "channels" and invite specific team members to each channel, depending on their role in the business. You can start by creating a different channel for each department—SEO and PPC, inventory management, etc.—for discussions with members who belong to those channels. You can also communicate with individuals or groups of people outside the channels via direct message. The channels allow you to restrict access to discussions to only the team members that you want involved in these discussions. This also cuts down on the amount of "chatter"—information that's important to some, but not others. Your SEO people don't want or need to see the inventory management discussions, right?

Think about your channels before you create them. You don't need a Slack channel for each product you sell, or you'll end up with too many channels. Make it clear to your people that their conversations need to happen in the correct channel. There's nothing more annoying than looking for a discussion and not finding it because it's in the "wrong" channel. An easy way to start is by opening a channel for each department that I mentioned before: SEO and PPC, inventory management, customer experience, product development and creative, and social media and launching.

As you grow, you can create more channels within these categories.

Other communication solutions exist. Try a few and see which one works best for you.

Decisions and Green Lights

Decision-making is a challenge for every entrepreneur. Some sellers make decisions based on guesses or gut feelings. Some do calculations to figure out their next step, but many times they don't document how they came to the decision. They might order 8,000 units because that gives them the lowest cost per unit and fills a whole container, for a lower shipping cost. If they took the time to figure out how many units they sold per day, and how much buying that many units tied up their cash flow and delayed their next launch, or how much it was costing them to store those units, they might have 2,000 units come in each month instead.

My decision-making process lives in spreadsheets that I've designed with calculations that inform my decisions. They guide my decisions based on numbers and facts instead of hopes, guesses, and hunches. Spreadsheets run on math, and math doesn't lie. Numbers do not lie. They don't have emotions either. Numbers give you the facts you need to make good business decisions. My Batch spreadsheet is a good example of this. It shows me how many units to order and which shipping method makes the most sense.

Here's an example: a seller tells me they have a new product, and they can't decide whether to ship it by air or by sea. Shipping by air, in this example, costs $2,000 more. To give them an answer, I need to know how much profit they will make from the sale of the product, and whether getting it there 30 days sooner by having it shipped by air will increase their profits by more than $2,000. If it does, then air makes sense. If not, then they should have it shipped by sea. That's an oversimplified example of how it works, but you get the picture. If they knew which data to look at and how to calculate it, they would always have their answer.

If they figured this out themselves and documented it, they wouldn't have to figure it out again the next time they had to make that decision. They could put all those calculations into a template or a spreadsheet and automate the math for future orders.

Goals, Tasks, and Calendars

I've talked about setting goals for yourself throughout this book. These goals can be long-term or short-term. They can be big goals like having total freedom with your time, or they can be financial goals. You might have a goal of launching 10 products this year. Every business owner must have goals, tasks that help them complete those goals, and a calendar to set timelines for meeting them. Monthly, quarterly, annual, three-year, and five-year goals take you where you want to be in your business.

Set your longest, biggest goals first. Dream big with these goals. You can accomplish a lot in five years, especially if you set a big goal. If you don't, you'll be completing tasks all the time with no clear direction. Those tasks have to take you somewhere within a certain time frame.

When I create tasks to meet a goal, I work backward. Say I want to launch a new product in 90 days to be ready with it for the holidays in Q4. This is a narrow window, so I'm going to choose a product that I can affordably ship by air. I know it will take 30 days for production and 15 days for shipping, so that means I have 45 days remaining to pick a product, find a supplier, get samples, approve a sample, and pay the deposit. While the product is being produced, I can work on my listing and launch plan. I break down those 45 days further by all the tasks and subtasks I need to complete to make the launch a success. Knowing this, and putting that goal on my calendar, and assigning those tasks to my team members, I know with confidence that I will be launching a new product in 90 days.

I set up 90-day goals for my business, and I expect my managers to set 90-day goals for their departments. This practice helps the company grow. They involve their team members, too, to get them thinking beyond their day-to-day tasks. This is important because if you're the only person setting goals, you're missing out on an opportunity to capitalize on the wisdom, experience, and insight of the talented people who are deeply entrenched in your business. They see things that you do not. They have ideas.

New sellers tend to be very disorganized with their time and work. They get out of bed in the morning expecting to accomplish so much, and by the end of the day they wonder where all the time went. Having a calendar of events and activities, and tasks to accomplish within certain time frames, makes you efficient. It prevents projects from slipping, keeps you on track, and ensures you're using your time wisely. This was another hard-learned lesson for me. When I quit my full-time job to be a full-time Amazon seller, I was excited to be working for myself. After a while, I realized that with no one holding me accountable, I had to hold myself accountable if I wanted my business to continue to succeed.

It doesn't matter which type of calendar and task-management tool you use, but use something. A calendar can be Google Calendar or any other online calendaring system. Put meetings and other events that happen on a particular day on the calendar and block out time for them.

Tasks may have a specific date or time that they're due. Task lists may accompany projects, such as a product launch, to ensure that each task is completed within the project. If one of your people learns a process within a project, they can use that process for the next product. Some project- and task-management tools have timers, so your employees can track their time for each task and project. Asana and ClickUp are popular task-management systems, and there are others. Some have free versions or are very inexpensive.

There is a learning curve to adopting a new task-management system. Expect all your tasks to turn red, signaling they're late, when you start out. It may take some time to correctly predict how long it takes to complete a task. The more you use the system, the better you'll get at setting deadlines and meeting them.

In my task-management tool, I divide the tasks by department. These departments are usually called "Projects": SEO & PPC, inventory, creative, product development, etc. I have three types of tasks for each department: recurring, backlog, and sprint tasks. Recurring tasks are repeated, usually daily, weekly, or monthly. A daily task can be "answering customer service in Amazon Seller Central." Backlog tasks are those that don't have a due date and aren't a high priority at the moment. I might want to research a new tool and make that a backlog task. I have a recurring task to review the backlog tasks once a month, to see if any of them need to be moved and acted on. Sprint tasks are currently being worked on and need to be completed soon. On top of those three types of tasks, I have templates for complicated tasks with a long list of subtasks. The template provides whoever completes the task with clear guidance on what to do and how to do it. Imagine all the steps for a new product from beginning to end, or for a new shipment. Each of those has a template, and every time we have a new product or a new shipment, we simply open the template, change the name of it, and we're off. This way nothing falls through the cracks, and everything is done in the right order.

Under a task, you can also put subtasks. A task can be getting new images for an existing product, and the subtasks can be something like this: (1) find a photographer, (2) find a graphic designer, (3) outline the images we want, etc. Every task-management system has its own special features that allow you to track things like milestones, communication, and dependencies. Some have places for documentation, or they integrate with Google Drive and your Google Site to some extent. This way, you can work inside the system and just click links to get all the information you need to do the work.

A calendar is less complicated than a task-management system. Use your calendar to keep track of upcoming events and your main goals for the year.

Task assignments let people know what they have to do, but this is a different kind of communication than what you'd put in a Slack message. Your communication channel, such as Slack, is for real-time conversations when you need to let someone know something right away, or you need an answer right away. Once you have all your organization, documentation, and task management set up correctly, you'll find yourself using real-time communication channels less frequently because people know where to find the answers to their questions. And if the information isn't readily available, they have specific communication channels where they can ask for help.

Once you have these categories all figured out—organization, information, communication, decisions, and tasks—you're on the right path. And again, it doesn't matter if at first it doesn't work out or if you switch software to test which ones work best for you. At the end of the day you're running a business, and you have to treat it as such. This is not a "side gig" anymore; this is it. This is what you're doing. It's your business.

Having said that, you're not building this business for the fun of it (although that's an added benefit). You're building it to reach your goals.

Meetings

Whenever I hired a new employee that reported directly to me, we talked and texted constantly every day. Over time, I realized how much these minor conversations were sucking away my time, so I decided to move almost entirely to text communication. That cut down on my team communication significantly.

I have two meetings a week with the managers via Slack texting. One meeting focuses on ongoing business such as new products we're developing, new product launches, and ongoing product listings. The managers meet together on their own before that meeting to organize their thoughts so when they meet with me, they're very prepared and only have to copy and paste the topics for discussion into a Slack message. I do the same, texting them the topics I want to discuss with them. We all come to the meeting very prepared. If we don't have anything launching, it can be a very short meeting; if we have a lot going on, the meeting can last an hour or longer. We don't have meetings for the sake of having meetings. We get things done.

The second weekly meeting is to review the goals we set in the first meeting to make sure everyone's on track. Then we discuss issues and opportunities around inventory management, optimization, and other topics—products that seem to be lagging and may need improvement, and those that are selling well and how we can leverage that success. This is typically a longer meeting, an hour to an hour and a half. Both of these calls are done in video from time to time, but usually it's just easier and more easily accessible later when done via text.

Each month, we have a video call for the whole team. This is more high level to talk about how everyone's doing and what we can do to improve the business and meet our goals. People can ask any questions on this call, and they come prepared to share their ideas. We see everyone face-to-face on the video call, and I can gauge the overall sentiment of the team. I like to know that my people are happy with their work, and seeing them on a call gives me a window into how they're feeling. I want them to know that I care about them, too, and not just for what they can do for me. If my people aren't doing well, I need to know that, and I need to know why.

That's the extent of my interaction for the most part, but the team members communicate among themselves regularly via the Slack channels. Someone doing keyword research can easily reach out to a copywriter, for example, without me orchestrating that connection. They build those relationships organically, as needed. The managers also set up team meetings and one-on-ones, and I leave those discussions to them.

Start building these communication channels early. You may not get them exactly right the first time, but you'll figure out what you need as you hire more people and launch more products. If you focus only on making money by launching more products, your business will suffer. The smaller you are, the easier it is to set something up and let it evolve naturally. If you wait too long, your business will get complex and more difficult to organize. If you're a midsize business and you try to set up everything perfectly before you hire more people, you will never get there. Your organization, information, and communication channels grow and change along with your company, so be open to that. You may be a perfectionist when it comes to your products and listings, but when people are involved, be flexible and learn as you go. Perfectionism is another word for fear—you're just afraid to fail. I'm here to tell you that there's nothing to be afraid of, and none of us were born CEOs. The same as you did with learning about Amazon, you just have to learn building and running a business as you go.

If you don't do these things, you'll hit a wall at some point, and either plateau or burn out. You need the support of your people, systems, and processes to scale, and that scale needs to be balanced.

Time Is Your Greatest Asset

When you think about why you want to be an Amazon seller, your ultimate goals, and which business structure best supports all of that, keep in mind that time is precious. It's your number one asset. You only have so many hours in a day, days in a week, and years in your lifetime. You can't earn more time by working harder or buy more time with more money. Think about how you want to spend your time creating your business and running it.

You may not want to put several years into being a seller. If you think you're going to sell your business in the next 12 months, then you don't need to hire a lot of people or create a lot of systems and processes. You just need to launch the right products, have a great listing, and take care of the PPC, customer service, and everything else that makes your business valuable to a buyer.

If you want to be a business owner for years to come by either running the same brand or by selling it and launching new brands, build a company that satisfies your "why," "what," "how," and "when." You'll have to put some effort into it up front. Doing that exercise and setting your sights on a goal will give you direction, and you'll be less likely to quit or end up with a business that doesn't make you happy. You'll end up exactly where you want to be.

BREAKERS

Visit my Breakers site at tomerrabinovich.com/breakers for more information about tools and services that will help you put your business on Autopilot.

CHAPTER 14

SELLING YOUR BUSINESS

"How lucky I am to have something that
makes saying goodbye so hard?"

—WINNIE THE POOH

When I started selling on Amazon, no one talked about selling their business. They didn't think of their business as something they could sell—they were focused on the freedom it gave them in terms of flexibility with their time. New sellers dreamed of working two hours a day and spending the rest of the time sipping piña coladas on a beach in Mexico. This should come as no surprise to anyone who's been doing this awhile—you might remember that was the "pitch" used back then by people selling courses about being an Amazon seller. Of course, a lot's changed since those times and now people who sell those courses are a lot more honest about their offerings. They tell people up front that being an Amazon seller can come with huge payoffs—but not without a lot of hard work.

The first time I heard of someone selling their business, I didn't believe it.

How could you sell your business? It's so complicated! I could never teach anyone else everything that I do.

Those were my thoughts. Even an experienced business owner would have a steep learning curve simply to pick up the business, never mind scale it over time.

Then this company came in that wanted to buy Amazon businesses. There were plenty of them out there too—and many were far from perfect. No people, systems, and processes. No automation. Some had terrible listings, poor reviews, low rankings, and lackluster sales. The PPC wasn't optimized, and inventory management wasn't as good as it could be. However, many of these businesses had good products. The owners just hadn't figured out all the other pieces necessary to take their businesses to the next level. This company saw a lot of opportunity in these businesses. They could buy them, fix them, and grow them. They could make them very profitable.

Early on, they bought businesses for low multiples, where the buyer looks at a company's profits for the past 12 months and pays a multiple of that number such as 2x, 3x, and so forth. Say a business had $1 million in revenue for the year and 20 percent profit ($200,000); the company might buy that business for 3x the profit, or $600,000.

Over the past few years, companies known as "aggregator companies" got involved in the Amazon business-buying business. There was no shortage of investors eager to put their money into these companies and reap the potentially enormous financial benefits. Aggregators have become a sort of "elephant in the room"—we may pretend they don't exist, but we all know they're there with big budgets.

These companies had many strategies, but some commonalities. They built teams of experts in every facet of the business: PPC, inventory management, sourcing. Some of them stuck with Amazon selling only, while others expanded their distribution to other retailers. Some developed what's called "microbrands," where they had dozens or even hundreds of brands curated from the many Amazon sellers whose businesses they had acquired. No matter what their strategy, they all acknowledged that Amazon would continue to account for a majority of their sales.

How Much Is Your Business Worth?

Today, everyone thinks about selling their business. New Amazon sellers often start out with a goal of selling their business within a certain amount of time for a certain sum of money—usually in just a few years for a few million dollars. Right after they sell their business, they start a new one, and why not? They have all the experience and knowledge to launch a business successfully that they can turn around and sell in a short time, just like the last one!

In recent years, I've been consulting for some of these aggregators and referring sellers to them. Working with their M&A (mergers and acquisitions) teams, I help the aggregator companies evaluate businesses for them to potentially acquire, and I connect Amazon sellers with good businesses to these companies. I also help the aggregators optimize their own brands on Amazon while launching new products to grow their brands.

I've seen another change in the business too: larger sellers, mainly in the eight-figure range, buying up smaller Amazon selling businesses, scaling them up, and then selling their own business (with the newly acquired and scaled ones) to aggregators. There are over 100 of these aggregators as I write this book, and they likely won't all survive. The market has matured, and it's becoming more organized and "corporate" rather than populated by individual sellers, like it once was. This can make it harder for new sellers to compete, but I believe that as long as you have a good product and know your way around Amazon—and you put in the effort—you can still succeed. There will always be a place for the individual seller on Amazon, which is why I continue to encourage people who are willing to do the work to pursue their dream and not be discouraged.

Multiples have also increased beyond the 3x mark, and I've seen businesses sell for 6x and 7x their last 12 months' profit. Aggregator companies sponsor Amazon events, and they look for people from the inside—highly successful sellers and former sellers—to bring on as consultants. They're on sellers' podcasts and they have their own podcasts. They know that the key to attracting the best sellers is through relationships, so they are everywhere sellers will be.

Aggregators have made selling your business very fast and easy. They've simplified it by taking only what they need. They don't want sellers' employees, systems, or processes. They want your product and your brands. Brokers have also sprung up—people who can get a seller's business in front of dozens of aggregators. Buyers bid in a sort of "silent auction," and the broker gets a cut, around 5 to 10 percent.

Aggregators are very skilled at convincing Amazon sellers that they're getting a good deal. So how do you know if you're getting what your business is really worth? First, speak with several of them to make sure you get a fair price. I also recommend talking to a trusted friend or fellow seller; ask them to refer you to a buyer or aggregator they have done business with and they trust. Ask the buyer for references, and talk to these other sellers. What were their experiences like with the buyer? Did they feel like they got a good deal? What about the payment structure? Was it to their advantage, or to their disadvantage?

Evaluate Your Business

Before you do any of this, evaluate your business and decide what you think it's worth, starting with your SDE, or seller's discretionary earnings. Here's how you calculate your SDE:

SDE = NET INCOME OF THE PAST 12 MONTHS + ADD BACKS

Net income is everything you receive from Amazon after fees and PPC, minus COGS and indirect expenses such as graphic design costs, salaries to employees, office expenses and overhead, and anything else you spend outside of Amazon and COGS. Your add backs are anything that the buyer won't need once they buy your brand. Most aggregators won't need your employees or the tools you use to run your business now. They have everything they need to run your business—all they want is your brand and product line. If there is anything you're paying for now that your buyer can get rid of and still run the business at its current level, remove those things from your total expenses, which adds to your profit, increasing your SDE. Here is what a buyer will pay for your business:

SDE × MULTIPLE (WHATEVER YOU HAVE AGREED TO) + GOOD INVENTORY

Good inventory means an amount of inventory (number of products) that is needed to run the business for a certain amount of time once it's sold. The buyer needs stock to keep selling, and they will pay for that stock. They don't want "dead" inventory of products that don't sell, or too much inventory because you ordered too much. As you go into the sale, make sure you have optimized your supply chain and inventory in Amazon to have the right amount of the right inventory when the sale is final—not too little and not too much. This includes products in storage at Amazon or anywhere else, products currently in production at the factory, and products on a ship or a plane between the factory and storage. This is all inventory that you have paid for or will have to pay for, so include it in your number.

Inventory can add up to a lot of cash, in the thousands and millions of dollars. Sellers are often unaware of how much money they have tied up in inventory until they go to sell their business. Sometimes, when they take the time to figure it out, they realize the money is equal to another multiple on top of the one they agreed to with the buyer. A good seller always knows how much money they have invested in inventory. If you don't know that now, add a task to your calendar to figure it out and come up with a process to monitor that number regularly.

Going back to figuring out the value of your business, let's look at an example. Say you made $1 million in revenue over the past 12 months at 25 percent net income, which is $250,000. We'll say you have add backs of $10,000, which you can add back as profit because the buyer won't need those resources. The buyer offers you a 4x multiple for your business, you have $150,000 tied up in good inventory, and your payout will be $1,190,000.

Here's the formula:

$$\text{NET INCOME} = \$250,000$$
$$\text{ADD BACKS} = \$10,000$$
$$\text{MULTIPLE} = 4X$$
$$\text{GOOD INVENTORY} = \$150,000$$

So, if you add the net income and add backs and multiply that amount times the multiple, then add in the value of your good inventory, you will get the payout—the amount you get paid at the time of the sale.

$$(\$250,000 + \$10,000) \times 4 + \$150,000 = \$1,190,000$$
$$\text{PAYOUT} = \$1,190,000$$

Taxes

Don't forget about taxes. The amount of taxes you pay on the sale of your business depends on the country you live in when you sell. Speak with your broker or a CPA for advice on the best way to manage this piece. Some brokers offer this as a service within their sales packages. Also, speak with other Amazon sellers in your country who have sold their businesses. Finally, consider talking to a tax attorney or other tax specialist. Taxes can add up to a lot of money and take a big bite out of your payout.

What's Your Multiple?

So, to review multiples: When you sell your business, you are usually paid a multiple of the profit your business made over the past 12 months. If you made $200,000 in profit and sold your business for a 4x multiple, you'd get $800,000. At a 5x multiple, you'd get $1 million. The multiple you get makes a big difference in your company's worth and what a buyer is willing to pay for it. Several factors contribute to the multiple.

Aggregators used to focus only on companies that had products with a lot of reviews—let's say more than 10,000 reviews. They didn't look closely at the product. As long as it was selling well and getting a lot of good reviews, they paid a premium for companies with these products. That's changed, and today, aggregators deciding what your business is worth look at several factors.

Growth Potential

Today, aggregators want more than a high-quality product that sells well and earns good reviews. They are looking for growth potential. If you have 50 percent of the market, but there's no room for you to grow to 60 percent, aggregators probably won't be interested in your product. They don't want to wait five years to get their money back—they want it back in two or three years, and they can only do that if they can grow your sales. They might be able to do this by getting more market share, or expanding into other markets around the globe, or by expanding your product lineup with variations of your product or new products within your brand. If you have already done all of those things and exhausted your growth potential, you are less attractive to an aggregator and not likely to demand a high multiple.

Timeless Categories

The typical Amazon seller looks for products that will sell for at least two or three years. If you're thinking of selling your business, think longer term. Your products must have the potential to sell for at least five to seven years.

Buyers look for Amazon businesses with products in "timeless" categories that won't be out of date in a short time. Timeless categories include home décor, sports gear, dog toys, and most pet items, for that matter. It's not likely that people will suddenly stop spending money on their homes or their pets. Electronics and electronic accessories, such as cell phone cases and chargers, can be out of date in a matter of months or a year, so that can be a tricky category. It's the same with seasonal products like toys, which sell well during the holidays but suffer a sharp drop in sales after the first of the year. Trendy products that come and go—like the fidget spinners that were all the rage in 2017, then seemed to disappear in the blink of an eye—aren't attractive to aggregators either.

Any business can be sold, but the timelessness of your category affects the multiple, and how much money you have in your pocket after the sale. Consider this when choosing products.

Business Size

The bigger the business, the more profit you make over a 12-month period, and the higher the multiple. A business that does $100,000 in 12 months might demand a 3x multiple. An Amazon business making $1 million in profits during the 12 months prior to a sale might demand a higher multiple, 5x, for example. Aggregators and other buyers want a company with legs and are willing to pay a premium for a high-profit company. There is much less risk than with a smaller business.

Sellers with small businesses sometimes combine their stores, or brands, for a better deal. Before you dismiss that idea, consider the potential of a 3x multiple versus a 5x multiple on the last 12 months of your profits. The numbers get big fast. I've seen eight- and nine-figure deals made by aggregators buying businesses put together by several sellers combining their brands.

Do Your Homework

All buyers will tell you they have your best interest at heart and that they will grow your business. But they could go bankrupt tomorrow. This is especially important if the buyer offers you an earn out, where part of the deal is based on the growth of the business from the sale until 24 months later. This can be risky. The buyer may not grow your business at all. My thoughts on earn outs is to think of them as a bonus—they should not make up a significant portion of the deal. Get as much as you can up front, "in closing." And make sure, when you close the deal, that the aggregator pays the amount you agreed to. Don't let them change the payment structure at the last minute (unless it's justified), especially if they try to pay you less in closing and push the rest of the payment to a later date, as an earn out.

This is why research is so important. Even if you go with a broker, you need to speak with other people about the end buyer or aggregator—the people buying your business. Get references. Talk to Amazon sellers you know who have sold their businesses. Ask them who they sold to and what the experience was like. Be specific. Where are they in the payout cycle? Did they get the money they expected? Did they get more? Remember, the Amazon seller-buying business is new. It could change dramatically over the next few years. Investors continue to pour money into these companies expecting a return, so aggregators are highly motivated to buy businesses. In the future, if they give in to that pressure and start overpaying for businesses that don't earn their investors returns, they could go bankrupt.

Sell Because You Want To, Not Because You Have To

I hate seeing a seller sell their business because they have to, so please don't put yourself in that position. If a buyer senses desperation, they will not offer you what your business is worth. I understand that people sometimes get in this situation, but try to avoid it at all costs. Run your business in a way that is sustainable so you aren't forced to sell it, or sell it sooner than you'd like.

YOU NEED TO BE IN A POSITION OF POWER WHEN YOU APPROACH A BUYER OR BROKER.

If they ask why you are selling the business, do not tell them you need the money. Do not tell them you're having personal problems, financial problems, or health problems—even if you are. Do not show any weakness at all. You need to present yourself as a seller who went into this with the goal of building a successful business and selling it at some point—maybe today, maybe tomorrow, maybe two years from now. Ideally, you really should be in a position where you don't have to sell. Don't accept less than what your business is worth. If you can't find a buyer you trust who gives you the deal you want, continue to grow your business until you do.

Strategies for Building a Business That Sells

Sellers tend to follow one of three strategies for building their business.

They build a brand around products they really like. These sellers usually don't intend to ever sell their business, or at least not sell it within the next 10 to 20 years, because in addition to their business being a source of revenue, it's also a passion project. They care deeply about the products, the brand, and the business.

The second strategy is building a business with the goal of selling it and then retiring. These sellers have a dollar amount in mind that they need to get to before they can sell. Some of these people don't actually retire—they just get into a different business.

The third strategy is "build and sell, build and sell, build and sell." Many sellers have turned to this model.

As you build your business, decide which strategy you want to follow, based on your goals. Otherwise, you could build a business that doesn't allow you to reach them, or you spend a lot of time on activities that aren't necessary for you to reach your goals.

A member of one of my masterminds, Albert, was working on setting up a lot of systems for his business. His goal was to sell the business, and I asked him when he planned to sell it.

"I'm thinking of selling it in six months," he said, "and then I want to get into the real estate business instead."

"Albert," I said, "if you're going to be out of the business in six months, don't spend that time setting up systems. Focus on selling; focus on maximizing your profits. Maybe launch another variation or two to show some growth. Don't do anything else."

If Albert were going to keep the business for a couple of years, my advice would have been different. I would have told him to hire an expert to help him set up systems and processes. That would have made sense, but to do that in a six-month time frame wouldn't benefit Albert enough for the time he invested in it. It probably wouldn't fetch him a higher price for the business, either, so it wasn't worth the investment of his time.

Likewise, if your goal is to sell your business and get out of the Amazon selling business completely, you shouldn't hire a lot of people who will just be let go once you sell. However, if you plan to build and sell, build and sell, you can always retain your team for your next business. Some sellers, while they are vetting buyers, are already building their next company with their team, working on new product launches that will not be included within the business they sell. If you don't do this, and you build a large business and then sell it, you will have to let all those people go and when you start building a new business, you'll have to start hiring and training a new team. So having that overlap between one business and the next, with your people working on both, makes for a seamless transition after the sale. You have all the people, systems, and processes in place for the new business, and you can focus on building a new brand. You also have the energy and the momentum. Taking an extended break between businesses can affect your drive, and you may never start another Amazon business again.

This was not always possible. Just a few years ago, when you sold your business, your people went with it. These days, buyers want your brand, your Amazon account, your trademark, and your products. They don't want your people and processes. They are not even buying your company per se—the umbrella under which you build brands. They are buying the brand and the right to sell everything within that brand on Amazon (and anywhere else they want to sell it). They may ask you to sign a noncompete agreement where you agree to not sell the same or similar products or work with the same suppliers or factories after they buy your business. This protects their investment.

It's All in the Timing

Exiting your business is like comedy: it's all about the timing. You want to exit when your business is on the rise, not when it's declining. That can be tricky.

Some sellers want to exit their businesses in 12 months, knowing the buyer's offer will depend on their sales for the year. They should be growing their business during this time, increasing sales, but too often they do the opposite. They're afraid to launch a new product that may not do well. They don't want to launch something that does well, then only enjoy a few months of the profits. They may not see a profit at all because their initial sales may only cover the costs for the first year of the launch. So they do nothing. They allow their business to stagnate. Sometimes they actually scale back! Their business declines. They may not see this, but the buyer sees it, because they're looking at the previous year's sales, too, and wondering why sales plateaued, or decreased. They will want to know why. This isn't to say you should go crazy with new launches, but you should aim to show growth.

You need to be in business for at least a year before you sell, preferably two years. Buyers want to see sustainability and growth.

What Buyers Want

Even motivated buyers tend to be particular about the businesses they buy. There are factors they see as "must haves," those they see as "should haves," and those that are "don'ts."

The Musts

You must have good products. If you don't, no one will buy your business. Products that average four-star reviews aren't good enough, unless everyone else in your niche averages three stars or less. Think about it from your buyer's perspective: Are these products they would want to sell? Will the products continue to sell for several years without them having to invest a lot of time and money to optimize the product or the listing?

You must have an Amazon brand. Good buyers want a solid brand that you've developed on Amazon that they can continue to sell on that platform, and also sell other places, such as other online sites and even brick-and-mortar retail. Make sure you have a trademark and Amazon Brand Registry. This was discussed in Chapter 2.

You must have your bookkeeping in order. Have your books organized by a professional bookkeeper, preferably by *accrual basis bookkeeping*. This method accounts for revenue as it's earned. This is different than the cash method of bookkeeping, where money changes hands before anything is recorded. With the accrual method, revenue is recorded when products are delivered and payment is forthcoming.

The Shoulds

You should have a few products that each generate more than $50,000 a month in revenue. You can get to $200,000 a month with just four products doing $50,000. If you have 20 products doing $10,000 a month each, that's a lot of work for the buyer to manage for the same revenue. You need to be hitting the $50,000 mark with a few products, but not too few. I know eight-figure sellers who have just one product, and even though they are generating a lot of revenue, their businesses are difficult to sell. There is just too much risk riding on that one product. You can sell businesses with products that don't generate $50,000 a month, and you can sell businesses that have just one product, but you will probably get offers of lower multiples because they are not as valuable to buyers, regardless of the revenue.

You should have optimized listings. To be clear, I mean optimized, but not perfect. Buyers want businesses they can improve and grow, so less-than-perfect listings are actually preferable over listings that have no room for improvement. If you're in the process of selling your business, don't spend any time on your listings. The buyers will test different images, bullet points, and price points after they buy your business. Let them see the opportunity for improvement—and greater revenue.

You should have social media pages and a DTC (direct-to-consumer) online website such as a WordPress or a Shopify site where you sell your products. Again, none of these needs to be fully developed. Good buyers know how to optimize social media and online sites, and they'll take what you've set up and make it great. That's what they do and how they grow businesses.

You should have a high market share in the niche. If the overall market is $4 million a month and your product is doing $400,000, you have 10 percent of the market. They will see how that compares with your competitors. Do they have higher or lower percentages? Are you number 1, number 2, or number 10 in the market? If you're close to number 1, how much will it take for them to get you there, and if you're already number 1, how much room is there for growth? These are all questions the buyer will be asking themselves when they're valuating your business.

You should have documented information on any products that most sellers see as difficult to sell, that you have researched and are selling successfully. If you spent time researching your products so you could sell them, share that with the buyer. Products that few competitors sell because of the research involved, which you are selling because you've done that research, can be valuable to a buyer as long as you are prepared to show them what they need to know to keep selling it. Expensive, heavy, and difficult to package or ship products, and products that require FDA approval fall into this category. So do products that you have design or utility patents for, which you can then pass on to the buyer.

You should have new products that you've researched but not launched. If you're selling in a year, yes, launch them. But if you're within a few months of selling, hang onto that research and present it to the buyer.

You should have considered global expansion. You don't need to be in the US, Europe, and everywhere else to sell your business. The buyer can do that and will want to have the opportunity to do that. Of course, if you are selling globally, you'll have more profit, which will increase the selling price of the business. You just want to leave plenty of room for more growth for the buyer. If you're within months of selling your business, don't even bother expanding into global markets. You can do some research to uncover the potential and have that in your back pocket to discuss with potential buyers, but unless you're keeping the business for a while, don't act on it. If you do, and it fails, that will not look good to the buyer. In case you plan on selling in 12 months or more, it might be a good idea to expand to a new marketplace to add more profit to your bottom line.

By the way, you should discuss all these "shoulds" with potential buyers. Tell them you see all the opportunity, but you would rather sell your business than invest more time and money into making it grow.

The Don'ts

Don't have a stagnant business. Aggregators buy businesses that they can improve and grow, and that will earn more profits for their investors.

Don't have short-term growth products. Some products may sell well today, but how well will they sell in two years? Face masks, for example, sold like hotcakes in 2020 and 2021, but once everyone acquired a few, the demand dropped and will likely continue to drop. Accessories for technology products such as cell phones also have limited growth potential because the products they support are always changing.

Don't launch products that are easy to launch such as variations on the product. Do your research and look at the potential and discuss it with buyers, but don't act on it if you plan on selling in a few months.

Don't have your own factory. If your product is produced in your own factory, a buyer will think twice about buying your business because they may also have to inherit your factory, adding a lot of complications to the deal.

Look for any areas of friction that can impede the ability of the buyer to take on your business and grow it. These can all affect their interest and the price they're willing to pay.

Your Mindset Matters

Whether or not you plan to sell your business, start it and run it as if you are going to sell it at some point. Select products that you can sell for at least five or six years. Look for opportunities for growth.

When you're an Amazon seller, think of every day as if it's day one. Pretend you just bought this business—your business. Look at your brand and products with a critical eye. What would you do differently? What can you do better? Seeing your business this way is especially important when you are trying to sell it. You need to see what the buyer, potentially the new owner, sees.

When you look at your own products on a macro level and analyze them, it's a lot easier to find what to improve. When I consult sellers in small mastermind groups, they are very quick to criticize each other's listings, but they are less strict with their own. It should be reversed:

you should be supercritical of your own business and open to criticism from others.

Think about selling your business the same way you research a new product. You see what's out there and decide whether you want to sell that kind of product too. Is this a product you want to launch? Now look at your business with the same critical eye. Is this a business a buyer wants to launch?

Like I said at the beginning of this chapter, timing is everything. If you're going to sell your business, a lot of the decisions you make should depend on when you will sell. The closer you get to the sale, the less effort you should invest, and the more opportunity for growth you should leave for the buyer.

BREAKERS

For more guidance on how to sell your business, visit my Breakers site at tomerrabinovich.com/breakers.

CHAPTER 15

FLOATING TO SHORE

"Life is like riding a bicycle. To keep your
balance you must keep moving."

—ALBERT EINSTEIN

One of my first speaking gigs was in Hawaii. The event producers flew me, my wife, Shani, and our five-month-old baby, Lavi, to the island of Kauai. They put us up in a beautiful resort that had a lot of activities, including helicopter rides all over the Hawaiian Islands. I wanted to try this, and so did my wife. The resort also had a babysitting service, so we could leave our son while we went for a ride. We had never left Lavi alone, and definitely not with a complete stranger. The thought made us very uncomfortable. But we really wanted to take that helicopter ride. When we expressed our concern to the company organizing the rides, they told us we could bring the baby with us.

They gave Shani and me earmuffs to protect our ears from the noise, and tiny ones for Lavi. I wondered if I was out of my mind, taking my child on a helicopter. Everyone around us took pictures of our little one in those earmuffs, like they had never seen a baby in a helicopter. That worried me more: *Was I a bad parent? What if my son cried the whole time? What if he was frightened? Or traumatized?* The helicopter took off and none of those things happened. Within five minutes, the little guy was fast asleep! And all my concerns were for nothing. My wife and I enjoyed a wonderful ride in the sky, and every worst-case scenario I had imagined never happened.

This may sound crazy, but that helicopter ride gave me a shot of confidence I had never experienced. That confidence infused itself in me, in my personal life, and spilled over into my business life. I came to accept that all the worrying I did over business decisions was usually for nothing. I could be uncomfortable taking a helicopter ride with my son, just like I could be uncomfortable making an important decision. But I could still do it, even though I was uncomfortable. I had to do it to grow. And it's those uncomfortable moments—the new experiences—that stick in my memory. They've made my life fuller, richer, and in a way, longer.

Add Years to Your Life and
Life to Your Years

If you have children, you know how impatient they are. The younger the child, the more impatient. For them, everything is new. Every day is a new day, literally, because they experience so many things they've never seen, heard, smelled, tasted, or felt before. For children, time passes slowly. It's the same when you're a new Amazon seller. You're learning every day, and time seems to slow down.

As your children grow and the days start to repeat themselves, time passes more quickly, and they become less impatient. Likewise, if you do the same things in your business day after day, the weeks, months, and years fly by. You'll have the same thoughts, the same ideas. The days blend together, with nothing to distinguish one from the next. If you've ever had an office job, you know what I mean. A year goes by, and looking back, there are few days that you clearly remember because they were all pretty much the same. If you take a vacation for just three days, and you come back to work, people will say that it seems like you just left. That's because they were doing the same thing every day. But you stuffed all kinds of excitement and memories into those three days. Coming into work feels like stepping into a foreign land.

If you don't expand your experiences, you will limit your life. It will feel short, like time is flying and you're missing out. I'm not suggesting you pack your suitcase and become a digital nomad. Only that you mix things up. Not just once in a while, but often. Go to events and make a point of meeting new people. It's easy and comfortable to navigate toward people you know from your inner circle of sellers, but you'll learn more breaking away to introduce yourself to a new group and seeing what they do, than if you don't. If you always work in the same room or office, rent an office space in a different building and see what that's like. If you eat at the same restaurants, make a point to try a new one every week. Set a goal to read more books, attend more conferences, and learn new skills.

These don't have to have anything to do with Amazon selling. You can read a book on knitting. Attend a conference on personal finance. Learn how to throw an ax or jump off a cliff. You are an entrepreneur, and you probably got into selling because you don't like the monotony that comes with the daily grind. Don't let that spark, that curiosity, that passion for learning and living life to its fullest wither away. It will, if you get so entrenched in selling and all the tasks that come with it that you forget to have other experiences.

When you start a business, there are certain tasks that must be done every day. There are regular meetings, calls, and emails. Getting into a rhythm and being consistent in your work is important to building a company. If you're going to sell your business, stick to that plan.

If you're going to run your business for many years, at some point, you have to stop the monotony. Keep trying new things, keep launching new products, and keep learning new skills. Keep it all interesting. Seek out bigger sellers to learn from and smaller ones to teach. Network with sellers and with people who have nothing to do with selling. Focus less on making money and more on making it a journey worth living.

The strange thing about new experiences is that the time you spend in them goes by slowly, in a good way. You're in the moment, taking it all in and noticing the details. Days, months, even years later, you remember those experiences. You can replay some moments in your head, like a movie.

When I think back on that helicopter ride, it seemed to last forever, even though we were in the air for just 30 minutes. I can still recall many of the details. Compare that to doing the same thing day after day. When you work in a cubicle, it seems like time stands still. Yet looking back at the years you spent in that same old cube, staring at the same computer screen, and doing the same work, your time seems to have flown by and you have few memories of it. Where did the time go? Where did your *life* go? By creating new experiences, you create a richer, longer, and probably happier life full of memories that last forever.

Fuel Your Ride

You can only go so far on your own, with what you know. If you want to keep learning, consider joining my Top Dog Community to continue your education with five levels of additional information and resources. You can find some of this on your own, and I offer much more. I give away a lot of the information and practices I've developed for free, and I charge a fee for the more advanced content and lessons.

Level I

The first level of information is what's free or very affordable online in blogs, articles, webinars, and videos. Other books on Amazon selling, in addition to this one, are also available as paperbacks or in digital format, or as audiobooks.

The market is saturated with this material, and some of it's useful, but some is not. When I started selling on Amazon, I had to dig around for information. I went out and met people and talked to them about their experiences. Now, everything is online or in a book. Look for content providers who are in the business and have valuable content to share. Avoid content from "experts" who have little or no real experience and are just trying to cash in on the popularity of Amazon selling. These people attract followers so they can monetize their sites, but they won't help you or your business.

Level II

The second level is all the information beyond this book that I can offer you for free, and it's a lot. You've seen the link to my Breakers resources throughout this book, and I hope you become a regular visitor to that site. You'll find lectures and other content that builds on each chapter in this book, and links to additional material beyond this book. Interacting with my site, you'll be aware of all the Level III, Level IV, and Level V content that I offer, which you may consider as you progress in your Amazon seller journey and career.

Level III

The third level is live events that you pay to attend, either physically or virtually. There may be hundreds or thousands of people in the audience,

and they are not all Amazon specific. Some focus on marketing, or entrepreneurship, or online selling in general. If you're starting out, these can
be a good way to meet people and build your sellers' network.

Level III members in the Top Dog Community take part in a lot of
online calls. These aren't just lectures—they're members interacting to
learn from each other.

Level IV

The fourth level is generally for people selling at a very high level and
people who are approaching that level. The conversations and presentations are more focused, and you can interact with a lot of people to get
your questions about the business answered. Level IV lectures, calls, and
other gatherings are limited to about 100 people. Sellers at this level are
experiencing challenges—and discovering opportunities—that aren't so
common with sellers who are just starting out.

Every year, I host the Top Dog Summit, which is open to all members at
Level IV or higher. The summit includes a lot of networking along with fun
activities aimed at building better, deeper relationships with fellow sellers.

Level V

Level V is much smaller and more intimate, with generally four to six people
in a group. Each group is a mastermind, where members share all the details
of their businesses, including company structure, brands, and product
information. Mastermind members help each other in any way they can,
understanding that by doing this they build trust, and they grow together.

My mastermind groups of four to six people experience a very intense
four to five months with me and my team. I provide them with personal-
ized guidance on methodologies, systems, processes, and everything else
I know about selling on Amazon. Members of a mastermind group are in

the same time zone so they can meet live every week. Each one has goals, and we work together to make sure they all reach them. A mastermind member may want to move their business to The Autopilot structure, or they may want to exit their business at a certain multiple. Whatever their goal, they have several very experienced sellers on their side, including myself, to help make it happen.

If you decide to start your own mastermind group or join one outside of my Top Dog Community, I recommend meeting at least once a month and preferably every week or two. Otherwise, groups tend to fall apart. People get busy and the momentum is lost. Join one with other people who are *not* in your niche, or start one and invite people not in your niche. People in your niche are your competition, and you don't want to share the intimate details of your success with sellers who can use that information to put you out of business.

Whether you join my Top Dog Community is up to you. Just don't finish this book and think you know everything about selling on Amazon. Things change, and I want you to keep up with those changes. Networking with active sellers on a regular basis is the best and easiest way to stay ahead of the game.

I have a selfish reason for inviting you to join my community, and it has nothing to do with money: teaching other sellers how to be successful is one of my passions, and the Top Dog Community helps satisfy that passion. I didn't know that helping other sellers would be one of my goals when I started selling on Amazon, but it has become one of my top goals.

Catching the Wave

When I started selling in 2015, people told me the business was dead. "It's oversaturated," they said, "too many people and too many products. You're wasting your time." They're still saying that. And I still don't listen to them. E-commerce is just beginning. In the US, it's responsible for just 10 percent of all sales. That's a very small percentage of sales, leaving a lot of room for opportunity.

Online retail isn't slowing down. It's growing. The ROI is better than any industry I know of too. When I speak to friends in real estate and other investment opportunities, they don't believe me when I tell them I'm seeing 50 to 100 return on investment in my business. Sure, some products fail, and you can have a momentary setback, but with those kinds of returns, you also recover quickly. Even if three products fail and the fourth is doing just OK, doing really well with the fifth product will cover your losses and make you a profit on the first four.

In my coaching career, I've spoken with many sellers who started with a $5,000 to $50,000 investment and became millionaires in two to four years. That doesn't happen in other industries. As a seller, you can work from anywhere. You can sell thousands of products without even touching them. That kind of opportunity was unheard of a couple of decades ago. If you are reading this book, in this industry, or just getting into the industry, you are in the best place possible to capitalize on the possibilities.

As you're starting a business or building the one you have, think about what comes next. Are you going to remain a Driver or change your business structure to Driving Instructor, Chauffeur, or Autopilot? What's your time frame for getting there, and what are you doing right now to make sure you arrive on time?

What are your goals? Maybe you want to be an eight-figure seller and make over $10 million a year in revenue. Maybe you're passionate about your products and want to build a real brand. All of these are terrific goals, and you can make them all happen. But then what? What's next for you? The world is a big place, and you can do more.

Your Next Wave

After graduating from college and building my business, I was invited to speak to my alma mater's entrepreneurship class. I asked people what they wanted to do with their lives. One woman, Ava, wanted to be a social worker. Ava wanted to work with children, and she had big plans for her career. When I asked her how she would be paid, she said she'd rely on donations. That was possible, I told her, and she'd probably be able to help other people with that money. But what about herself? She'd be scraping by, unable to make any of her other dreams come true. Serving people is a good cause, don't get me wrong, but I don't believe we are here to suffer through life with no pleasures of our own.

What if, I asked Ava, she helped herself first? What if she put herself in a position where she had the time and money to help many people and have the life she dreamed of too? Ava could do that as an entrepreneur. That would enable her to meet all her goals in social work. She could donate a lot of money to her favorite charity. She could even start and fund her own foundation for a cause she was passionate about.

Money is not the end, it's the means to an end. Business is how that money is generated. Without it, achieving goals is an uphill battle. With it, you can achieve your life's goals and enjoy the journey.

Once you reach your goal, and you have all the money you need and lots of time to enjoy your life, there has to be a next step, another wave. I can't tell you how many sellers I know who had goals, reached them, and just kept going. When they started, remember, they pictured themselves someday sipping piña coladas on a beach in Mexico. They could do that, but they don't. They start another adventure, or they build another brand on Amazon.

I'm not faulting them for that, or for skipping the beach. Entrepreneurs aren't very good at sitting still, and I can't imagine any one of them lazing on a beach for more than a week or two. If they're truly passionate about their products, their brand, or their company, and that's their life's mission, I completely understand why they commit every thought, every breath, to being an Amazon seller.

Most people have other dreams beyond selling. I like to help people. I like to teach. I love showing people how to do something and seeing that lightbulb go on when they get it. I love seeing them put what I've taught them to work and seeing them find success. That makes me very happy. My business has allowed me to do that on a level that would never have been possible without my business and the freedom it's allowed me.

You probably have dreams too. You have passions. Something you do makes you very happy. While you're building your business, be aware of the happy times. Be aware of those times when you're so intensely fulfilled that you think you might want to do that thing—whatever you're doing—every day. With the freedom you gain from your business, you can do that thing.

If you think having a lot of money in the bank will make you happy, think again. Creating something from nothing is a lot more fulfilling. Starting a business, growing a business, helping other people—whether they're needy, like in the social worker's case, or they're sellers who need your guidance—that will make you happy. Making a change for the better in another person's life will bring you more happiness than all the money in the world.

Enjoy the Ride

I'm sure that, before you became an Amazon seller, you had different hobbies and different friends than you have now. In your previous life, you might have hung out with cynical people who complained about how terrible their jobs were, while falling asleep exhausted in front of the big red "N" on their TV screen. Now, you probably don't have those pastimes, or those friends, or that kind of life anymore. You actually enjoy waking up in the morning and can't wait to keep building your little empire—but that can't be your entire life. You can't let your business take ownership of your life. That doesn't mean you rekindle those old friendships and hobbies, especially if they didn't make you happy, but you should find new ones.

Think ahead to the day that you stop running your business. What will you do then? If the business stopped today, for whatever reason, what would you do every day? Or if you sold it for a figure with a lot of zeroes, what would you do the next day? I see sellers investing all of their time into their business, and even those who sell it usually jump right back in. Why? Because they have nothing else that drives them, nothing else that they're passionate about. Passion takes time to create. Learn a new skill, master an instrument or a new language, play a new sport, spend time with your family, take a cooking class, or see the world. Whatever it is, find more passions for yourself. Today, you're a completely different person than you were when you started this journey. I think we can both agree you like this version of yourself much more. Having other passions in your life allows you to grow your business even further and faster, because you have something to live for outside of your business.

Think about why you started your business. You had goals for your life. What were they? Now that you have the time and the money, go after those goals. And don't fall into the trap of trying to monetize them. You did that with your Amazon business. Enjoy hobbies, travel, time with your friends and family because it makes life richer and more enjoyable. You don't need to be turning a buck with those hobbies. Just do them because you want to.

Your business is not the goal. Selling your business is not the goal. Having a better life is the goal.

Your Dream, Your Life

AS YOU FINISH THIS BOOK, LOOK BACK AT WHY YOU STARTED YOUR BUSINESS IN THE FIRST PLACE. NEVER LOSE SIGHT OF THAT. KEEP CHASING IT.

Sellers get so caught up running their business, they lose sight of their real dream, the one that motivated them to launch that first product, make that first sale, and build that first brand. You can achieve your ultimate goals. The sooner you plant the seeds and nourish them with hard work, the sooner you'll reap the fruits of your labor.

Use this book as a guide. The more you learn about selling on Amazon, the more ways you'll discover to succeed. And whichever path you take, the journey will be your own. Remember to enjoy it as much as you will eventually enjoy all the business gives you. It gave me the lifestyle I dreamed of as a young newlywed. Some days, I cannot believe I discovered this business—the best business in the world—so early, and with nothing more than my hard work, leveraged it to make all my dreams come true.

Being an Amazon seller is a unique opportunity that only comes along once in a generation. It's like a gold rush, or an oil strike. It's making people millionaires who never believed they would have that much money—not in a million years. It wasn't the internet that made online selling such a fantastic entrepreneurial opportunity. It was Amazon. Sites like eBay required you to have your own warehouse and your own supply chain. There were no marketing tools, selling tools, sophisticated customer support tools, or analytics. Amazon perfected the customer experience. Then they invited other sellers to utilize their platform, selling our products to Amazon's happy customers.

If Amazon went away or another site opened to compete with them, sellers would still have their brands and their products. They can sell their private label products and other products anywhere else. So they have the advantage of leveraging the present online powerhouse, but they aren't tied to that retailer.

Prepare yourself to be a seller. Know what you're stepping into. You won't be a millionaire in a month or even a year. You won't even pull a salary at first. It's a real job and a real business, and you as the owner can set it up and run it however you want.

Learn everything you can about listings, PPC, inventory management, and all the other details, but first, have a great product. A great product will make up for a lot of mistakes, but doing everything else right will never make up for a problematic product. You may spend months preparing your next launch and have everything ready to go. Just before you place your order with the supplier, you ask for another sample, just to be sure. And you realize it's not that good. You have to be honest with yourself and admit it's not good, and it's not right for you. You have to have the courage to start over.

Put yourself in the customer's shoes. They receive your product. What does it look like? How does opening the package make the customer feel? When you open your product, remove the packaging, and use it for the first time, do you smile? Or are you disappointed? Your product must deliver a Six-Star Experience every time.

Look at the competition—their listing, their product. The images, the bullets, and all the copy. Compare it to yours. Whose product would you click on? Which would you buy? If the answer isn't "My product, of course," then you have more work to do.

You'll be eager to launch a product. Every seller is. But take your time and get it right. Give yourself a fighting chance—a chance to win. Don't rush into it. Set it up, optimize it, and have a killer launch.

Start thinking about the kind of business you want early on. Will you have employees or do it all alone? Get organized and create systems and processes to make the work repeatable. Make your business easy to scale right from the start. Do this when you're small. I know eight-figure sellers who work sixteen hours a day because they have to. They've gotten so big, and are doing so much, they can't delegate anything. Making even a small change in their business requires a major effort. They wish they could go back in time and set up their companies the right way, but they're in so deep, they can't change.

If you need more help, just look for me. I'll be online at tomerrabinovich. com. Listen to my podcasts. Read my blogs. Much of my online content is free. Like I said, I love helping other sellers reach their goals and change their lives. I can't wait to show you how to change yours.

BREAKERS

Visit these online resources for more guidance on floating to shore: tomerrabinovich.com/breakers.

ABOUT THE AUTHOR

TOMER RABINOVICH is an Amazon seller who has created and launched multiple private label brands. His first product went live in March 2015, and he became a seven-figure seller within his first year. A sought-after speaker, Tomer's addressed thousands of people around the world. His audiences range from intimate mastermind groups to national and global conventions and trade shows.

Though he's still an active online seller, Tomer's real passion is helping other sellers and online retailers scale their businesses. As the founder and owner of Top Dog Global, Tomer launched Tog Dog Community, an online network of entrepreneurs, and an annual in-person event, Top Dog Summit. He's grateful for the life-changing opportunities he's earned as an Amazon seller and enjoys nothing more than seeing other people fulfill their dreams by following a similar path.

Tomer lives in Israel with his wife, Shani, and their three children. He still carries a deck of cards everywhere he goes and if you ask, he'll show you a magic trick or two. Tomer can be reached at tomerrabinovich.com.

Made in the USA
Monee, IL
25 July 2023

39878676R00187